A WORD TO SAY

THE STORY OF THE MARITIME FISHERMEN'S UNION

Sue Calhoun

FOREWORD BY ROMÉO LEBLANC

NIMBUS
PUBLISHING LTD

Nimbus Publishing Limited
P.O. Box 9301, Station A
Halifax, Nova Scotia
B3K 5N5

Cover Design: Jay Rutherford, Halifax
Interior Design: Steven Slipp, Halifax
Map: Arthur Carter, Halifax
Cover Photograph: MFU protest, Caraquet, N.B., 1979
(CEA Collection l'Evangéline E5752)

Canadian Cataloguing in Publication Data

Calhoun, Sue

A Word to Say

Includes bibliographical references and index.
ISBN 0-921054-64-5

1. Maritime Fishermen's Union—History.
2. Trade-unions—Fishers—Maritime Provinces—History. I. Title
HD6528.F652M37 1991 331.88'1392'09715 C90-097700-0

Printed and bound in Canada

CONTENTS

To Gilles and Raphaëlle,
mes amours

ACKNOWLEDGEMENTS

WHEN I MOVED from Halifax, Nova Scotia, to Shédiac, New Brunswick, in 1983, I remember being surprised by how much the Maritime Fishermen's Union (MFU) dominated the media, especially the French-language media. In contrast, the Eastern Fishermen's Federation had caught most of the attention of the conservative Halifax *Chronicle-Herald*. Because I was living with Gilles Thériault and quickly becoming friends with Réginald Comeau, Omer Chouinard, and Guy Cormier, among others, I began to learn something about how and why the MFU had been formed. It was a fascinating story, a story that, it didn't take me long to realize, deserved to be told.

The problem, of course, was finding someone with the time and the money to tell it, something easier said than done. The Sobeys and Jodreys and National Seas of the world have all had their stories told for one simple reason: they had the money to hire someone to do them. The MFU, on the other hand, had gone from one financial crisis to another in its relatively short life. At times, it didn't even have the money to pay its staff. It is not an uncommon problem, and it is why our history is dominated by presidents and corporate executives, not by ordinary men and women.

So I decided to undertake the project myself. I wanted to write an honest evaluation of the MFU: where it came from, why it started, and what it has accomplished. Perhaps it cannot be said, as Gordon Inglis did of the Newfoundland fishermen's union, that the MFU has altered the social fabric of the region, yet it has played a major role in the momentous changes in Canada's fishery since the mid-1970s. Not least of all, it has given inshore fishermen "a word to say" about their industry. As the only union in the country made up strictly of inshore fishermen, the MFU is unique. I hope, therefore, that this book will fill a gap in the history of the organization of fisheries workers in Canada.

In writing a history of labour struggles, it is difficult to do justice to the role of everyone. Over the years, the MFU has touched thousands of lives, not only those of fishermen and their families but also of bureaucrats, politicians, and academics. For this book, I have had the help of many of them, and they appear in its pages. To those who have been left out, I apologize in advance.

I would like to thank the following for their time and interest in being interviewed: Tim Andrew, Leonard Aylward, Léandre Babineau, Jim Bateman, Stuart Beaton, Michael Belliveau, John Andrew Boyd, Clifford Chiasson, Réal Chiasson, Omer Chouinard, Junior Coffin, Kevin Coffin, Réginald Comeau, Bernie Conway, Alphonse Cormier, Guy Cormier, Antoine Daigle, Xavier Daigle, Mabel DeWare, Adrice Doiron, Maurice Doucet, Jamie Ellsworth, Ed Frenette, Linda Gallant, Graeme Gawn, Charles Gaudet, Ted Gaudet, Jean Gauvin, Gastien Godin, Louis Godin, Jean-Eûdes Haché, Réginald Haché, Percy Hayne, Jr, Valmond Johnson, Johnnie Jones, John Kearney, Aldéa Landry, Jean-Jacques Lanteigne, Maureen Larkin, Raymond Larkin, Roméo LeBlanc, Michael LeClair, Hasse Lindblad, Edison Lumsden, Terrence MacDonald, Marion MacDonald, Alvin (Bill) McIntyre, Jamie MacKenzie, Frank McLaughlin, Allister MacLeod, Jean-Guy Maillet, Paul-Aimé Mallet, Harold Manuel, Elmer Martin, Alain Meuse, Con Mills, Jim Morrow, Marcel Muise, Carl Myers, Herb Nash, Paul Nowlan, Reg Pauley, Rod Pauley, Robbie Paynter, Fred Pigott, Basil Reilly, Eloi Robichaud, Herménégilde Robichaud, Zoël Robichaud, Antoine Sippley, Ivan Shaw, Sandy Siegel, Ellie Smith, Oliver Smith, Kevin Squires, Stuart Squires, Ron Stockton, Henry Surette, Gilles Thériault, David Viebert, Rick Williams, and Fred Winsor.

Many people also critiqued the manuscript. Their help was indispensable in making the book as complete and as accurate as possible. They included Michael Belliveau, Omer Chouinard, Wallace Clement, Réginald Comeau, Guy Cormier, Adrice Doiron, Maureen Larkin, Raymond Larkin, Roméo LeBlanc, Clarence LeBreton, Jean-Claude LeClair, Jean-Guy Maillet, Mario Thériault, and Rick Williams. Needless to say, any errors that remain are my own.

I would also like to thank the MFU staff for allowing me access to files and photographs. In most cases, the name of the photographer has been lost, and I apologize in advance to those not credited. Thanks as well to staff of the Centre d'études acadiennes, at the University of Moncton, for access to archival material and photographs, and to the Department of Fisheries and Oceans and Valerie Mansour for research assistance.

I am thankful to Nimbus Publishing, in particular Dorothy Blythe, whose initial enthusiasm spurred me to finish the project, and Nancy Robb, who edited the book and tracked down some of the photographs.

I am grateful as well to the Canadian Council on International Co-operation for expense funding. Finally, my work would not be possible without the excellent work of Bertha Berryman and the staff of the Ciel des Petits Day Care in Shédiac.

Gilles Thériault was very involved in this book, from reading and criticizing drafts on a regular basis to providing moral support to continue with this project, which, at times, seemed overwhelmingly complex. Probably one of the most controversial aspects of this book will be Gilles' part in it. Some people have already told me that he is too present; others have said that I understate his contribution to the union. Although Gilles' role in founding the MFU and providing leadership over the years was crucial, the union could never have accomplished what it has without the support and dedication of other staff and of fishermen across the Maritimes.

I realized early on that I wouldn't write a book that everyone agreed with 100 percent—even, maybe especially, those closest to the story. Perhaps I should say, as Gordon Inglis did about his book, that what follows is my story of the Maritime Fishermen's Union.

This, then, is a story of inshore fishermen in the Maritimes. They aren't rich. They aren't powerful. Many aren't educated. Their strength, when and if they have had any, has come from working and fighting together. They are ordinary people who have done extraordinary things.

Sue Calhoun
Shédiac, New Brunswick

FOREWORD

S UE CALHOUN HAS WRITTEN an important story—the history of some east-coast fishermen who found the courage to overcome their divisions, to face the indifference if not the hostility of their provincial governments and, perhaps more important, to resist their temptations to despair and give up.

My first memory of the Maritime Fishermen's Union is of a wintry Sunday-afternoon meeting in Richibucto, New Brunswick. A backbench MP, I sat with a few local officials of the federal Fisheries Department. The fishermen cheered and jeered as their well-educated young spokesmen denounced the officials, the politicians, and other associated villains.

But a few fishermen spoke as well. Their frustrations were so intense and their pleas for help so eloquent that the impact of that meeting has never left me.

I understood what they were talking about. I grew up on a marginal farm in rural New Brunswick. My brothers sold milk, hay, potatoes, pulpwood, and logs. They took the "given" price—they did not negotiate the value of their work—and they never knew how the "given" price was set.

I have often wondered why society values so little its primary producers—the farmers, the woodcutters, and the fishermen. Why are they usually denied or so grudgingly conceded the rights enjoyed by doctors, lawyers, police officers, and civil servants, that is, the right to defend together the collective interests of their group?

As far back as 1929, Father Moses Coady of St Francis Xavier University in Antigonish, Nova Scotia, met inshore fishermen in Shippegan, New Brunswick. He and Father Livain Chiasson of

Bathurst preached the virtues of co-operative action. During the Depression and World War II, co-ops multiplied. Many fishermen and plant workers saw their lives improved. But post-war prosperity eroded the fishermen's will to work together, and co-ops gradually lost their significance.

Inshore fishermen compete among themselves for good fishing grounds. They resent boats from the next village, and they show a strange mixture of subservience and suspicion to their local fish buyers. Their traditional enemies were fisheries officials, wharf engineers, and experts of all stripes.

Yet they risk their lives to help in a storm, and given a voice, they often speak collectively with great wisdom.

Sue Calhoun's book brings out these contradictions and these virtues. In describing events, she reveals the strengths and the doubts of many actors—and even the weaknesses and the mistakes.

The young university-educated *animateurs* are revealed with some of their hang-ups and mixed motivations. The chapter on the communist link, for example, is important and informative. Whispering campaigns against the union arose, and some of my old Liberal friends warned me against "those people." But I was somewhat immunized, having known the major role played by the British Columbia fishermen's union and their veteran leader Homer Stevens, a communist. In the case of the British Columbia union and the MFU, I knew that what these people *did* was more important than what they supposedly *were*.

In trying to be fair, Sue Calhoun, in my view, understates the causes of the exhausting battle waged by inshore fishermen. Most provincial politicians betrayed their responsibility to protect the rights of all their citizens. Leaders of public opinion were muted—with some exceptions. The courageous Bishop James MacDonald denounced in 1983 a plebiscite to determine if Prince Edward Island fishermen had the God-given rights that "flow from the dignity of the human person."

Father Moses Coady would not have applauded the tactics of some leaders of eastern co-ops who had forgotten the Coady doctrine of fraternal solidarity.

When Prime Minister Pierre Trudeau asked me to become minister of fisheries in 1974, I had only one question: "Do you accept that my first duty will be to speak for the fishermen?" With his clear approval, I felt very secure. Except for the nine months of the Clark government, I was minister of fisheries until 1982, and during that time, the MFU matured far beyond the apparently modest gains of its fight for legal recognition.

The MFU accepted the challenge to help my department manage the fishery, to make changes in licensing, quality improvement, and a whole array of issues.

One issue that concerned me when I became minister was the fragmentation of fishermen's groups. I saw how some fisheries officials used this division among groups and among regions to delay changes. The herring fishery was a glaring example.

I knew that no credible fishermen's group would accept government money, and I did not like paternalism. In 1979, squid were plentiful, and the Japanese were paying a good price. As companies were selling their quotas, I thought, "Why not give fishermen a quota as well?" They could sell the squid and use the money to finance an east-coast fishermen's federation. All groups were invited to participate in the new umbrella group, though the MFU, in the end, withdrew, to my regret.

I made two mistakes in this initiative. The time needed to bring the groups together was too short—the 1979 federal election was imminent. And my "neutrality" prevented me from giving a leading role to the MFU, the best-led group at the time. I accept some blame for this decision, and, in fact, the book brings out aspects that I had not understood until today.

Sue Calhoun gives credit to a lot of people. She is right to do so, for the credit deserves to be widely distributed. Fishermen themselves—Adrice Doiron, Guy Cormier, Jean-Guy Maillet, and Paul Nowlan of New Brunswick, Hasse Lindblad and Percy Hayne, Jr, of Nova Scotia, Jamie Ellsworth and Terrence MacDonald of Prince Edward Island, and so many more—kept hope alive. They also remained supportive of dedicated staff like Gilles Thériault, Réginald Comeau, and Omer Chouinard. Money was scarce in those days, and even the warmth of friendship does not pay the rent.

Perhaps the MFU's greatest legacy is not the battles that it fought for legal recognition but the respect that it earned for the fishermen from the people who knew them. Today, the fishery is being better managed because fishermen, through the MFU, play a role in managing it.

Sue Calhoun has told the fishermen's story well. When I closed the book on the final page, I felt proud and moved at the thought that I had known so many of them.

The Honourable Roméo LeBlanc, P.C.
Former Federal Fisheries Minister
January 1991

Campbellton

Bay of Chaleur

L.

Caraquet   Shipp

ACADIAN   Tracadi
PENINSULA

Neguac

Miramichi River   Baie-Ste-

Kouchibouguac Mimine
National Park

Richibucto Village

NEW BRUNSWICK

Cocagne
Shédiac

Moncton
Memramcook

Fredericton

Bay of Fundy

Digby

Lunenbu

Meteghan

Yarmouth

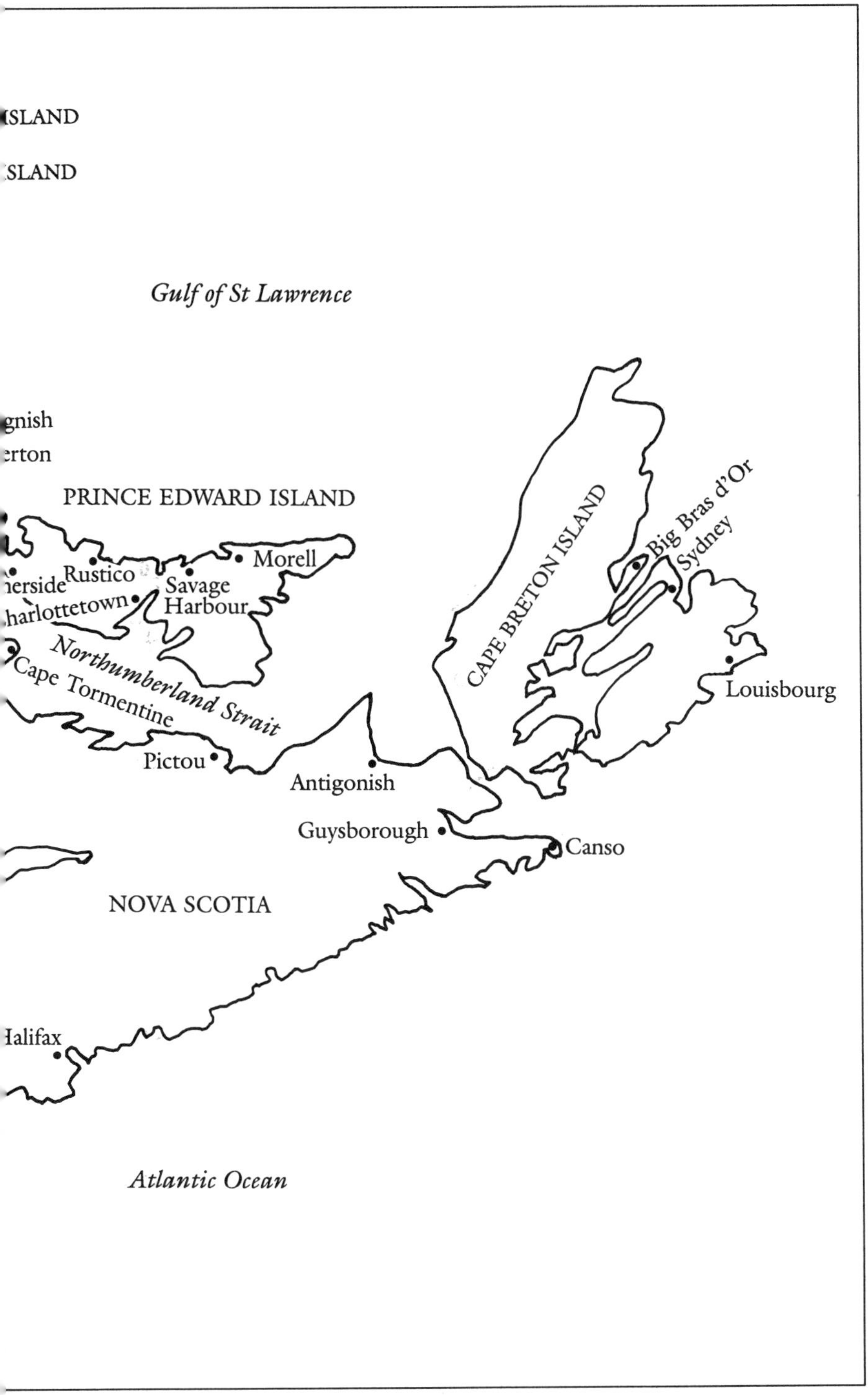

ISLAND

SLAND

Gulf of St Lawrence

gnish

erton

PRINCE EDWARD ISLAND

Morell

erside Rustico   Savage
harlottetown   Harbour

Northumberland Strait

Cape Tormentine

CAPE BRETON ISLAND

Big Bras d'Or

Sydney

Louisbourg

Pictou

Antigonish

Guysborough

Canso

NOVA SCOTIA

Halifax

Atlantic Ocean

A UNION
OF FISHERMEN

"There are people who are going to try and break the union. There are companies who are going to do everything to see that the union doesn't work. We're going to have to fight!"
—Gilles Thériault, March 20, 1977—

THE DAY BEGAN EARLY as Gilles Thériault quietly closed the door of his Moncton apartment, got into his ageing Datsun, and headed north. In his late twenties and already balding, Thériault was nervous, preoccupied with how the events of the day would unfold. Forty-five minutes later, he stopped in Richibucto to pick up a couple of fishermen and the reams of paperwork before continuing on to Baie-Ste-Anne. As he drove the long stretch of rough road, along the barely inhabited coast and through snow-covered peat bogs, he thought about the incredible amount of work that had been done in the past few years to bring fishermen together. If things went as planned today, inshore fishermen from New Brunswick, most of them Acadian, would form a union. It would be the first union of fishermen in the province's history. The date was Sunday, March 20, 1977.

For centuries, Acadian fishermen had had little control over their industry. The companies had paid what they wanted, and the fishermen could take it or leave it. Then, in the late 1960s, fishermen seemed to have even less control as the federal government became more involved in managing the industry. In the early 1970s, more and more regulations were introduced at a time when landings were dropping dramatically, and the fishery was heading for a crisis. The companies, on the other hand, continued to expand. It wasn't long before fishermen began to feel that it wasn't all just coincidence. Many believed that there was a deliberate plan, on the part of government and industry alike, to wipe out the inshore fishery, long touted as inefficient and unprofitable, in favour of the growing offshore fleet.

Over the years, inshore fishermen had started co-operatives and joined associations, but neither had given them much strength.

More recently, they had begun to talk about a union, believing that only a union could give them a word to say about the price of fish and about their industry in general. Fishermen had begun to demand input into how their industry was run.

As one of the union's organizers, Gilles Thériault had been supporting and encouraging this changing mentality since the early 1970s, and he thought about it as he headed towards the centre of Baie-Ste-Anne. It was a brilliant morning. The sun bounced off the snowbanks, though the shore was still jammed with ice, and the wind blowing in off the Gulf of St Lawrence was bitter.

Baie-Ste-Anne is located at the mouth of the storied Miramichi River. Consisting of a smattering of houses along a stretch of highway, it has always depended on the fishery—on the lobster, fished spring or fall; the herring, which come each year to spawn; the cod, once abundant in the gulf; and the salmon, caught in Miramichi Bay. As in many New Brunswick fishing villages, life in Baie-Ste-Anne was uncertain and at times dangerous, conditions that many took for granted as a consequence of living by the sea. In June 1959, for example, Baie-Ste-Anne made international headlines when it was struck by a major storm. Fifty-four fishermen had put out to sea in the evening to drift-net for salmon, and 35 of them, in 22 boats, never returned. "They were people who had grown accustomed to accepting the hardships and cruelties as well as the blessings of the sea," Roy Saunders wrote in an account of the event.

At that time, Baie-Ste-Anne was known throughout the province as a rough place, a place where a stranger was unwise to venture alone. This was Yvon Durelle country, the hometown of the fighter who almost became the light-heavyweight boxing champion of the world. As Durelle had told his biographer, "If you're from Chatham and you come to a dance down here we wouldn't allow that, we beat you up. Not just Chatham, anywhere, we didn't allow strangers here. Even the Escuminac people, only three miles down the road, they were different people, we didn't allow them in Baie-Ste-Anne. We go there they beat us, they come here we beat them."

Such aggressiveness towards strangers was, in fact, typical of many Acadian communities. After the Deportation of 1755, Acadians had intentionally settled in isolated areas to avoid contact with the English. It wasn't until two centuries later that the isolationist mentality began to break down. Louis Robichaud's government

Every year, Baie-Ste-Anne residents hold a ceremony to mark the anniversary of the 1959 disaster, when 35 salmon fishermen were lost at sea during a major storm. (JEAN DAVID/CEA COLLECTION L'EVANGELINE E563)

reforms throughout the 1960s—the restructuring of health and education systems and the financing of both through Fredericton—reduced the influence of the Roman Catholic Church, leading to a secularization of Acadian society. A new kind of Acadian nationalism created a new sense of openness. Gilles Thériault was a product of that nationalism. In his work with Acadian fishermen, he convinced them that they needed to look beyond the boundaries of Acadia and to join with fishermen in other parts of the Maritimes if they were to confront governments and companies effectively.

Thériault had grown up in Baie-Ste-Anne, a son of a fish merchant-turned-politician. Norbert Thériault was first elected to the provincial legislature in 1960 and later became a cabinet minister in Robichaud's Liberal government and the man responsible for piloting many Equal Opportunity reforms through the legislature. He had a reputation as a good scrappy debater. He was on the left of his party. In another time and another place, he might have belonged to the NDP.

His wife, Josée Thériault, came from one of the poorest families in Baie-Ste-Anne. She married young and worked in her husband's store while raising 11 children. As her family got older, she learned to socialize with the influential in Fredericton and Ottawa and travelled the world with her husband after he was appointed to the Senate in 1979. But she never forgot her roots. In Baie-Ste-Anne, she is seen as a woman with an indomitable spirit who lends a helping hand to all.

Norbert Thériault's political skills and Josée Thériault's innate sympathy for working people rubbed off on Gilles and his brothers and sisters. Growing up, Gilles hung around with the sons and daughters of fishermen. One incident in particular, when he was in his early teens, gave him firsthand experience with the danger and uncertainty of a fisherman's life. Again, the salmon fleet was out when an unexpected storm blew up. The fishermen decided to wait it out, rather than take a chance and run for shore. Thériault, helping out on one of the boats, spent a queasy, terrifying night below deck as the vessel tossed and rolled with the waves, not knowing when or even if he would ever feel his feet on solid ground again. By early morning, the storm had blown itself out. Fishermen arrived home to find the entire village waiting at the wharf. Thériault's parents had spent the night at the church, praying for his return. "When you grow up in that kind of environment," Thériault says today, "you develop almost a subconscious realization that something has to be done to help."

After high school, Thériault left Baie-Ste-Anne for Moncton. He spent four years studying political science and economics at the University of Moncton, then alive with left-wing student activism. By the time he graduated in 1971, he had become a strong Acadian nationalist and committed socialist. But he wasn't an academic. He decided to apply his knowledge and his theories to the people he knew best. He began to organize inshore fishermen, those people, still mostly men, who fish out of small boats close to shore and usually return home within 24 hours.

Thériault's home village had been chosen for today's meeting because it was halfway between the province's northeast and Cape Tormentine, on the Nova Scotia border. Privately, Thériault was also hoping that holding the meeting there would make Baie-Ste-Anne fishermen more supportive of a union.

Gilles Thériault, MFU executive secretary, 1977-87, grew up in Baie-Ste-Anne, the son of a fish merchant-turned-politician. (CEA COLLECTION L'EVANGELINE E40, 739)

They seemed to epitomize the accepted stereotype of fishermen: independent and individualistic in the extreme, hard-working and hard-drinking, sometimes opportunistic. Baie-Ste-Anne fishermen had supported the idea of an organization a few years ago when it meant getting better compensation for the loss of their salmon-fishing rights, but today, they weren't loath to throw an organizer off the wharf if they didn't like the union's position against lobster poaching.

Thériault knew that if Baie-Ste-Anne fishermen could be talked into joining a union, fishermen anywhere in the region might be convinced to do the same.

The decision to form a union had actually been made at a meeting in Shédiac during the winter of 1973. But first, fishermen wanted the provincial government to change the existing labour legislation so that they could legally unionize and obtain the right to negotiate fish prices collectively. (Fishermen were not covered by the province's Industrial Relations Act because they were not considered to be in a traditional employee-employer relationship.) They held demonstrations and marched on the Legislative Assembly, but the government refused to listen, insisting that the fishermen who favoured a union were in the minority.

So fishermen decided to go ahead and establish the union, anyway, and to fight for legislation afterwards. "We said, 'To heck with government,'" Thériault recalls. "'We're going to set up this organization whether government wants it or not, and we'll see what happens from there.'"

Between late 1973 and early 1977, nearly 1,000 fishermen signed union cards, but Thériault wasn't sure how many would actually show up for the meeting today. He was pleasantly surprised as he pulled into the gravel driveway of the Baie-Ste-Anne high school shortly before nine o'clock. The registration line was already forming.

Two hundred and fifty fishermen had come from most parts of the province. Some were English, most were French. All were small-boat inshore fishermen who wanted a strong organization to give them a united voice. Many had already been involved one way or another—attending meetings, participating in demonstrations, going door to door and wharf to wharf to convince fellow fishermen to sign union cards. They were here today for a singular purpose—

to found the Maritime Fishermen's Union officially. There was an aura of excitement, even a sense of new-found confidence. At one point, Gilles' father, Norbert, then the MLA for the area, dropped in to see what was happening. Fishermen politely but bluntly told him to leave. The meeting was for them only.

It was to be an all-day meeting whose agenda included the adoption of a constitution and the election of a president. Documents had been prepared beforehand. "But of course none of us really knew how to proceed," says Thériault. They decided to go through the constitution clause by clause. Many fishermen also had a lot of questions about how the union would actually work. How would it force the companies to negotiate? Would co-op fishermen also belong? And if they did, would they be able to bargain with their own co-op for the price of fish? The constitution would have to clarify these kinds of issues, as well as matters of procedure.

"We tried to answer as best we could," Thériault recalls, "but even some of the organizers weren't too sure how to respond." It was a slow process, even with simultaneous translation. Omer Chouinard, another organizer, later recalled that the event "was very amateurish in the sense that we only had a few hours to adopt a whole constitution." It was a lot to ask of fishermen, some of whom were illiterate and not used to meetings, others who knew little about rules of order.

By two in the afternoon, the job was done. With the constitution finally accepted, the election began. It was the highlight of the day. There was a strong sense of regionalism among fishermen, so there had been a lot of behind-the-scenes courting of candidates. Those in the northeast had nominated Rodrigue Brideau of Tracadie; Baie-Ste-Anne fishermen had chosen Harold Manuel; and fishermen from Cape Tormentine, the largest anglophone port in eastern New Brunswick, had picked Rod Pauley. Richibucto Village fisherman Vincent Richard was also in the running. Never again would there be so much competition for the union's top job. Perhaps it was the excitement of the moment, or maybe, as some say, it was the salary—$15,000 a year, more than most fishermen could make from the sea.

In the end, the election was carried by Rodrigue Brideau, who hadn't been involved in laying the groundwork for the organization. Brideau didn't fish full time—he had only a mackerel licence—

At the MFU founding meeting in March 1977, four fishermen ran for the presidency (left to right): Vincent Richard, Rodrigue Brideau, Harold Manuel, and Rod Pauley. Never again would there be so much competition for the union's top job. (CEA COLLECTION L'EVANGELINE E9095)

and there were rumours that he was interested just in the money. But he had spent three years at university, and he was confident and articulate, the only candidate who had prepared his speech beforehand. To many fishermen, it seemed that Brideau would make an impressive leader. Manuel came second and became the secretary-treasurer.

In a few short months, Brideau would be gone, let go when fishermen realized that he wasn't able or wasn't prepared to provide the kind of leadership that they wanted. His concluding remarks at the meeting should have served as a warning. "We must avoid confrontations which will hurt us," he told the fishermen. "The companies will not give us a second chance. If they can break us in half, they will. By being careful in our negotiations, we can survive and come out on top."

Executive secretary Gilles Thériault also had a message for the fishermen, one that was more in line with the mood of the day. "A union isn't going to change our situation tomorrow," he warned. "There are people who are going to try and break the union. There are companies who are going to do everything to see that the union doesn't work. We're going to have to fight!" It was an ominous prediction, but the fishermen applauded, knowing that he was right.

Later, with the speeches finished, the fishermen filed out of the school and were met by the media waiting in the parking lot, hungry for some detail about the new organization. It was a historic event, and one editorial writer would later call it "a new adventure for fishermen."

Brideau's election and subsequent firing would be a minor setback for the newly founded group. Leadership would remain a problem in the years to come, but the Maritime Fishermen's Union would indeed be a new adventure for fishermen. It would be—and still is today—the only union in Canada made up strictly of inshore fishermen. That fact alone would bring with it innumerable problems because of distance, isolation, the seasonal nature of the work, and the relative poverty of the membership. Other fisheries unions had plant and trawler workers in their ranks to give them clout.

Started by Acadians, the MFU would quickly expand to include anglophone and francophone fishermen from across the Maritimes. It would fight for both to have the same rights as other workers. The union would challenge the accepted wisdom that fishermen were self-employed businesspeople and would embark on a long fight for legislation that would succeed in New Brunswick in 1982, when that province became one of only two in Canada to grant inshore fishermen collective bargaining rights. Along the way, the MFU would definitely influence the price of fish.

It would also become involved in questions of resource management. Through endless battles with the federal Department of Fisheries, marked by demonstrations and occupations, the union would make major gains for its membership and, in the process, stave off the destruction of the inshore fishery. Ultimately, the MFU would give fishermen more than a word to say.

As the fishermen piled into their cars on that Sunday afternoon, many faced with a long drive home, they realized that the task ahead would not be easy. But they also realized that they had no choice. If inshore fishermen from New Brunswick and across the Maritimes were ever to have some control over their industry, after centuries of exploitation, the time had come to join and fight together.

THE ACADIAN FISHERY: A HISTORY OF EXPLOITATION

There is probably no part of the world in which such extensive and valuable fisheries are to be found as within the Gulf of St. Lawrence. Nature has bountifully provided within its waters the utmost abundance of those fishes which are of the greatest importance to man, as affording not only nutritious and wholesome food, but also the means of profitable employment.
—Moses Perley, 1852—

JUST AS IT WAS COD that first brought Europeans to the Grand Banks of Newfoundland, it was cod that encouraged them to pursue the fishery farther inland, in the Gulf of St Lawrence. As far back as the early 1600s, cod was fished at Miscou, at the mouth of the Bay of Chaleur. Moses Perley, hired by the New Brunswick government in the late 1840s to study the province's fishery, noted that the Bay of Chaleur "literally swarms with fish of every description." Perley, however, went on to lament that these riches were benefiting not the local population but the Americans and especially the Jerseymen.

The history of the Acadian fishery is inextricably tied to the history of the Jerseymen in North America. Fish traders from the tiny island of Jersey, a British colony at the mouth of the English Channel, they had been involved in the cod fishery off Newfoundland since the mid-1600s. European vessels arrived each year, cleaned and salted their catch on deck, then returned to home ports. Later, the French developed a *pêche sédentaire,* which involved drying the cod on shore before taking it home in the fall. In time, a third type of fishery evolved—a resident fishery—as people began to settle in the New World.

Until the 1760s, the fishery in the gulf was dominated by the French. But with the Treaty of Paris in 1763, the French were forced to abandon their fishing operations, except for those around the islands of St Pierre and Miquelon and along the French shore of Newfoundland. This left a vacuum, and the Jerseymen moved in

In the late 1840s, the New Brunswick government hired Moses Perley to conduct a study of the province's fishery. (PROVINCIAL ARCHIVES OF NEW BRUNSWICK, P8-236)

to fill it. In 1765, the Jersey firm Robin, Pipon and Company established a base at Arichat, on Cape Breton Island, under the management of Jacques Robin. A year later, Jacques' brother Charles established a second base at Paspébiac, Québec, on the north shore of the Bay of Chaleur.

There already was a resident population in both places. According to historian Rosemary Ommer, Charles Robin's diary indicated that there were about 200 Acadians in the area after 1755. Robin bought cod and furs from them and in turn sold them salt.

Robin also recruited "considerable numbers of planters," about 400 Acadian settlers who had been deported to the St Malo region in France. But, says Ommer, the presence of these Acadians created a situation "fraught with difficulty for an entrepreneur attempting to maintain control over *his* resource base."

The solution was what came to be known as the "truck" system, which had already come into use in Newfoundland. Instead of paying wages, the merchant provided gear and provisions at the beginning of the fishing season in exchange for the fisherman's catch, salted and dried, at the end. No money changed hands, and the "price" paid—that is, the amount of supplies that a fisherman received—was decided by the merchant himself in Jersey. The "price," of course, was never quite enough, and the fisherman often depended on credit from the company store to carry him through the winter.

For the merchant, the truck system worked well. It allowed him to control the supposedly independent fisherman and, through him, the resource. For the fisherman, however, it was a form of slavery. As Moses Perley wrote, "All the settlers at Point Miscou complained bitterly of their poverty and state of bondage. They said they were completely in the hands of Jersey merchants to whom they were indebted and who dictated their own prices and terms of dealings."

The Jerseymen's methods of operation reinforced this "bondage." The company established "rooms," or fishing stations, along the coast and imported "skilled" labour from Jersey to run them. These employees had to sign contracts for periods of three to five years, and their lives were completely controlled by the company: alcohol was not allowed, and intermarriage with Acadians was strictly prohibited.

Acadians, on the other hand, provided the "unskilled" labour to bring in the catch, using their own small boats and fishing with handlines close to shore. If a fisherman was too poor to own a vessel, he could rent one from the company. The catch was usually taken home and salted by women and children before it was delivered to the company's station in the fall.

The American War of Independence temporarily suspended the operations of Robin, Pipon and Company, and in 1778, Charles Robin sailed for home. He returned in 1783 with his own firm, the Charles Robin Company. By the turn of the century, the cod fishery on the Gaspé coast and in the Bay of Chaleur had become a major commercial enterprise. Other Jersey firms sprang up. William Fruing established several stations in the Gaspé region in the 1820s and, later, on Lamèque Island in northeast New Brunswick. John and David LeBoutillier built an operation next door to the Charles Robin Company in Paspébiac in the 1840s. Fruing and the LeBoutillier brothers had learned their trade as Robin employees, and both their companies operated in the same way.

But neither was really able to compete with the Charles Robin Company. Although Charles Robin had retired in 1802, leaving the firm to three nephews, the company that he founded had a virtual monopoly in the gulf by 1850. According to Bernard Thériault, who researched the Jersey presence in Acadia, the Robin firm owned a dozen fishing stations on the Gaspé Peninsula, 10 on the north shore of the St Lawrence River, one at Caraquet, New Brunswick, and several in Nova Scotia. The company was interested exclusively in cod, and all its profits were sent home. "[The Jersey companies] conduct their business very admirably but solely with a view to their own profit, without regard to the interests of New Brunswick," Moses Perley concluded in his report. "They expend their earnings in Jersey or elsewhere; they make no investments in the province, and they do not aid in its advancement."

*   *   *   *   *

Acadians had only moved to the New Brunswick coast in any numbers after the Deportation of 1755. By now, the story of the Grand Dérangement is well known. After a century and a half of trying to remain neutral, as France and England battled over North America, Acadians, the original settlers of peninsular Nova Scotia, were given an ultimatum: swear unconditional loyalty to England or risk being deported. Refusing to take oaths of allegiance, they were put on ships bound for England, France, and the American colonies. It was a sombre period in Acadian history. Families were split up, and many people died from unsanitary conditions or lack of food and water on board or when ships were lost at sea.

When hostilities between England and France ended in 1763, Acadians were allowed to return, but they found that their lands in Nova Scotia had been taken over. Some settled in other parts of Nova Scotia or on Prince Edward Island, while others moved into what would, in 1784, become the province of New Brunswick. Many settled in Memramcook or headed north to Caraquet and Miscou Island. As historian Jean Daigle writes in *The Acadians of the Maritimes*, "... acting on their desire to get as far away from their enemies [the English] as possible, the Acadians chose to settle in remote areas. Their ultimate goal was to re-create in isolation a country in which their values would be preserved without outside interference." Eventually, the New Brunswick coastline stretching from the Nova Scotia border in the southeast to the Bay of Chaleur in the northeast became the new Acadia.

In Nova Scotia, Acadians had been mostly farmers, developing a system of dike agriculture that was unique in the New World. In coastal New Brunswick, however, the soil was not fertile enough and the climate was too harsh, so Acadians, particularly in the northeast, turned to the sea for their livelihood. The rise of a resident population at Caraquet and Shippegan and on Miscou Island, along what would eventually become known as the Acadian Peninsula, coincided with the arrival of the Jerseymen. This triangular bit of land was particularly suited to the cod fishery: cod was abundant on the shore, and the peninsula was also within a few days' sailing of several rich fishing banks in the gulf.

In the southeast, the story was different. (The New Brunswick fishery in the Gulf of St Lawrence falls naturally into two districts separated by the Miramichi River.) When Moses Perley arrived, he found no Jersey fishing "rooms" established to the south of the Miramichi. From Point Escuminac to the Nova Scotia border, he wrote, fishing was carried out only by the resident population. It was a subsistence activity: as a rule, fish were not cured for sale. (There is also a third fishing region in the province, the Bay of

Fundy. Today an anglophone fishery based on sardines, lobster, and groundfish, it is dominated by Connors Brothers Ltd, a subsidiary of the giant Weston corporation.)

There were several reasons why the fishery in the southeast was slower to develop. First, the land in the southeast was more fertile, and Acadians were able to continue their traditional *métier* as farmers. Second, the southeast coast, bordering as it does on the warmer waters of the Northumberland Strait, was less abundant in cod, which prefers colder waters and was the only species that interested the Jerseymen. Third, the forest industry was more extensive in the southeast, though Acadians there had to do a bit of everything—farming, fishing, woodcutting—in order to survive.

It wasn't until the mid-1800s that a commercial fishery arose in the southeast, and then it was a lobster fishery, not a cod fishery. Lobster had always been abundant along the eastern shore of New Brunswick, so abundant that it was considered a nuisance and used as fertilizer. But the discovery, in the United States in the early 1800s, of a way to can lobster precipitated a later-day gold rush in the province and throughout the Maritimes. The first lobster cannery was established on the Miramichi River in the mid-1840s, and by the turn of the century, there were more than 200 in New Brunswick. The value of lobster quadrupled during that time.

The boom, however, did not last. Jean Chaussade, in *La pêche et les pêcheurs des provinces Maritimes du Canada,* maintains that by 1885, the lobster fishery was already on the decline; by 1920, landings across the Maritimes would drop by half. As quickly as lobster canneries had appeared on the horizon, they began to disappear, victims of poor quality control, increasing competition, and a dwindling resource. Lobster had been seriously overfished.

Nonetheless, the lobster fishery remained important to inshore fishermen along the coast. (Even today, it accounts for half of the income of many fishermen in eastern New Brunswick.) Régis Brun, in *La ruée vers le homard des Maritimes,* says that the lobster fishery changed the face of Acadia. In almost every village, a lobster cannery opened, providing paid employment for the first time to women and young people. At a time when many New Brunswick Acadians were leaving to find work in the cotton mills of New England, the lobster fishery had a stabilizing effect. It showed fishermen, at least to a certain extent, that they could make a living

By the turn of the twentieth century, Acadian fishermen in the Bay of Chaleur were beginning to free themselves from the grip of the Jerseymen.
(PROVINCIAL ARCHIVES OF NEW BRUNSWICK, P38-342)

by staying home. For Acadians, staying home meant one thing—being able to preserve their language and culture, being able to forestall assimilation into an English-dominated society.

But again, it was a subsistence living. Fishermen were little more than salaried employees for companies like W.S. Loggie that paid partly in wages, partly in goods from the company store. The companies advanced money to fishermen to buy boats or, to those fishermen already too far in debt, rented vessels for a season in exchange for the fishermen's catch. Although it was a looser kind of truck system than the Jerseymen's in the northeast—at least some money was changing hands—it still bound the fishermen to the company.

Many have written about the effects of the truck system on the areas in which it was practised. Historian Rosemary Ommer maintains that in northeast New Brunswick, it seriously hindered the development of a local economy. Given the nature of the cod fishery, the Jersey companies needed only a strip of land along the coast to dry fish. They did not need to build processing facilities or roads or other infrastructure.

When Moses Perley visited Miscou Island, he found that there were no schools. Nor had a priest or a magistrate ever visited the area. Gary Hughes, in a history of Miscou and Lamèque islands, points out that there was a school at Shippegan in 1861. But it had no authorized schoolbooks, and classes were taught by an un-trained teacher who, "like as not, received payment in potatoes or other produce from the parishioners, in addition to a small pittance from the government." Some believe that the Jerseymen actively opposed schools. Historian Harold Innis noted a letter that Phil-ippe Robin, father of Charles, sent to one of his clerks in 1836. "Schools are ruled out. They have no need of education," Robin wrote. "If they were educated, would they be any cleverer as fishermen?"

The truck system also hindered the diversification of the fishery itself. Fishermen complained to Moses Perley that despite the abundance of herring and mackerel in the gulf, they were unable to buy salt from the Jersey companies for any fish other than cod.

Fishermen lived from season to season, always in dread of a poor catch that might put them even further in debt. Before 1900, they had little time and little opportunity to consider how to fight back collectively. As Gary Hughes writes:

> The Robin Co., together with its satellite competitors and other Jersey firms, exercised a near total control over many of the coastal inhabitants of the Bay of Chaleur, Miscou and Lamèque and else-where. So much so, in fact, that a situation was created whereby the company (or companies) became the sole determinant of the quality of life. Those in debt to the Jersey Houses were held to the coastline, virtual prisoners, at least until the second half of the nineteenth century.... In consequence, much of the area's populace developed a chronic sense of dependence on the Jersey houses and/or the English speaking merchants, a process which, to say the least, stunted the initiative of those affected.

*　　*　　*　　*　　*

Little did Moses Perley know, as he prepared his report in the early 1850s, that the Jersey empire of which he wrote so disparagingly was already on the wane. Rosemary Ommer maintains that the demise of the Jerseymen began with the Reciprocity Treaty of 1854, a free-trade agreement between the United States and

Britain that lasted for more than a decade. Under that agreement, Americans were allowed to fish in Canadian waters and, as a result, began to break the Jersey import-export monopoly in the Bay of Chaleur and the Gaspé region. At the same time, several English fish traders arrived on the Acadian Peninsula, and by the end of the nineteenth century, they were also buying fish at Caraquet. Acadian fishermen were beginning to free themselves from the grip of the Robin company.

A series of events on Jersey also spelled doom. In the late 1850s, Jersey banks suffered financial losses, forcing the Charles Robin Company to affiliate with the J.E. Collas Company under the name Robin, Collas and Company. In 1886, another bank crash on the island undermined that company's financial base and forced it to close its warehouse at Paspébiac and its station at Caraquet. In 1910, the company was finally sold to Canadian interests in Halifax, and it became the Robin, Jones and Whitman Company. "In an age of improved communications and speedier transportation," Gary Hughes writes, "it had become increasingly difficult to manage the firm's interests in Canada from the Island of Jersey."

About 1940, several American companies whose traditional supplies of European fish were being cut off because of World War II came to New Brunswick looking for new sources. In 1938, Gorton-Pew Fisheries of Gloucester, Massachusetts, announced that it would build a plant at Caraquet. Although Americans had been fishing in the Gulf of St Lawrence for two centuries, they didn't open a fish plant in New Brunswick until this time.

While the Robin, Jones and Whitman Company was still salting fish, transporting it home in sailboats, and operating on a truck system, the Americans had moved into the twentieth century. The Americans began processing frozen fish, using speedier trawlers to transport their product, and paying cash to both fishermen and plant workers. All these changes taken together, Hughes says, "marked the beginning of the end for the Robin, Jones and Whitman Company in New Brunswick." The company found it more and more difficult to compete. By the 1950s, it closed its doors.

Until World War II, the fishery in eastern New Brunswick was mainly an inshore fishery. According to Delbert Gallagher, the fishing industry in the northeast was depressed before and during the war because it was "too individualistic.... Each fisherman had to fend for himself...." Fishermen were earning $300 per year. There was plenty of fish, Gallagher notes, but fishermen couldn't catch it in quantities large enough to compete with American trawlers and to capitalize on growing United States and Canadian markets for frozen cod fillets.

Although the coming of the Americans had loosened the grip of the Jerseymen, it had, in essence, replaced one exploiter with another. Despite the increase in the number of companies, theoretically creating competition, inshore fishermen in reality remained subject to the whim of the buyers. The companies continued to dictate the price of fish, and often fishermen were not even told the price until well into the season.

If neutrality was the original form of resistance by Acadians—and when that failed, after the Deportation, isolation—in the 1930s, another form of resistance arose. During the Great Depression, Acadians turned to the co-operative movement, which had already started to make inroads into New Brunswick. Inshore fishermen in particular began to realize that they would remain powerless unless they learned to work together.

From its beginnings at St Francis Xavier University in Antigonish, Nova Scotia, the movement headed by Moses Coady would sweep the Maritimes, organizing farmers and fishermen and, some say, significantly changing their lives. Many writers would credit the co-op movement with giving inshore fishermen their first taste of economic liberation.

CO-OPERATION, CONCENTRATION, AND REGULATION

*Our co-operatives must centralize and amalgamate because this is
an age of amalgamation and centralization.*
—Cornerstone of Co-op Fisheries Movement—

T IS A STORY that has been told and retold. On July 1, 1927, as Canadians gathered across the country to celebrate the sixtieth anniversary of the founding of the nation, Nova Scotia fishermen and their families flew the flag at half-mast at a rally in Canso. "What have we to rejoice about?" they asked. "What has Confederation done for us?" These questions were taken up first by priests from the Diocese of Antigonish, later by priests from fishing villages across Cape Breton Island. Resolutions were drafted, calling on the federal government to come to the aid of fishermen—to implement a program of education and to encourage fishermen to organize one big union. In August 1927, the government responded with the MacLean Royal Commission, the first royal commission on the fisheries. The commission's report less than a year later recommended that "fishermen be assisted to organize co-operatives and that an organizer be appointed to carry out the work."

In 1929, the task was given to Father Moses M. Coady, who had just been appointed founding director of the extension department at St Francis Xavier University in Antigonish. A charismatic man, Coady believed that ordinary people, if given a chance, could take control of their lives. "The world calls loudly today for a real democratic formula to bring life to all its people," he once wrote. "It is not going to be done by guns, marching armies or bombs but by a program in which the people themselves will participate."

Coady and his cousin Canso priest Jimmy Tompkins had given courses to adults, helping them to understand their social and economic problems and how to deal with them. Now they began stomping from village to village, preaching the virtues of education and co-operation to inshore fishermen throughout the region. They found a captive audience. As one document later noted, "A 20th century 'John the Baptist,' Dr. Coady said to these fishermen: 'I've come to organize you,' and this he did!"

In February 1929, Coady spoke to fishermen in Shippegan. Perhaps it was here that he met Father Livain Chiasson, a Bathurst priest who became a pillar of the co-op movement in New Brunswick. In early January 1930, Coady travelled to Campobello and Grand Manan islands. Later, he went to Moncton and began a tour of the north, meeting with fishermen from Campbellton to Shédiac and recruiting representatives for

Bathurst priest Father Livain Chiasson was an early proponent of the co-op movement in New Brunswick.
(CEA COLLECTION L'EVANGELINE E26,186)

the founding meeting of an organization called the United Maritime Fishermen (UMF).

That meeting, held in Halifax in October 1930, kicked off a flurry of activity across the Maritimes. In 1932, the first fishermen's co-op in New Brunswick was founded at Shemogue, with the aid of the local priest, Father Camille-André LeBlanc, and of a Barachois priest, Father Edgar LeBlanc, who would help set up more than a dozen fishermen's co-ops. In 1935, Father Chiasson, who had been trained in the principles of co-operation at St Francis Xavier, was hired by the extension department. A year later, a branch of the department opened in Shippegan, and Chiasson became the director.

From the beginning, the clergy, particularly in rural, Catholic areas, played a major role in the co-operative movement. This is perhaps not surprising, as priests were often the most educated people in the community. They saw the establishment of co-ops as a way to keep young people in the villages and to maintain the authority of the church. In Acadia, they also viewed it as a way to preserve the French language and, for all intents and purposes, to ward off outside influences.

*   *   *   *   *

The UMF was established as an umbrella group to teach inshore fishermen how to develop local co-ops. Its original mandate was education, though by 1934, it had moved into marketing. It believed that lack of access to world markets was keeping inshore fishermen divided and oppressed. By marketing together through a central organization, fishermen would have more control over the price of fish. "The UMF is not a fish buyer," a UMF document noted. "It is a marketing agency through which the organized groups are enabled to place their products on the world's markets and receive for these products the highest prevailing prices in keeping with quality." At first, divisions were clear. Local co-ops would process their members' fish; the UMF would provide gear and supplies, as well as market the products. The UMF did not buy fish directly from fishermen or process it. It was there to work *with* local co-ops, not to compete *against* them. Fishermen could be members of the UMF only if they belonged to a local co-op.

Lobster became the backbone of the co-operative movement. By 1942, there were 67 co-operative canneries in the Maritimes, about 30 of which were in Acadian New Brunswick. Some also began to process groundfish and herring. By this time, the UMF boasted about 4,500 members. (The UMF had counterparts in other parts of the country. The Prince Rupert Fishermen's Co-operative, for example, was founded on the West Coast in 1939 with the help of St Francis Xavier's extension department. In Québec that year, Les Pêcheurs Unis was established as a federation of 31 co-ops located along the shores of the Gulf of St Lawrence.)

Richibucto Village, north of Moncton, was typical of the times. During the 1930s, men there fished at the Cap-Lumière wharf three miles away and sold their catch to the local store. The store owner, in turn, supplied fishermen with gear and with credit during the winter. As in many places, fishermen seldom saw cash. They dealt in vouchers and usually began the fishing season already in debt to the local merchant. As Pierre-Yves Pepin noted in a report to the federal government in 1967, "Living and earning conditions

Following the founding meeting of the United Maritime Fishermen in October 1930, co-ops sprang up across the Maritimes.
(PUBLIC ARCHIVES OF NOVA SCOTIA)

have not always been decent, and it was the co-operative which saved the village. In 1935, lobster sold for three cents a pound and the fishermen were exploited. It was then that Father Coady of Antigonish and Martin Légère of Caraquet came to tell the village about co-operatives."

In the fall of 1937, after the fishing season ended, fishermen in Richibucto Village asked the local priest, Father Zoël Landry, to organize a meeting on co-operation. Held on November 30, with Father Chiasson as speaker, that meeting, says historian Alvin Richard, caused a "real revolution" in the community.

During the winter, fishermen set up a study group, similar to study groups elsewhere, to learn the principles of co-operation. In March 1939, the fishermen's co-op in Richibucto Village was incorporated with 44 members. Each member had a say in the running of the operation, and all profits were shared. That summer, fishermen built a lobster cannery at Cap-Lumière. One of the most modern lobster canneries in the province, according to Richard, it cost slightly more than $2,000 to build.

By processing their own lobster and selling it to E.P. Melanson, a private company in Cocagne that handled the marketing, fishermen began to see better returns. In 1941, they received 18 cents for market-sized lobsters, 11 cents for canners. For the first time, they saw cash at the end of the season. Although the co-op depended on lobster, it also bought and sold anything that local fishermen caught—hake, gaspereau, mackerel, scallops. It wasn't long before most of the fishermen at the Cap-Lumière wharf joined the co-op. In 1952, the co-op expanded to include a herring smokehouse.

The fishermen's co-op in Richibucto Village remained independent, selling to E.P. Melanson, for 20 years. But in 1959, it decided to affiliate with the UMF. At this time, the UMF was expanding its activities—education and marketing—to include processing. It asked the Richibucto Village co-op to affiliate because it had identified Cap-Lumière as an ideal spot for processing fish trucked in from northeast and southeast New Brunswick, as well as from Prince Edward Island. The UMF wanted to build its own processing plant at Cap-Lumière. To members of the Richibucto Village co-op, that meant more jobs for the community.

The UMF had decided to go into production because of what it called "changing market conditions." Since World War II, a UMF document noted, new competitors had come on the scene, and they were building large, centralized plants to serve the entire region, not small ones in every village. This resulted in a large volume of production that permitted companies to reduce costs. They could attract the best employees because by processing lobster in both spring and fall, they could offer wages over a longer period. Better equipment and improved processing techniques contributed to greater efficiency. As a result, companies were able to pay prices for fish that fishermen could not receive from their small local organization. The UMF decided that it would have to follow suit. "Our co-operatives must centralize and amalgamate because this is an age of amalgamation and centralization," the UMF document said.

By the early 1960s, the UMF owned six facilities throughout the Maritimes. In Cap-Lumière, it had built a lobster cannery alongside the existing one owned by the Richibucto Village co-op. The UMF's was three times the size. The two operated side by side, with the UMF facility processing fish that it bought from other co-ops, as well as any surplus that the local co-op could not handle. "Having the plant there meant a lot of work for the women," recalls Léandre Babineau. "I remember the UMF had a school bus that went all over the area picking up women to work in its plant."

A tall, quiet man and one of the best fishermen in Richibucto Village, Babineau had begun fishing with his father in 1953 at the age of 16. In 1962, shortly after the local co-op became a UMF affiliate, he started fishing on his own. "I believe [the affiliation] meant more money," he says. "The price to the fishermen went up." Antoine Daigle, another Richibucto Village fisherman, agrees. "The UMF wasn't *buying* our fish," he emphasizes. "They were taking it and putting it on the market. They were our *agent*. So any money they got for it came back to the fishermen." Daigle, too, had started fishing on his own in the early 1960s. He was also one of the best fishermen in the village. (In some parts of the region, he would be called a highliner, though Acadians do not use this word.) Both he and Babineau became leaders in the community, and both served on the local co-op's executive for more than a dozen years.

The relationship between the Richibucto Village co-op and the UMF was good for 20 years. It would only be in the 1980s, when the UMF was on the verge of bankruptcy, that Richibucto Village people would begin to understand what the long-term effects of their UMF affiliation had been. "Having that huge cannery there stopped our local co-op from developing," one resident says. "The local co-op was eating its assets. Rather than expanding, investing in new equipment, et cetera, to handle the fish supply that existed, it just depended on the UMF to absorb its surplus." In 1988, when the UMF went bankrupt, the future of the local co-op seemed grim.

Despite their apparently good relationship with the UMF co-op, Richibucto Village fishermen had not been unaffected by the changes happening within the UMF structure. The decision to move into processing made some fishermen feel that the UMF was now in competition with local co-ops. This view was reinforced in the late 1960s when the UMF, as part of its program of centralization, bought two wooden draggers in order to have a year-round supply of fish at its plant in Alder Point, Cape Breton. This was the UMF's first venture into offshore technology, a fact not lost on its inshore-fishermen members, by now feeling increasingly threatened by the offshore sector. By 1975, UMF membership had dropped to 2,000, and only a handful of independent co-ops remained, including, in New Brunswick, those in Richibucto Village, Baie-Ste-Anne, Cocagne, and Lamèque (made up primarily of midshore fishermen). The weaker ones had been absorbed into UMF operations.

To inshore fishermen, including those in Richibucto Village, all of these developments had seemed to alter drastically what the co-op movement was supposed to be about. As Carleton University professor Wallace Clement says in *The Struggle to Organize:*

> The UMF came more and more to resemble other corporations in the fishery, not because profit was lacking (which was true) but because increasingly management became distant from the membership.... The Co-op ceased to be the extension of the person who fished; it did not bring the fishers and their product closer to the consumer or their fellows as it once had. Membership loyalty became a serious problem as more and more members drifted away. The Co-op leadership, instead of coming closer to its membership, was attempting to run in a race where private capital set the pace.... By entering this race the United Maritime Fishermen lost what had been special to it.

*   *   *   *   *

In order to understand what went wrong with the fisheries co-operative movement—and why inshore fishermen would look around for another organization to represent them—it is necessary to understand the context of the times. After 1940, three trends began to affect the fishery, and inshore fishermen in particular. One, like the United Maritime Fishermen, fish companies were becoming bigger and more concentrated. The 1950s and 1960s were indeed a time of "amalgamation and centralization." Two, the fishery was heading into a crisis. In 1968, landings began to drop dramatically. By 1974, the fishery would be in its worst state since the 1920s. And three, the federal government became more involved in regulating the fishery, and those regulations were making life difficult for inshore fishermen.

Under the British North America Act of 1867, the Dominion government had been given responsibility for the management of the fishery. It issued licences to fishermen and for boats, and it set regulations. In the mid-1870s, for example, with the lobster fishery

Richibucto Village fishermen Léandre Babineau (left) and Antoine Daigle started fishing at an early age. Both became strong supporters of their local co-op. (CEA COLLECTION L'EVANGELINE E35,213; COURTESY MRS ANTOINE DAIGLE)

The Richibucto Village co-op was one of only half a dozen independent co-ops that survived into the 1970s. (CEA COLLECTION L'EVANGELINE E21,472)

on the decline, it set size limits and made the catching of egg-bearing females illegal. Later, it established seasons.

In reality, however, Ottawa intervened very little in the fishery during the second half of the nineteenth century and the first half of the twentieth. Many believed that it wasn't necessary. The resource seemed to be limitless. Fishing was seen as an occupation of last resort. When times were tough, a person could always go fishing. Even as late as the 1960s, anyone could buy a lobster licence—or any fishing licence—for 25 cents.

According to Gene Barrett, in *Atlantic Fisheries and Coastal Communities*, the outbreak of World War II marked a significant change in the government's role in the fishing industry. "Federal war purchasing and demands for increased production and efficiency focused attention on the deficiencies of the fishing industry," he writes. Both levels of government began to invest money in modernizing fleets and plants so that Canada could compete effectively with the United States in meeting the demands of a growing market for frozen fish.

In 1941, for example, the federal government gave approval for the province of New Brunswick to divert three-quarters of a $100,000 grant to Gorton-Pew Fisheries to build a cold-storage plant in Caraquet. "This was to be the forerunner of state schemes for fast development in later years," Barrett notes. "With the appointment of Ernest Bertrand as minister of fisheries in 1942, the modernization policy mushroomed with subsidies for dragger construction and schooner conversion to trawler gear."

Also in New Brunswick, in the late 1940s, loans were available to fishermen from a newly established provincial loan board on a percentage pay-as-you-earn basis. Loan payments amounted to roughly 12 percent of a fisherman's catch. If a fisherman caught nothing, he paid nothing. This flexible system encouraged fishermen to get involved in improving the fleet.

The money was available to fishermen throughout the province, though preference was given to fishermen interested in building bigger boats to catch larger quantities. In Acadian areas, fishermen in the northeast, rather than those in the southeast, began to develop what would become known as a "midshore" fleet. This was simply a consequence of geography: as noted earlier, the Acadian Peninsula was close to several rich fishing grounds, and cod was more plentiful than in the southeast. As well, ports in the northeast tended to be deeper.

By 1955, there were about 50 draggers on the peninsula, 48- to 65-foot vessels worth between $30,000 and $40,000. In a six-month season, one dragger could catch a million pounds of groundfish valued at $31,000; at the time, an inshore fisherman was lucky to make $300 per year. (In fact, one of the biggest UMF affiliates was the Lamèque co-op, dominated by midshore fishermen.) Midshore vessels were owned by individual Acadian captains, had crews of five to seven, and could spend up to 12 days at sea before returning home. Today, the "midshore" designation usually includes vessels between 50 and 100 feet. Inshore vessels, in contrast, are owned by individual fishermen who have one or two helpers and usually return to port every 24 hours. Inshore vessels are mainly considered to be those under 45 feet.

Before the war, almost all fish in New Brunswick had been landed by the inshore, but by 1953, Delbert Gallagher says in his masters thesis, 80 percent of cod was landed by the midshore.

The growth of the midshore fleet in New Brunswick was a direct result of government subsidy programs, and its creation was welcomed by people in the northeast. By the 1980s, some Acadian captains, especially those lucky enough to have a snow-crab licence, would be millionaires.

The rise of the midshore, however, created an illusion of wealth among fishermen that didn't exist for the vast majority. From the Bay of Chaleur south to the Nova Scotia border, the Acadian fishery remained by and large an inshore fishery. Thousands of fishermen worked several months of the year, weather and ice conditions permitting, and depended on lobster and herring and, to a lesser extent, groundfish, scallops, and mackerel. For the inshore sector, fishing continued to be a hard life.

Elsewhere in the Maritimes, an offshore fishery began to evolve. (New Brunswick has never had much of an "offshore" fleet, though some midshore vessels do venture offshore.) The most significant development in the post-war period, according to Gene Barrett, was the creation of National Sea Products Ltd. Through wartime contacts in Ottawa, Halifax businessman Ralph Bell, who had been a member of the Joint War Production Committee for the Department of Munitions and Supply, put together a syndicate to amalgamate the three largest fresh- and frozen-fish processors and 21 other, minor companies in the Maritimes. The result was National Sea, and within six years, it purchased a second plant in North Sydney, entered into a joint venture with Gorton-Pew Fisheries in Louisbourg, and built seven trawlers.

At the same time, the federal government was subsidizing provincial programs to develop an offshore fleet to compete with foreign countries fishing in the Northwest Atlantic. Before the war, only Canada, the United States, and half a dozen European countries fished off the East Coast, but eventually, Soviet Union and other Eastern Bloc vessels began to arrive. During the 1950s and 1960s, what Barrett calls "the golden age of modernization," there was an "amazing degree of consensus" between the provincial and federal levels of government. From 1947 to 1960, for example, the Nova Scotia Fisheries Loan Board, with federal assistance, funded the construction of 125 longliners and 34 draggers. Overall, federal subsidy programs saw the number of offshore vessels (more than 50 tons) increase from 211 in 1959 to 558 in 1968. Today, offshore vessels are owned by large companies, are more than 100 feet, have crews of 12 to 15, and stay at sea for up to 30 days.

Throughout this period, there were also financial incentives for consolidation of smaller plants, construction of larger plants, and vertical integration of companies. As Jean Chaussade points out in his book on the Maritime fishery, the number of plants dropped from 350 before World War II to 270 by 1955 and to 180 by 1975.

Despite these developments, Gene Barrett says, Canadian landings of groundfish in the Northwest Atlantic increased by only 6 percent between 1960 and 1965; Soviet landings more than quadrupled. In reality, the Canadian share of groundfish dropped from 29 to 20 percent.

The growing Canadian offshore fleet and the increasing number of foreign vessels eventually had an adverse effect on the resource itself. By the early 1970s, many observers began to realize that stocks were not limitless. Groundfish landings in the Northwest Atlantic, which had been 1,499,000 metric tonnes in 1955, had jumped to 2,829,000 metric tonnes in 1965. By 1974, landings had dropped to 1,743,000 metric tonnes. A similar decline occurred in the herring fishery. Herring landings by all countries peaked at

After World War II, both levels of government began to pump money into the construction of offshore trawlers. (COURTESY DFO HALIFAX)

967,000 metric tonnes in 1969 but dropped to 433,000 metric tonnes by 1974. These reductions reflected an overexploitation of the resource, not a reduction in effort. Fleets were fishing as hard as ever. They just weren't catching as much fish. Observers became concerned that stocks in the Northwest Atlantic were being seriously depleted.

Yet even as the fishery moved into a crisis, the large companies continued to expand. National Sea, for example, purchased a fish plant in St John's, Newfoundland, in 1971 and ordered six new trawlers in a bid to move into groundfishing off Labrador and Greenland. "More than any previous expansion," Gene Barrett writes, "this one was largely financed by subsidies from the Newfoundland and federal governments." Such subsidized expansion, in the face of declining landings elsewhere, gave National Sea a new lease on life.

For inshore fishermen, it meant less and less power in a situation already heavily weighted in favour of the companies. Many inshore fishermen had already begun to see themselves as a threatened species. In New Brunswick, their numbers had dropped by almost half in two decades: from 9,600 in 1955 to 4,900 in 1974. In Nova Scotia, the number of fishermen went from 14,000 to 10,000 during the same period. Since the 1960s, landings by inshore fishermen had declined steadily. In New Brunswick, for example, lobster landings decreased by more than 50 percent between 1960 and 1974. And prices weren't keeping up with the cost of fuel and gear.

At the same time, the federal government was introducing more and more regulations. In 1967, for example, the concept of "limited entry" was applied for the first time in Canada to the Maritime lobster fishery. That meant that not everyone who wanted to fish lobster could get a licence. A person now had to buy one from a retiring fisherman or inherit one from his father. A year later, licences were limited in the British Columbia salmon fishery and, still later, the Atlantic herring purse-seine fishery.

By 1973, most major Atlantic-coast fisheries were limited-entry fisheries, and regulations were increasingly placed on the type of gear and the number of traps. Inshore fishermen, who had previously had no trouble adding another licence to their boat, began to find it impossible if they hadn't historically fished the species in question. "I have a 44-foot lobster boat," says Nova Scotia fisherman Graeme Gawn, "but in the 1970s, when I went to put a licence on it for groundfish, I found I couldn't get one. The licences had been frozen. At the same time, we were being pushed out of the herring by the seiners. So if lobster went down to the point that we couldn't make a living, I would have been out of business altogether."

Meanwhile, the federal Department of Fisheries began to put into place a structure that would allow participation in management decisions by the industry. Prior to 1971, the only consultative mechanism had been the Federal/Provincial Atlantic Fisheries Committee, which had been set up originally to co-ordinate federal and provincial involvement in modernizing the fleet.

In 1972, the first advisory committee—the Atlantic Herring Management Committee—was established. Made up of federal and provincial officials and industry representatives, the committee included no inshore representative, even though herring had traditionally been an inshore fishery. The "industry" at that time, as far as government was concerned, consisted of the large companies involved in the offshore sector, represented by the Fisheries Council of Canada. As a federal fisheries document noted, "Inshore fishermen in most cases were poorly organized, and unable to take part effectively." Roméo LeBlanc, a rookie MP from the Acadian Shore in New Brunswick, sat on the advisory committee. "I realized that Adrice Doiron [an inshore fisherman from New Brunswick] and his crowd were not at the table but that National Sea and B.C. Packers were, and were treated with some deference by the department."

In 1974, the Offshore Groundfish Advisory Committee was established. Again, as its name suggests, it was open only to the offshore sector. (The name was changed two years later to the Atlantic Groundfish Advisory Committee.) A number of other consultative committees were created, though inshore fishermen had little involvement in them.

At the time, the United Maritime Fishermen was the only organization representing inshore fishermen on a Maritime-wide basis, and fishermen began to look to it to get involved in questions of resource management. Some fishermen believed that the UMF had no clout in Ottawa. Others felt that UMF management wasn't listening. "I remember in those days, going to annual meetings," says one fisherman, "and fishermen being cut off at the microphone by the executive.... At the UMF level, there was no sense of co-operation."

The UMF's *raison d'être* had been education, marketing and, later, production. UMF management clung to that mandate despite appeals from its members to change. "Resource management was a big issue back then," says one fisherman, "but the UMF stayed out of it." The UMF's failure to take a position on resource issues represented for many fishermen its failure to defend the inshore fishery, the foundation of many communities—what allowed many coastal villages, in fact, to survive.

Fishermen began to realize that they needed a strong organization to fight on their behalf if they were to have input into government decisions. Even Léandre Babineau and Antoine Daigle of Richibucto Village, who remained fiercely loyal to their local co-op and the principles of co-operation, knew that another organization was called for if fishermen were to have a say. Spurred by "social animators" active at the time, they, along with fishermen like Adrice

Doiron from Barachois, formed an association bringing together fishermen from across southeast New Brunswick.

Today, many people say that the association, and eventually the Maritime Fishermen's Union, arose to fill a gap left by the UMF, though it wasn't so clear-cut or evident at the time. "It wasn't something that happened overnight," says former MFU executive secretary Gilles Thériault. "During the 1960s, everyone was aware that the co-op movement didn't have a majority of fishermen, so an association was a way of getting fishermen together. Of giving fishermen a voice." The association, and eventually the MFU, was a new form of resistance, a product of the 1960s and 1970s, a way for inshore fishermen to fight the destruction of their industry.

A NEW
ACADIAN
NATIONALISM

"In 1968, it was the first time in Acadia that there was an open confron-
tation between the generations.... The idea of the generation before us was
to say, 'shut your mouth and try to manage.' We were saying, 'no, we're
not going to do that any more.'"
—Artist-filmmaker Herménégilde Chiasson, 1989—

T HE SIGNIFICANCE of the co-operative movement in the Acadian community went far beyond fishermen's co-ops organized under the umbrella of the United Maritime Fishermen
(UMF). The first Acadian co-op, Assumption Mutual Life Insurance Company, had been established in Waltham, Massachusetts, in
1903 by Acadians who had migrated to New England looking for
work. The company was originally set up as a beneficial society for
the poor, sick, widows, and children. A nationalist organization, it
sought to regroup all Acadians under their flag, "to conserve our
language, our customs, and our religion."

Monique Gauvin, in her masters thesis, maintains that during the
first half of the twentieth century, a new Acadian "petite bourgeoisie" arose. Made up of priests and intellectuals, it provided leadership, organizing not only fishermen's and farmers' co-operatives
but also *caisses populaires* (credit unions). By 1946, there were more
than 90 Acadian *caisses populaires*. They brought economic stability
to communities, though one that was controlled by the clergy. As
University of Ottawa professor Yvon Thériault wrote in 1980, "On
dépose à sa caisse populaire comme on va à la messe, les deux
d'ailleurs sous la direction du curé. [People deposited money at the
caisse populaire in the same way that they went to mass: both were
under the direction of the priest.]"

Before long, life in many Acadian villages was centred economically, spiritually, and socially on a cluster of buildings: the Catholic
church, the *caisse populaire,* the co-op store, and the UMF co-op.
By the end of the 1950s, these, along with Assumption Mutual Life

(once it had moved its headquarters to Moncton) and the French-language daily *l'Evangéline,* had become the dominant institutions in Acadian life. Their boards of directors were intertwined, made up of a small group of people who saw the co-operative movement and themselves as *les gardiens de la vie nationale.*

It was a nationalism that some considered elitist but that few dared to criticize openly. Michel Roy, an Acadian from northern New Brunswick, was one of the first to do so. His book *L'Acadie perdue* shocked many people when it came out in 1978. In it, Roy says that throughout the twentieth century, an elite made up of clergy and professionals had dominated Acadian society with their "narrow views," through colleges that were "bastions of conformity." By the "irritation of its silence or a call to repression," this elite opposed any form of popular movement that arose occasionally in Acadian society.

Through its domination, Roy continues, the Acadian elite condemned the population to a life of second-class citizenship. This created "a sense of servility" among ordinary Acadians who were willing to work for low pay and without complaint in fish plants and pulp-and-paper mills run by anglophone-owned multinationals. Roy maintains that one had to look only at the existing social and economic situation to see that this was the case.

New Brunswick in the late 1950s was a chronically depressed province. As Della Stanley notes in *Louis Robichaud: A Decade of Power,* "Emigration rates were high, incomes were low, unemployment was high, literacy levels were low, industrial development was limited and expenditures on health and education were well below the national average." Yet if things were bad for anglophones, they were worse for Acadians, who made up about one-third of the province's population. Along with serving as a reserve labour force for factories and fish plants, Acadians worked mainly in the primary sector, as fishermen, farmers, woodsworkers. The employment was seasonal, the pay was low. In winter, after the program came into being, they lived on unemployment insurance benefits. Compared with their English-speaking counterparts in the south of the province, Acadians had higher unemployment rates, lower income levels, and less education. Poverty wasn't limited to Acadian areas, though it was more prevalent and more deeply engrained.

After he was elected premier in 1960, Louis Robichaud hoped to counter such inequities with his Equal Opportunity Program. Until then, taxation and funding of essential services such as health and education were controlled by county councils. It was an archaic system that meant more-inadequate services in poorer areas of the province. Schools in Acadian areas, for example, often could not afford to pay their teachers for a whole year. By the time Robichaud came into office, the system was on the verge of collapse. Despite sometimes fierce opposition, he completely overhauled it with a series of social reforms that were probably the most radical ever implemented in Canada. By the time he was finished, all major services were funded through Fredericton, the capital.

While such reforms helped the Acadian population, they also undermined the position of the Acadian religious hierarchy, which had previously funded and thus controlled schools, hospitals, and colleges. As University of Ottawa professor Yvon Thériault pointed out in an article in *Egalité*, this led to a secularization of Acadian society that resulted in a collective Acadian identity crisis. In trying to deal with this crisis, Thériault argued, younger Acadians began to espouse a new kind of nationalism.

An element of the secularization was the creation of the University of Moncton in 1963. An amalgamation of three clergy-run colleges, it was the first secular institution of higher learning for francophones in the Maritimes, and it would produce the first generation of Acadians with a non-religious university education. Despite its remoteness from major centres, the University of Moncton was not untouched by student revolts under way on campuses across North America and Europe during the 1960s. It was the era of the Quiet Revolution and the rise of nationalism in Québec, of Martin Luther King and Kent State in the United States, of May 1968 in France.

In Moncton, Leonard Jones inadvertently helped young Acadians struggling with their identity to focus their dissent. Mayor of the city since 1963, Jones was a lawyer—and staunchly anti-French. He insisted on running an English administration in a city that was almost 40 percent French-speaking. During the 1960s, a new city hall, constructed ironically by the venerable Assumption Mutual Life, was adorned with an English-only plaque. The sign sparked a wider debate about the lack of bilingual services at city hall, and it became a rallying point for students on the University of Moncton

Students at the University of Moncton did not go untouched by revolts under way at campuses across North America and Europe. (THE TIMES-TRANSCRIPT)

campus. Students made national headlines when, during a sponta-neous march following an Acadian "frolic" on campus, they paraded to Jones' house and deposited a pig's head on his doorstep.

Perhaps one of the most striking comments on the Robichaud era came from Michel Blanchard, a student activist whose mother is a fiery union organizer in northern New Brunswick. "Louis Robichaud and his gang wanted us to feel at home in New Brunswick," Blanchard said in the National Film Board documen-tary on Robichaud, produced in 1989. "They told us we were *chez nous*. But when we came to Moncton to go to school in the 1960s, we found out that we weren't *chez nous*. This wasn't our province. We couldn't speak our language here." For Blanchard and other younger Acadians, that represented a betrayal by the older genera-tion.

In fact, the late 1960s in Moncton were as much about conflict within the Acadian community as they were about conflict between Acadians and anglophones. "In 1968, it was the first time in Acadia that there was an open confrontation between the generations," Herménégilde Chiasson, who wrote and directed the Robichaud film, told *Atlantic Insight* in 1989. "We were confronting the Acadian elite as much as we were confronting Anglophones. The idea of the generation before us was to say, 'shut your mouth and try to manage.' We were saying, 'no, we're not going to do that any more.'"

In a sense, the "neo-nationalists" were taking on the "elite nationalists" who dominated the boards of directors of Acadian institutions, including co-operatives and the University of Moncton, which responded by expelling students like Michel Blanchard and by shutting down the sociology department (considered the hotbed of dissent). The nationalist fervour, however, was not quelled. In February 1972, more than 3,000 Acadian students marched from Victoria Park to Assumption Place in downtown Moncton. Several carried a coffin marked "fear," and they were surrounded by young people carrying funeral torches. The implication was clear—the fear of speaking out, the fear of being heard, was dead.

The new generation of Acadians would not remain servile and isolated, would not remain hidden in the bushes of New Brunswick, as their ancestors had done so long ago after the Deportation.

*   *   *   *   *

The rise of the new Acadian nationalism is important to the story of the Maritime Fishermen's Union for two reasons. One, the 1960s were formative for several individuals who later played key roles in founding the MFU. Two, unlike the elite nationalism, which had been rooted in religion and culture, the new nationalism was rooted in a socioeconomic analysis of Acadian society. Intellectuals began to theorize that Acadia would survive only if the people who were at its economic base—the farmers, the fishermen, the woodsworkers—also survived.

This analysis became the underlying motivation for those leaving the University of Moncton to get involved in organizing primary producers, fishermen in particular. "One of the strongest criticisms of the elite during this time," says Gilles Thériault, "was that the approach that they had taken was paternalistic, that it had never included empowering the grass roots. So out of that criticism, the next most logical step was to attempt to give power to those who had none."

Thériault had arrived on the University of Moncton campus in 1968, when the radical student movement was at its height. At first, he was a face in the crowd, afraid even to open his mouth. Acadians from Baie-Ste-Anne, because of the village's isolation and the presence of a small clique of anglophones who control the economy, have developed over the years one of the most distinctive accents in the province. The words are French, but the pronunciation is English. Thériault felt self-conscious about the way he spoke. Other students thought that he was an anglophone trying to speak French.

Nonetheless, it didn't take him long to get involved in student politics, though he was an anomaly: he also played hockey with the university's renowned Blue Eagles. He became a frequent sight on campus, rushing from hockey practice to political meeting. By the time he graduated in 1971, Thériault was committed to radical social change. He had other attributes that would serve him well in the coming years: he was pragmatic and inextinguishably optimistic, and he knew how to talk to politicians. Through his father, Norbert, the MLA for Baie-Ste-Anne, Thériault had been exposed early to political life. For example, after the 1959 storm, when 35 salmon fishermen died, federal Liberal leader Lester Pearson visited the village to extend his sympathy and had lunch at the Thériault home.

After Thériault left the University of Moncton, he moved to Ontario to enrol in a masters program in international relations at the University of Ottawa. One year later, he returned home. By 1973, he had emerged as one of the prime movers, other than the fishermen themselves, behind the Maritime Fishermen's Union.

Two other men on campus during this period also played major long-term roles in organizing the MFU: Réginald Comeau and Omer Chouinard.

Chouinard went to the University of Moncton in 1964. At a time when students like Michel Blanchard were leaders, Chouinard stayed in the background. He was an analyst, the *grand penseur* who always knew what the next move should be. In 1969, he enrolled at Laval University in Québec, where he did a graduate degree in fisheries development on the Gaspé coast. He was working for a social development council in Montréal in the early 1970s when he began to hear tidbits about a fishermen's union in New Brunswick.

Born in northeast New Brunswick, Réginald Comeau first attended the University of Moncton in 1968. He was fascinated by the student activism under way but was too shy and insecure to participate fully. He didn't feel comfortable in an academic environment, so he dropped out a year later and went to Montréal, where he worked in a textile plant. There, he met a Hungarian immigrant who convinced him that working conditions in the plant were not what they should be. The two attempted to organize a union, without success as it turned out, and both were fired. For Comeau, however, it was his first grounding in the principles of trade unionism. Soon after, he returned to the University of Moncton and graduated in 1972 with a degree in education.

Other people on campus in the 1960s were important, though more minor characters in the MFU story: Paul-Eugène LeBlanc, who worked with southeast New Brunswick fishermen in the early 1970s; Jean-Marie Nadeau, an Acadian from the northwest of the province who helped bring fishermen in the northeast into the union; Jean Gauvin, who, as New Brunswick's fisheries minister during the late 1970s and early 1980s, spearheaded a drive in cabinet to pass collective bargaining legislation for inshore fishermen; and Denis Losier, provincial fisheries minister in 1990 when a bill requiring all fishermen to pay dues to an organization was finally passed. To a certain extent, Acadian nationalism underlay the motivation of each.

It was a nationalism of refusing to accept the status quo, though it wasn't consciously thought out at the time, nor is it well articulated even today. Jean Gauvin expresses it this way: "If you go back to St Francis Xavier, the co-operative movement had a role to play, but they weren't able to follow the social evolution. With ... the Maritime Fishermen's Union, what we saw was an awakening of the population. Popular participation started from there. And that's where the power of the church, the co-ops, and the *caisses populaires* started to slip." Others state simply that the MFU didn't have support within certain sectors of the Acadian community because it was a challenge to "those guys."

The challenge was eventually played out in 1982, in the fight between the United Maritime Fishermen and the Maritime Fishermen's Union when the MFU was trying to get certified as a bargaining agent. The co-operative movement maintained that its fishermen didn't need a union. But some believed that its opposition ran deeper, that it went to the root of what kind of leadership was needed in Acadia. Many saw the MFU as a popular movement, something that, as Michel Roy points out, had always been suppressed by the Acadian elite.

The fight between the co-operative movement and the MFU in New Brunswick would be, by no means, the primary one. Ultimately, the companies were not interested in dealing with fishermen on an organized basis—it was obviously in their financial interests to keep fishermen divided—and for a long time, they had the support of government. But it was important because, as one observer noted, it pitted two social movements against each other, two *Acadian* social movements that started out with the same purpose—to better the economic conditions of inshore fishermen.

But all that was yet to come. In the early 1970s, as activists began to leave the university, they found an outlet for debate and political involvement in the Parti Acadien (PA). Founded in 1972, the PA was a product of the new nationalism. Its 150-page manifesto announced its intention to instil in francophones pride in their own culture, thereby renewing the French language and ending regional disparity for Acadians. The PA advocated the creation of a separate Acadian province. In the 1974 provincial election, it ran candidates in a dozen ridings, including Gilles Thériault in Kent North (meanwhile, his father ran in Bay-du-Vin next door) and Jean-Marie Nadeau in Madawaska-Les Lacs. Overall, the party took 4 percent of the popular vote, though it didn't elect any candidates. (In the 1978 election, the PA's share increased to 12 percent.)

Along with becoming involved in the PA, some University of Moncton activists went to work for regional development councils, which had been set up by the federal government during the 1960s. These became the structures through which young Acadian nationalists attempted to empower the poor and the powerless at the bottom of Acadian society.

*   *   *   *   *

The Maritime provinces had faced severe economic problems almost from the time that they had joined Confederation in 1867. But it wasn't until the 1960s that the Canadian government began to do something about it. In 1960, the Diefenbaker government unveiled the Agricultural Rehabilitation and Development Act (ARDA), which, according to economist Donald Savoie, was "an attempt to rebuild the depressed rural economy." Originally aimed at farmers, ARDA was later expanded to encompass other sectors of the rural poor, including fishermen.

ARDA was the first of many acronyms for government departments, legislation, and agencies that would attempt and largely fail over the years to alleviate underdevelopment in Atlantic Canada. At the time, however, it was welcome news for the region. Sixteen months after the bill was promulgated, the first federal-provincial ARDA agreement was signed in New Brunswick, paving the way for the creation of five regional development councils. In francophone areas, these *conseils régionaux d'aménagements* became known by their acronyms—CRAN in the northeast, CRASE in the southeast, and CRANO in the northwest. (Two councils were also set up in anglophone areas.)

Their original mandate was to get people involved in working with government to develop the region socially and economically. From 1964 to 1969, the councils attempted to achieve that goal. But then, says Greg Allain, a University of Moncton sociologist, people became frustrated because of "the complete failure of most planning efforts, due particularly to lack of government implementation mechanisms." In 1970, the three francophone councils radically changed their orientation from working *with* government to organizing broad segments of Acadian society to *confront* government.

None of the francophone councils had to search for issues. In the northeast, at a time when unemployment was about 30 percent, the government closed the unemployment insurance office in Bathurst in a bid to centralize operations in Moncton. Thirty-four people lost their jobs at the same time that there were massive lay-offs under way in industry. In February 1972, 100 people occupied unemployment insurance offices for 24 hours until the RCMP finally cleared the building and arrested a dozen people. Meanwhile, in the northwest, CRANO was organizing welfare recipients.

In the southeast, Kouchibouguac became the focal point of CRASE. During the 1960s, the federal government had decided to create a national park in Kent County, one of the most beautiful counties in New Brunswick. Tourist development, it was thought at the time, would help eliminate pockets of poverty. (Kent County was also the province's poorest county.) The selected area spanned roughly 90 square miles and included a 15-mile crescent of beaches and sand dunes along the shores of Kouchibouguac Bay, at the northern end of the Northumberland Strait. The area was rich in animals, fish, blueberries, cranberries, and even wild orchids. But there were also people: 228 families, 85 percent of them Acadian, lived in eight small villages inside what would become the park's boundaries.

The story of how land was expropriated and people expelled in order to create Kouchibouguac National Park is a story of government insensitivity, ineptitude, and paternalism. The expropriates were poor, and many of them were illiterate. A special inquiry into the Kouchibouguac affair in October 1981 pointed out that 81 percent of the families had incomes of less than $3,000, compared with 24 percent in Canada as a whole. Of the 145 houses surveyed, only 23 percent had inside toilets, 22 percent had hot running water, 22 percent had a bathtub or a shower, and 36 percent had only cold running water.

Yet people in the park area didn't judge their economic well-being strictly by their material possessions. The inquiry report went on to point out that "... though the conditions under which they lived may have seemed intolerable by middle class standards, many of the residents of the park appear to have been reasonably content with their mode of life. They particularly like being near the water and the opportunity for fishing." Another report said, "They felt rich, culturally speaking, because the park area was their home." When the government began the process of expropriation in the late 1960s, clearing park boundaries and evaluating properties without telling the inhabitants what was going on, it didn't take long for an anti-expropriation movement to form.

The CRASE office in Richibucto was handy to the park, and in 1971, CRASE staff person Paul-Eugène LeBlanc helped organize two citizen's committees, one in the village of Cap-St-Louis, headed by Oscar Doucet, and one in Claire-Fontaine, headed by Jackie Vautour. A father of 10 and former amateur boxer, Vautour was a scrappy jack-of-all-trades who stubbornly refused to move his family out of the park. Before long, he emerged as the main spokesperson for the expropriates. Vautour went on the CRASE payroll and began to work closely with CRASE staff, who helped the expropriates confront government with their grievances.

At the heart of the struggle were the fishing rights of the approximately 200 fishermen who had lived within park boundaries. Fishing, in fact, had been the main occupation of the residents, and Parks Canada wanted to eliminate fishing in Kouchibouguac, as it had done in other national parks. A 1969 agreement between the federal and provincial governments provided for the continued use of the wharf at Cap-St-Louis, but still, fishermen had to travel farther afield to fish. Wharves in other villages inside park boundaries would be removed, and the government would compensate fishermen for their lost rights.

The proposal satisfied no one. Fishermen considered the compensation inadequate and its application inequitable. As well, fishermen in Cap-St-Louis did not want outsiders using their wharf. CRASE took up the case. In May 1972, about 80 fishermen occupied park offices. In the meantime, two barns, an abandoned house, and a wooden bridge went up in flames. Jackie Vautour reportedly

The Kouchibouguac affair was marked by occupations, demonstrations, and fires. In December 1979, fishermen occupied park offices to protest the loss of their fishing rights. (CEA COLLECTION L'EVANGELINE E8404)

told the press that the fires were set by people who supported the residents' cause. "There could be a black park before this finishes but I hope it doesn't happen," he was quoted as saying.

It was the beginning of violence that marked the Kouchibouguac affair throughout the decade. In 1973, four people were charged with assaulting the park superintendent during a demonstration. In 1976, exasperated with trying to get Vautour out of the park, the government bulldozed his house and moved him and his family into a nearby motel. They were evicted a few months later for not paying rent, and Vautour and several of his sons were charged with assaulting a police officer. Meanwhile, the fires continued. Park cars were vandalized, and park officers received threatening phone calls. One of Vautour's sons was arrested one Christmas Eve after the park superintendent had been assaulted. In 1980, 100 protesters occupying park offices overturned two RCMP cruisers and smashed the windows and lights. Six people were eventually convicted on charges arising from the incident.

Although most Acadians did not condone the violence, they understood the frustration of the expropriates. To them, Kouchibouguac had become an Acadian cause célèbre. The thought of Acadians being forced from their homes was reminiscent of an earlier, painful period that had never really left their collective consciousness: the Deportation of 1755. The comparison was a frequent theme, and it drew supporters from across the province. Jackie Vautour became an Acadian folk hero.

The *Report of the Special Inquiry on Kouchibouguac National Park* later said that the government had made serious errors, especially in the beginning, in the way it had treated the residents. Because of the experience, government policy would change so that today residents are no longer forced to move to make way for a new national park.

The intended ban on fishing in the park remained an issue until 1980, when the government finally backed down and agreed to allow former residents to continue fishing within the park boundaries. The rights of the residents also remained an issue, though by then, only Jackie Vautour and one other family still lived in the park.

Vautour had moved back in 1978, building four small shacks to house his family. Despite primitive conditions and even after the provincial government cut power to his home in early 1987,

Vautour stood firm. Even Richard Hatfield couldn't convince him to leave. As one of his last acts before going down to defeat in October 1987, the premier signed an agreement with Vautour, giving him $250,000 and a piece of property elsewhere in exchange for leaving the park. Vautour took the money, used it to buy a mobile home, and remains in the park today.

* * * * *

The original focus of CRASE had been to get people working with government to improve social and economic conditions. During the 1960s, its mandate included sponsoring leadership training courses, and many fishermen enrolled in these courses. Later, about 1970, CRASE turned to organizing disadvantaged Acadians to challenge government. Kouchibouguac and the fishing rights of those who lived in the park were natural issues.

But as CRASE got more involved in working with fishermen, its focus again began to change. Sociologist Greg Allain attributes this change to "the result of a diagnosis of the populist 1970-72 period as having been, after all, somewhat scattered, bearing few if any long-lasting effects." In 1972, Paul-Eugène LeBlanc was replaced at CRASE by Gilles Thériault. "We realized," says Thériault, "that with Kouchibouguac and unemployment in the north, we were just reacting to the issues of the day, and it wasn't leading anywhere. We made a conscious decision that if we were going to give long-term power to people in the community, we had to give them structure. We had to build organizations that involved the rural population."

Much later, Dalhousie University professor Rick Williams, who spent years working voluntarily with the Maritime Fishermen's Union, wrote that the nationalism of the 1960s had evolved by the mid-1970s into a "highly politicized effort" to mobilize Acadian primary producers to fight regional underdevelopment.

ACADIANS
ON THE MARCH

*"At a certain point, the fishermen realized that they had to live
in an organized world. Plumbers were getting organized, carpenters
were getting organized. But the fishermen were there, still hopeless.
They finally said, 'Why not us, too?'"*
—Barachois fisherman Adrice Doiron—

ONE OF THE FIRST FISHERMEN to take a CRASE leadership course was Adrice Doiron of Barachois, near Cap-Pelé, on New Brunswick's southeast coast. Doiron had started fishing with his father at the age of 12 and had worked as a helper for 20 years until he was finally able to buy his own boat in 1952. Although there was a co-op in Cap-Pelé at the time, Doiron wasn't a member. The co-op didn't have the financial means to provide cash up front for fishermen to buy boats.

"Being a fisherman's son," Doiron recalls, "your dream was always to go fishing one day with your own boat. But you had to have advances, cash to buy yourself gear. So, as a rule, whichever fish buyer paid for your boat, you'd go out and fish for that company. First of all, at that time, you didn't even know what you were getting for your fish. You'd take your fish over to the company, they'd weigh it, then give you a slip for so many pounds. Most of the time you'd know the price of fish only after the season. You would sell your lobster for two months, and then on October 15, they'd tell you that the lobster was worth 22 cents a pound."

Like other inshore fishermen along the coast, Doiron participated in what was called a "multipurpose" fishery. In the spring, once the ice moved out, he geared up for herring. When that finished at the end of May, he fished mackerel. Then, in mid-August, he went after lobster, though he landed most of his catch in the first few weeks of the season. When lobster season ended in mid-October, he fished smelts. After the weather turned bad, he laid up his boat and spent the winter repairing his gear. By the 1960s, Doiron, in his mid-forties, was a solid, respected fisherman who knew his way around the fishing grounds—and understood the problems that fishermen faced.

At this time, fishermen were still isolated. Often fishermen from one village did not know fishermen from another 10 miles down the road. If they did, they may have viewed them as enemies, competitors for the same, sometimes scarce resource. It was a zero-sum game. "What you got, I didn't," recalls Doiron. "It's not as if you were a farmer or a labourer. You work with other labourers, and you're all getting the same pay. It's not the same with fishing. If there's a bunch of fish somewhere, well, the fisherman who finds it would rather keep it for himself. So we're competing with one another. You can't argue with that."

It was a situation—and an attitude—that made the first attempts at organizing difficult. Doiron was different from most fishermen in that he knew fishermen in other villages. In the mid-1960s, he signed up for a CRASE leadership course at the Memramcook Institute near Moncton. The course provided basic information on the fishery itself, as well as on programs offered to fishermen through the federal Department of Fisheries. It also taught fishermen how to conduct meetings, how to get other fishermen involved, and how to deal with the media.

At the course, Doiron met fishermen like Antoine Daigle and Léandre Babineau from Richibucto Village. Through these contacts and through the network that CRASE developed once it began pushing its way into communities in the southeast, a group of fishermen formed what would become the nucleus of an association bringing together inshore fishermen in that region. Along with Doiron, Daigle, and Babineau, the group included Xavier Daigle from Pointe-Sapin, Paul Nowlan from Ste-Anne-de-Kent, and Alvin (Bill) McIntyre from Baie-Ste-Anne.

Already in his fifties, Xavier Daigle was the oldest member of the group. He had been a long-time supporter of the co-operative movement, and he was a member of a co-op in Pointe-Sapin. In 1938, he had taken a leadership training course at St Francis Xavier University in Antigonish, Nova Scotia, and had come back to organize a *caisse populaire* in his village, serving on the *caisse* executive for years. Considered a community leader, Daigle was a strong believer in the need for fishermen to work together. He became the association's first president.

Paul Nowlan had quit school at the age of 14 to fish with his father. As the only boy of five children, he was expected to help support the family. Like many Acadian fishermen along the shore, Nowlan also went to Saint John to work during the winter months. At one job he held there, in a fertilizer plant that no longer exists, he caught his right hand in a conveyor belt. It was crushed, and he spent five months recovering in hospital. There was a union at the plant, but it did nothing to help him. Partially disabled, Nowlan, then in his early twenties, continued to fish. When CRASE began, he became a volunteer, and through the organization, he met Gilles Thériault, who took up his case with the Workers' Compensation Board. Nowlan received a lump-sum payment, as well as a monthly disability allowance. Thériault would go back to the board on Nowlan's behalf several times in the coming years to have the monthly allowance increased. That touched Nowlan. "Gilles was a good fighter for the fishermen," he says. "It didn't matter what it was or what time of day it was. Gilles would do it."

Bill McIntyre was also a CRASE volunteer. An Acadian from a long-ago assimilated English family in Baie-Ste-Anne, McIntyre was considered one of the best fishermen in the village. He had been a long-time member of the local co-op. When government regulations started to become severe during the late 1960s, he decided to "put in some time," as he says, to help other fishermen. At the same time, McIntyre, like many fishermen, was strongly individualistic and competitive. He was known to idle his boat on a school of herring— and even go below deck and take a nap—waiting for other fishermen to finish for the day and go home, rather than haul the fish aboard and in the process alert others to his good fortune. Yet it was because of McIntyre's support—even when a position taken by the Maritime Fishermen's Union worked to his own financial disadvantage—that many Baie-Ste-Anne fishermen joined the association and, later, the union.

In 1969, McIntyre, Nowlan, and Xavier Daigle—together with Adrice Doiron, Antoine Daigle, and Léandre Babineau—set up the Professional Fishermen's Association of Southeast New Brunswick, a fledgling organization with 48 members out of a possible total of 1,400. "At a certain point, the fishermen realized that they had to live in an organized world," says Doiron. "Plumbers were getting organized, carpenters were getting organized. But the fishermen were there, still hopeless. They finally said, 'Why not us, too?'" By the late 1960s, fishermen were also beginning to anticipate a crisis in the fishery, and growing monopolization in the industry.

The association's members came from nearly a dozen fishing communities. In the beginning, the organization had no staff, though CRASE provided help and, later, money for organizers. The objectives of the group were straightforward: to act as the official voice of fishermen, to inform the public at large of fishermen's needs, to obtain benefits such as group-insurance and pension plans. Its constitution reflected the co-operative backgrounds of its members:

> The Association favours the study of the principles of cooperation because cooperation gives a sense of solidarity and a conception of the community that are totally different of those of the bourgeois conception. The Association believes that in order to avoid adopting the habits and ideas of the "bourgeois" it is necessary to inspire the people in such ways as to improve education which develops collective convictions and thoughts, and thereby brings the members together in a true collectivity.

In 1971, CRASE loaned staff person Paul-Eugène LeBlanc to work with the association. A year later, LeBlanc, due to ill health, was replaced by Gilles Thériault. A priority was to develop leadership among fishermen. "To build a strong organization, we had to have strong fishermen leaders from all the communities," says Thériault.

Leadership—and the lack thereof—was a constant problem for the association and would continue to be for the Maritime Fishermen's Union. Fishing, a solitary occupation by definition, breeds not only competitiveness but also an independence of spirit. In those days, illiteracy was high, and fishermen lacked confidence. While they could express themselves in no uncertain terms to fellow fishermen at the end of the wharf, they found it difficult to communicate with company officials or, worse, with bureaucrats and politicians. "It was always hard to find people to take leadership jobs," says Adrice Doiron. "We were aware that we were not qualified in education to take on those jobs. But we didn't have the money to hire qualified people. A job like that, where we wanted to

In the early 1970s, fiery union organizer Mathilda Blanchard spoke at an annual meeting of the Professional Fishermen's Association of Southeast New Brunswick. *Left to right:* Paul-Eugène LeBlanc of CRASE, Adrice Doiron, Bill McIntyre, Blanchard, Léandre Babineau, and Lionel Gallant, also of CRASE. (CEA COLLECTION L'EVANGELINE E26940)

have an educated man, it would have cost us thousands of dollars. That's why it's hard for the poor to get organized. The rich have no problem. I guess what saved us was the government at certain times lending a helping hand, with job employment programs, CRASE, et cetera."

Although leadership training was important, there was also work to do. People like Gilles Thériault encouraged fishermen to focus their energies. The association helped get wharves built and channels dredged. It also convinced government to provide compensation to Baie-Ste-Anne and Escuminac fishermen who had lost lobster traps during Hurricane Beth in 1971. Little by little, fishermen began to see concrete results from working together.

One of the biggest issues in New Brunswick during the early 1970s was the ban on the commercial salmon fishery. The Miramichi River was at one time, and, some say, still is, the best salmon-fishing river in the world. The magnificent salmon that winter in international waters off Greenland and return home each spring to spawn have attracted anglers from around the world, including the likes of Ted Williams of Boston Red Sox fame, who has a cabin on the river. For commercial fishermen at the mouth of the Miramichi, the salmon fishery was a significant source of income. Almost one-fifth of the fishermen in the area had died in the Baie-Ste-Anne disaster of 1959, yet even this tragedy did not diminish the importance of the salmon fishery.

Catching the first salmon of the year was a thrill unlike any other. "Salmon fishing wasn't hard work compared to other fisheries, although you had to put in a lot of hours. And that first salmon was never sold. It went right here," says Bill McIntyre, slapping the supper table in his Baie-Ste-Anne home.

But in the early 1970s, salmon stocks not only in the Miramichi River but in Atlantic Canada generally were in serious trouble. In 1967, east-coast fishermen caught 200,000 salmon. But in 1971, they took only 30,000. The same year, the Danes landed 500,000 salmon off the coast of Greenland. Fishermen in both Newfoundland and New Brunswick, where the major salmon rivers are located, believed that foreign fishermen were intercepting the fish before they could get home to spawn.

In 1971, federal fisheries minister Jack Davis announced a freeze on commercial salmon licences in Atlantic Canada and made existing licences non-transferable. That meant that a retiring fisherman couldn't pass on his licence. A year later, Davis banned commercial salmon fishing in Atlantic Canada altogether. (He had also wanted to ban recreational salmon fishing, but the anglers' association, with provincial government support, rallied enough opposition that Davis backed down. New Brunswick natural re-sources minister Wilfred Bishop pointed out that salmon anglers were taking only 2 percent of the fish but represented a $3.5 million business. In contrast, he noted, the economic contribution of commercial fishermen was only a fraction of that. The battle over the economic importance of recreational versus commercial fishing raged for nearly a decade. The anglers—many of them American— would eventually emerge the victors.)

After almost a year, Gilles Thériault succeeded in negotiating compensation for each of the roughly 120 commercial salmon fishermen in the Baie-Ste-Anne/Escuminac area. This was, in fact,

Thériault's first major accomplishment. "For me," he says, "just coming out of university and going back home to a fishing community, I was kind of like a prophet in my own country. 'What does he know about fishing?' That was the attitude of some fishermen. So negotiating for them was an enormous challenge.

"There had been individual settlements in other parts of the Maritimes," he continues, "but we were the first to negotiate a collective settlement. That was a new idea at the time. We didn't have a problem selling the majority of fishermen on the idea, although some of them, the highliners like Bill McIntyre, would have done better if they had negotiated individually. For the good of the community, and the good of the association, Bill agreed to accept what everybody else got."

The settlement was an annual payment of $3,300 for five years, the expected life of the ban. Little did fishermen realize that the ban would be renewed for a second five-year period and that they would never really resume fishing salmon as they had before. Nor did Thériault realize that one of his last tasks with the MFU, in the mid-1980s, would be, again, to negotiate compensation under a government salmon-licence buy-back program.

At the time, however, fishermen saw the compensation package as an accomplishment of the association—the result of banding together. After 70 fishermen from the Bay of Chaleur area met with New Brunswick MP Herb Breau in 1972 to express their fears about the future, Carson Daley, one of a dozen part-time salmon fishermen who had received notices that their licences were being cancelled, told the press, "The Acadian people are on the march. We're not going to the fisheries department and tear the door off, but we must do something."

*   *   *   *   *

During the early 1970s, the federal government funded several employment programs for young people (a response, in large part, to left-wing activity taking place on campuses). The Professional Fishermen's Association of Southeast New Brunswick began to make use of them. In 1971, with a Local Initiatives Program (LIP) grant, the association hired 12 fishermen to knock on doors, and membership subsequently climbed to 600. The following year, the association received a second LIP grant to conduct a survey of fishermen's problems. The two major ones, fishermen said, were lobster poaching—which had been rampant for years and cut into efforts by honest fishermen to make a decent living—and the inability to have input into price. Then, as they had two centuries earlier, companies dictated the prices that they paid—and fishermen were expected just to accept them. In 1973, the association got a third LIP grant, this time to hire 11 fishermen, one in each of the major ports in the southeast, to study the possibility and financial feasibility of a union. The project was co-ordinated by Adrice Doiron.

Meanwhile, grants were also available from the Company of Young Canadians (CYC). In 1974, Jean-Guy Maillet, a young fisherman from Richibucto Village, was hired to work winters on a contract that would be renewed three times. Two years later, Guy Cormier of Cap-Pelé was hired as well. Both Maillet and Cormier would play key roles in the MFU, and both had remarkably similar backgrounds. Both were in their early twenties and well educated by fishermen's standards, both had fished from an early age, and both had fathers who were strong co-op members yet had discouraged their sons from becoming fishermen.

"After Grade 12," Maillet recalls, "my father literally drove me to the community college because he was very skeptical about me making a living as a fisherman." Maillet became a welder and worked for four years around the Maritimes (in the process becoming a member of the United Steelworkers of America) before returning home to fish. Cormier had also finished Grade 12, and worked for the RCMP and, later, Massey Ferguson in Saint John before deciding, in 1971, to follow his heart and go fishing.

Cormier joined the Cap-Pelé fishermen's co-op and also became a member of the fishermen's association. His father and grandfather had both preached co-operation and organization from the time Guy was old enough to help out on the boat. It was a lesson that he learned well, a lesson that was reinforced when he began fishing and became better acquainted with Adrice Doiron, who lived up the road. To Cormier, Doiron was like a second father. To Doiron, Cormier seemed like a younger version of himself. Both were natural leaders—articulate, intelligent, respected by other fisher-

In 1974, the CYC hired Richibucto Village fisherman Jean-Guy Maillet, who would go on to play a key role in the MFU. (COURTESY MFU).

men. Cormier's weakness, if he had one, was that he took fishermen's problems too seriously. He was an emotional man, always worried about what kind of future inshore fishermen faced in the world as the 1970s unfolded.

"Guy is such a good-hearted fellow," says Jean-Guy Maillet, "the kind of guy who can't understand politicians making decisions against inshore fishermen, who can't understand people in the industry who don't give a shit about the inshore. He felt that everyone should have the same heart as him." This quality made Cormier a pessimist and thrust him over the years into moods of despair. At the time, however, many fishermen didn't know that side of him. They saw Cormier as a leader, someone capable of representing their interests. In 1980, Cormier would be elected president of the MFU, a position that he would hold for three years.

*   *   *   *   *

In all the work that they did, fishermen involved in the Professional Fishermen's Association of Southeast New Brunswick continued to be bothered by one issue: price. "There were a lot of fishermen who were convinced we should know the price of our fish when we came to the wharf," says Adrice Doiron. "Fishermen couldn't accept the fact that when they went to the market to buy fish, the company knew the price it wanted. When they went to buy gear, the company knew the price beforehand. But when they tried to sell their fish to the same company, they couldn't have the price."

After the survey of 1972, in which fishermen had identified price as an important issue, some began to think that maybe a union could force the companies to negotiate. Association members started to discuss the idea among themselves. Gilles Thériault, by then working full time with the group, encouraged them. He also began to research how a fishermen's union would function. One of the purposes of the third LIP grant, in 1973, had been to find out how fishermen across the southeast felt. The response was positive enough that at a meeting in Shédiac that winter, fishermen voted to turn their association into a union. (The association continued to operate until the MFU was officially founded in 1977.)

That they did so is perhaps a measure of the frustration that fishermen were feeling. Some of the most active fishermen didn't know how, or even if, a union of fishermen would work. "To tell you the truth, I didn't think it could work," says Léandre Babineau of Richibucto Village. "Fishermen are too independent. At the same time, I always supported it, always paid my dues. I knew that a union would give us a word to say that we didn't have with an association. A union was more power." Adds Antoine Daigle, "If there hadn't been unions starting up all over, we maybe wouldn't have needed a union. But when I went to buy an engine, it was made by union labour. When I went to buy a rope, it was made by union labour. I had to pay union rates, but I couldn't afford it with the price I was getting for my fish." In fact, according to government statistics, 60 percent of fishermen in Atlantic Canada made less than $5,000 (gross) in 1973. Prices they received for lobster—around 90 cents a pound at the time—were not keeping up with rising costs.

Fisherman Guy Cormier of Cap-Pelé joined Jean-Guy Maillet on the CYC payroll. In 1980, Cormier became president of the MFU. (COURTESY MFU)

Some of the early association leaders, especially the older fishermen, never really believed philosophically in the idea of a union. Shortly after the decision, Xavier Daigle retired from the association. Adrice Doiron began to drift away. Bill McIntyre, always an independent soul, eventually owned three boats and left the union after members passed a resolution that inshore fishermen could own only one.

For the time being, however, fishermen had great hopes and great expectations. By now, many were disillusioned with the United Maritime Fishermen (UMF) because of its refusal to become involved in issues of resource management and to speak out on behalf of its membership at a time when the federal government was increasingly regulating the resource and the offshore sector was rapidly expanding. "It was only in the mid-1970s that fishermen began to openly confront the UMF, to openly challenge the leadership," says Gilles Thériault. "Many saw guys like Arthur LeBlanc [head of the UMF] as being too entrenched and not interested in their problems. The union became the voice that could articulate what many had been feeling for a few years." Adds Léandre Babineau, "Once we started talking about negotiating the price of our fish, UMF management was always against us." Many inshore fishermen remained committed to the principles of co-operation and to their local co-op, but they turned to the Maritime Fishermen's Union to defend their economic interests.

As the fishery headed towards the crisis of 1974, with landings dropping, fishermen became adamant that they should have the right to negotiate price. By then, the association was attracting a younger generation of fishermen, including Jean-Guy Maillet and Guy Cormier, many of them with trade-union experience. Leaders were emerging among fishermen in the northeast of the province as well.

Strong leadership was also being provided by non-fishermen such as Gilles Thériault (and, later, others) who, because of their nationalist ideals, were prepared to work for the fishermen for next to nothing.

Together, these people embarked on a voyage to give fishermen a word to say about the price of fish and about the management of the inshore fishery. They would eventually succeed, making history in New Brunswick in the process, though it would take them the better part of a decade.

IN SEARCH
OF A MODEL

"On the West Coast, they really reinforced what we were feeling. That you can do it on your own, you don't need to join a big union."
—Gilles Thériault—

T HE FISHERMEN were late arriving for their lunch date. Their flight had been on schedule, and the taxi had brought them straight to Parliament Hill, but they had got lost looking for the dining room. Gilles Thériault had left them, just for a moment, to look up a friend. The fishermen, most clad in jeans and woollen jackets and several unable to speak English, felt far from home and slightly out of place. The feeling increased as they finally found their destination and were ushered into a private room off the main dining room in the Centre Block.

The group included Adrice Doiron, Léandre Babineau, Paul Nowlan, and Bill McIntyre, four of the founding members of the Professional Fishermen's Association of Southeast New Brunswick. They were accompanied by Rodney Walton from Murray Corner, the only anglophone, and two fishermen from the northeast, Fernand Mallet of LeGoulet and Herménégilde Robichaud of Val Comeau. The men were on their way west to meet with representatives of the United Fishermen and Allied Workers' Union (UFAWU) in Vancouver, a trip organized by the association's executive secretary, Gilles Thériault, and financed by the federal Secretary of State.

Their stopover in the nation's capital was a courtesy visit. It wasn't often that fishermen went to Ottawa, and New Brunswick MPs Herb Breau and Roméo LeBlanc were anxious to wine and dine their constituents. They had reserved a special room. The fishermen, however, began to wonder if it was a good idea when they saw the confusing array of silverware and glass on the tables. It wasn't like the restaurants back home. "The waitress brought us beef consommé in a two-handled cup," recalls Herménégilde Robichaud. "I drink my tea black, but everybody else started putting sugar and milk in it. They didn't know it was soup. Herb finally said, 'Hey, did you know it's consommé?'"

Later, the fishermen met with federal fisheries minister Jack Davis, a meeting arranged by LeBlanc, who would replace Davis as minister a few months later. Davis had arranged for a photographer to take his picture with the fishermen—each fisherman would get a copy in the mail—but he didn't have time to chat. He answered a couple of questions, then left. "He had no respect at all for fishermen. We were a big zero," says Robichaud. "Roméo was embarrassed by it. Davis didn't treat us any better than if we were a group of students. In fact, he probably would have spent more time with them."

When fishermen in southeast New Brunswick decided to transform their association into a union, in the winter of 1973, they were motivated by a vague idea that, as Léandre Babineau had said, a union meant "more power." For one thing, they believed, a union would give them the right to sit at the table with the companies and negotiate the price of fish. For another, they thought, a union, financed by dues collected from its own members, would be more independent in its fight with government over questions of resource management. The association, on the other hand, was financed largely by government grants.

But in reality, the fishermen didn't know much about unions. Although a few had been union members in the past, most had gained their experience from the co-operative movement. They knew how co-ops functioned, but they had a lot of questions about how a union would work and what form it would take. So shortly after making the decision to unionize, they went looking for answers.

In Canada, two unions had inshore fishermen in their membership. The youngest was the Newfoundland Fishermen, Food and Allied Workers Union (NFFAWU). In the fall of 1973, Gilles Thériault had written a letter to its president, Richard Cashin, who, along with Father Des McGrath, had been one of the original organizers. "The Fishermen's Association has just given me the mandate of conducting a study with them on the possibility and feasibility of forming a union," Thériault wrote. "As soon as this study is finished, and if positive, we would like to proceed immedi-

During their stopover in Ottawa, New Brunswick fishermen met with Fisheries Minister Jack Davis (standing, right), but he didn't have time to chat. He stayed long enough to have his picture taken with the fishermen—each would receive a copy—and to answer a few questions. (CEA COLLECTION L'EVANGELINE E26942)

ately to organize such a union." He asked Cashin for all the material he had "in terms of constitution, structure, legislation, etc." He also asked for a meeting. New Brunswick fishermen wanted to go to Newfoundland to see for themselves how a union of fishermen worked.

Thériault also wrote to representatives of the UFAWU in British Columbia. Although there were inshore fishermen and trawler and plant workers in both unions, there were at least two striking differences between the NFFAWU and the UFAWU. The British Columbia union, founded in 1945, didn't have collective bargaining legislation for its inshore members. It had, however, built a reputation as a militant union and, through a series of boycotts, strikes, and demonstrations, had succeeded in winning voluntary recognition from the major fish companies. It negotiated contracts with them for the price of fish. As the union's secretary-treasurer Jack Nichol explained to Gilles Thériault in a letter in 1973, "With respect to [inshore] fishermen, all of the Union's jurisdiction has been established without benefit of labour legislation but by the determination of the fishermen membership to strike if the companies and/or owners refuse to bargain. Consequently, we have had many strikes in our history but we also have the highest standards for fishermen anywhere."

On the other hand, the Newfoundland union did have collective bargaining legislation. Cashin and McGrath had begun organizing inshore fishermen in 1969. In 1970, the Northern Fishermen's Union was founded on the St Barbe coast with a membership of 100. As in British Columbia, fishermen in Newfoundland were not legally allowed to unionize because, under the Labour Relations Act, they were not considered employees. But the union made legislation a priority, and incredibly, in June 1971, not long after the union began, Joey Smallwood's Liberal government passed the Fishing Industry (Collective Bargaining) Act, which gave negotiating rights to self-employed fishermen. At the time, it was hailed as the most progressive and comprehensive labour legislation in Canada. In the union's newspaper, *Union Forum,* Richard Cashin wrote, "That was a historic day for Newfoundland fishermen, for it finally, after centuries of helpless exploitation, placed firmly in their hands the means by which they can control their own destiny."

The second major difference between the two unions was affiliation. Within six months of its formation, the Northern Fishermen's Union merged with the Canadian Food and Allied Workers Union (CFAWU) to become the NFFAWU. The CFAWU was an affiliate of the Amalgamated Meat Cutters and Butcher Workmen, a powerful American union headquartered in Chicago. The international (read American) affiliation meant an immediate influx of funds with which to organize, but it was obviously not without critics, even among NFFAWU members. In August 1971, Cashin wrote, "Even in this short time, we have been given ample opportunity to prove to those who criticized the connection with a powerful international union that without that union's strength and influence we could never have tackled the enormous challenge that faces us."

The UFAWU in British Columbia, in contrast, was staunchly independent and prided itself on being the only union in Canada dominated and therefore controlled by workers in the fishing industry. "True some fishermen are organized," Jack Nichol wrote to Thériault, "but the unions to which they belong are principally occupied in other fields." (The UFAWU was also a much more radical union. Its president, Homer Stevens, was a communist. Gordon Inglis, in his book on the Newfoundland union, maintains that Cashin and McGrath considered joining the UFAWU at one point but decided against it for that reason. "Cashin and McGrath were alarmed by the B.C. union's reputation for being Communist-led," Inglis writes.)

These were some of the issues and questions swirling around in New Brunswick fishermen's heads as they boarded an Air Canada 727 for St John's, Newfoundland, on a sunny day in mid-January 1974. The group included Léandre Babineau, then president of the Professional Fishermen's Association of Southeast New Brunswick, Bill McIntyre, Gilles Jacob from Petit-Cap, Rodney Walton from Murray Corner, and Gilles Thériault. They spent four days meeting with the Newfoundland union's executive and visiting fishing communities to talk to union members.

The Newfoundland union was still young, still in the throes of organizing, though it already had 2,000 inshore fishermen, 800 offshore fishermen, and 5,000 plant workers in its membership. There was a lot of enthusiasm and a lot of excitement as Newfoundland fishermen told the visitors about the gains the union had made. Two years earlier, the companies had paid 15 cents a pound for shrimp; today, 22 cents. Two years earlier, the price of cod had stood at 5 cents a pound; today, 13. The New Brunswickers, who had been getting 6 cents a pound for cod, looked at each other and shook their heads. They were impressed and encouraged.

At the same time, they were uncomfortable about the union's international affiliation. For too long, the Acadian fishery had been controlled by foreigners, first by Jerseymen, then by Americans. If inshore fishermen were finally going to take some control—and this was still only a dream—they weren't about to turn around and pass that control to someone else, not even to a union. Most of the delegation didn't speak English. They were already a minority and couldn't imagine being part of a union where fishermen—especially French-speaking ones—would be even more of a minority. They were genuinely afraid of outsiders trying to tell them what to do. Richard Cashin confirmed their worst fears when he offered help in organizing. "Cashin suggested that if we wanted to organize a union, they could have somebody sent down from Toronto to help us," recalls Gilles Thériault. "Just that notion sort of left the fishermen reluctant."

Two months later, with fishermen from the northeast in their group, the New Brunswickers went to British Columbia, where they met with the west-coast union, a visit that was more reassuring. "On the West Coast, they really reinforced what we were feeling," says Thériault. "That you can do it on your own, you don't need to join a big union."

The British Columbia union's Jack Nichol also didn't think that New Brunswick fishermen needed to worry about getting collective bargaining legislation. His union's members didn't have it but negotiated with the companies, anyway. On that question, the New Brunswickers were less sure. The UFAWU had not only inshore fishermen but also plant and trawler workers in its membership. It had the numbers, and it had the power to shut down the industry.

In the Maritimes, the industry was already fragmented. Some trawler workers in Nova Scotia and Prince Edward Island were members of the Canadian Brotherhood of Railway, Transport and General Workers; others belonged to the Canadian Food and Allied Workers Union. Many plant workers also belonged to the CFAWU or the Canadian Seafood Workers Union. In southeast New Brunswick, plant workers were not unionized.

While New Brunswick fishermen could dream and even talk about "one big union," for the moment they didn't think that it was realistic. They believed that their union should remain a union of inshore fishermen only—at least for the foreseeable future—which they preferred, even though they realized that it placed limitations on their bargaining power. Without plant and trawler workers in their ranks, they probably *wouldn't* be strong enough to shut down the industry if the companies refused to negotiate. Forcing them to negotiate because they were obligated by law seemed to be the next best thing. When the fishermen reflected on how fast Newfoundland had passed legislation, they didn't think that it seemed like such a difficult challenge.

Nevertheless, the visit to British Columbia was exhilarating. By day, the New Brunswickers met with the union's executive and visited fishermen along the coast. By night, back in their Vancouver hotel rooms, they discussed and debated the issues. "The fishermen were really fired up," Thériault recalls. "We were all determined to go home and to go to every village in the region and tell fishermen what this—what a union—could do for them."

They also realized, however, that their union would have to include fishermen from across the Maritimes, because the fish companies bought fish in all three provinces. Otherwise, one group of fishermen could be played off against another. If fishermen in New Brunswick went on strike, for example, a company could just increase its purchases from fishermen in Nova Scotia. For Acadian fishermen to make such a concession represented a major break from the isolationist mentality of the past.

After a week on the British Columbia coast, the fishermen flew home, determined more than ever to organize a union of fishermen.

*   *   *   *   *

The first major task facing the fishermen on their return was to get a majority of fishermen on-side. By late 1973, the Professional Fishermen's Association of Southeast New Brunswick had claimed a membership of 600 out of a possible total of 1,400 inshore fishermen and helpers in the region. There were another 2,000 in the northeast and 1,500 in the Bay of Fundy, not to mention thousands more in Nova Scotia and Prince Edward Island. Expanding their base would be a slow process.

There were two major hurdles. One was the threat of having to go on strike. Fishermen throughout the Gulf of St Lawrence were, and still are, mostly lobster fishermen. In some places, on Prince Edward Island in particular, lobster accounts for up to 80 percent of a fisherman's income. Often, most of the catch is landed in the first few weeks of the season. "That's the only time we could hurt the company by striking," Adrice Doiron explains. "But the fishermen were scared. How in hell could they strike when the fish are here?"

While fishermen in Newfoundland are mostly cod fishermen and after a strike can just pick up where they left off, lobster fishermen in the Maritimes, and especially in the Gulf of St Lawrence, can't do that. Seasons are short and, as a rule, can't be extended. There are two seasons in the gulf. In northeast New Brunswick, along the Northumberland shore in Nova Scotia, and in the eastern part of Prince Edward Island, lobster season runs from the beginning of

May to the end of June. In July, lobsters begin to moult in order to expand their size. They then grow a new shell that in the beginning is soft and full of water, which makes them unappealing to consumers. In southeast New Brunswick, in western Prince Edward Island, and on the western side of the Northumberland Shore, the season goes from mid-August to mid-October, when the weather begins to turn cold and the gulf starts to freeze. (Lobster season on the Atlantic coast of Nova Scotia and in the Bay of Fundy runs for six months, beginning in late November.)

Many fishermen feared that if they missed the first few weeks of lobster season, they would, in all likelihood, lose the whole season and, with it, most of their year's income. It was a fear whose importance was vastly underestimated by union organizers at the time. The unwillingness of lobster fishermen to strike—probably more than any other single factor—would undercut the bargaining power of the Maritime Fishermen's Union in the years to come.

The second hurdle involved geography and logistics: how to organize fishermen who were spread out in hundreds of isolated villages. It was even difficult at the time to pinpoint who was an inshore fishermen because there were so many part-timers.

In a strike at a company, employees walk out of the plant and put up a picket line that, in theory at least, keeps others from working and the company from operating. This shutdown—and potential loss of income to the company—is supposed to convince the company to negotiate. "With our fishermen, there are hundreds in the southeast, and they're all spread out along 300 miles of shoreline with about 50 landing places. If you go on strike, how do you control that?" asks Adrice Doiron. There was no guarantee that any company could be shut down and no guarantee that fishermen would even stick together when faced with the possible loss of nearly a year's income.

Association members decided that recruitment would have to go hand in hand with an education program that taught fishermen something about union solidarity. Members organized information sessions, using the University of Moncton campus and recruiting the help of academics who knew something about the fishery, union history, and organizing.

In the spring of 1974, on the heels of their visit out west, association members decided to test the strength of support for a union and organized a vote among inshore captains in the 11 main fishing ports in the southeast.

The association had calculated that there were 915 boat-owning fishermen in the southeast. Of these, 578 came out to mark a ballot: 466 of them said yes, in principle, to a union; 112 said no. That meant that slightly more than 50 percent of all boat-owning fishermen in the southeast were prepared to support the concept. Association executive secretary Gilles Thériault, along with members of the association executive, went ahead and drafted a model of what the union would look like. "The biggest fear at that time was that the fishermen wouldn't have control of the union," says Thériault, "so our challenge was to come up with something that would guarantee them control. We took some things that we liked from the models in Newfoundland and B.C., but we adapted them to our own situation. In the end, we came up with a model that provided local autonomy but in a centralized organization."

The model was this: Each village where a majority of fishermen favoured a union would form a local, and each local would then have a representative on a regional council. There would be a regional council for each of the three fishing regions in the province (northeast, southeast, Bay of Fundy). In turn, two representatives from each regional council would sit on a provincial council. The provincial council would also have a full-time paid elected president and secretary-treasurer.

The union would also have committees—for example, one that would negotiate with companies for the price of fish. At first, the fishermen thought that negotiating could be done company by company. Later, they realized that given the number of companies in New Brunswick (more than 100) and the number of species (some fishermen were involved in a dozen fisheries), bargaining with every company for every species would be an impossible and never-ending task. It would make more sense to negotiate one contract per species across the board with all the buyers in one region. (This is the process that was eventually adopted. Once the MFU was certified as the bargaining agent in the northeast and southeast, the companies set up a buyers' bargaining association to negotiate on their behalf.)

The proposed structure of the union was democratic in the extreme. Every year, for example, each local would have the opportunity to vote again on whether to continue its membership, something unheard of in other unions and something that could lead to the union's demise after only a year. It was also a model that would prove cumbersome and unworkable. (There were 19 locals in New Brunswick when the MFU was officially founded in 1977, and any major decision required a meeting of each. They were amalgamated later that year into one local in the northeast and one in the southeast. Later, when locals were formed in other provinces, a Maritime council was set up, and its membership included the executive of each local, plus a president, vice president, and secretary-treasurer. The council met every three months to deal with business arising between annual conventions.)

For the time being, however, it was a structure that fishermen liked. It seemed to promise village autonomy, something that fishermen treasured. It also seemed to guarantee fishermen a voice. If they didn't agree with what was happening in the union, they could simply withdraw in the annual vote.

In the spring of 1975, a second vote was taken. This time, 70 percent of inshore fishermen in southeast New Brunswick said yes to forming a union.

* * * * *

It wasn't long after fishermen in the southeast had decided to transform their association into a union that they began to make contacts with fishermen in the other two regions of the province. As early as 1974, fishermen like Adrice Doiron travelled to southwest New Brunswick, to hold meetings with fishermen in the Bay of Fundy. A year earlier, Bay of Fundy inshore fishermen had formed a weir fishermen's association, and initially, there was some interest in merging with the Professional Fishermen's Association of Southeast New Brunswick. Several meetings were held over the next couple of years. "Fishermen from the Bay of Fundy seem to agree with the idea of a *regroupement*," Gilles Thériault wrote in one of his reports.

After the Maritime Fishermen's Union was officially founded, Thériault returned to the Bay of Fundy several times. At one point, 200 fishermen there signed union cards. But attempts to bring them into the union would eventually fail for several reasons. Fishermen in the Bay of Fundy didn't speak the same language as the majority of fishermen in eastern New Brunswick. The fishery there was also dominated by offshore herring seiners: workers on the larger vessels outnumbered inshore fishermen by four to one. Perhaps most important, fishermen from the Bay of Fundy didn't share the same fishing grounds. As a result, their working conditions—their seasons, their quotas, even their methods of fishing—were different from those of fishermen in the Gulf of St Lawrence. When it came to fighting the federal Department of Fisheries over specific issues, fishermen in the Bay of Fundy had more in common with their counterparts across the bay in Nova Scotia.

Fishermen in southeast New Brunswick, for their part, began to realize that it made more sense to develop links with fishermen in "the same puddle"—the Gulf of St Lawrence. The most logical next step was to bring fishermen in the northeast of the province into the union.

In the late 1960s, fishermen on the Acadian Peninsula had also organized an association, the Association Professionnelle des Pêcheurs du Nord-est (APPNE). APPNE brought together not only inshore fishermen but also midshore captains. Fishermen had help in organizing the association from Father Pierre Beaugé, a priest from France who worked as a "social animator" for the northeast regional development council (CRAN), as well as from Eustache Duguay and Réal Chiasson, both of whom worked for the extension department of St Francis Xavier University. Although founded with great enthusiasm, the association of inshore and midshore fishermen didn't last. Within a year, some of the inshore members began to drift away. They believed that their interests couldn't be properly represented in a group that included and, in fact, was dominated by trawler captains.

Nonetheless, there remained pockets of active, interested fishermen who did not abandon the idea of an organization for the inshore sector. Val Comeau, a village of several hundred, was one. In 1972, fishermen there organized an association that brought together 110 skippers and 90 helpers from villages in the surrounding area. The group got a grant from the Company of Young Canadians (CYC) and hired Réginald Comeau, who was working part time for the local school board.

Born and raised in Val Comeau, Comeau was one of nine children. His father was an inshore fisherman, a life that provided few amenities for a growing family. One of Comeau's strongest childhood memories is a box that came every Christmas from an aunt in Montréal. It was filled with oranges, clothing, sometimes a few toys. "For us, that was Christmas," Comeau recalls. "We looked forward to that box."

Comeau's father was a doer, a founder of the Val Comeau *caisse populaire* and president of the APPNE local in the village. "He was always involved in something," Comeau says, "and he gave us the desire to get involved in the community as well." But Comeau and his brothers and sisters were discouraged from going into the fishery. "My parents placed little value on manual labour," he says, "especially work in the fishery. At that point, fishing was still something you did if you weren't capable of doing anything else. They wanted us to get an education." All of the Comeau children received technical or university training after high school.

After he graduated with an education degree from the University of Moncton in 1972, Comeau became interested in what he calls "political work" with fishermen, rather than in teaching children. He was well suited to the job. Quiet and unassuming, he was liked immediately by fishermen in the northeast. He was one of them— his father, after all, was a fisherman. Comeau became the organizer in the northeast, the friend of the fishermen, the person they called for information or for help with their taxes, the one they depended on to help them deal with government. He became a pillar of stability, for the fishermen and for the union.

When Comeau was hired by the fishermen's association in Val Comeau, his first assignment was to establish a co-operative in the village. The fishermen wanted to take over a fish plant whose owner was about to retire. Not only would the plant buy and market their fish, but it would also provide employment for their families. The United Maritime Fishermen, however, well into its centralizing phase, wanted Val Comeau fishermen to join the co-op in Lamèque.

So the idea was dropped, though Réginald Comeau continued to work with fishermen in his home village to build their association. Fishermen in the Caraquet area had also shown an interest in forming an association. In early 1973, fishermen Louis Godin of Maisonnette and Paul Chiasson of Anse-Bleue—both of whom had helped set up APPNE five years earlier—invited Comeau to speak at a meeting, and a second fishermen's association was formed. Later that year, fishermen from the Pigeon Hill area also formed an association. The following winter, a fourth association sprang up on Miscou Island and a fifth in the Pointe-Verte/Bathurst/Petit-Rocher area. As in the southeast, the impetus for the formation of all these associations was increasing government regulation and a growing desire on the part of fishermen to have input into the price of fish.

By 1973, CRAN, like CRASE, was moving towards organizing the sectors that formed the basis of the Acadian economy. Following a "day of reflection" organized on the peninsula after two sister vessels sank within months of each other, CRAN decided to focus its energies on the inshore, not the midshore, fishery: there were more inshore fishermen, and they were worse off. In 1974, CRAN hired Réginald Comeau full time to organize inshore fishermen. He was joined a few months later by Jean-Marie Nadeau, a University of Moncton graduate who had been working for the CYC. That summer, Comeau and Nadeau went to a CYC conference where they met Gilles Thériault and Fred Winsor, another CYC worker, who was organizing fishermen in Nova Scotia.

In 1975, CRAN and CRASE set up the Centre de Formation au Développement (CFD), an adult-education centre that conducted research on the fisheries. Its board members included Gilles Thériault and Paul-Eugène LeBlanc, an original employee of CRASE and, later, of the Professional Fishermen's Association of Southeast New Brunswick. The same year, the board hired Omer Chouinard to do research out of the CRASE office in Richibucto.

Chouinard was born in Anse-aux-Gascons, on the Gaspé Peninsula. His father, a fisherman, wanted his sons to follow in his footsteps, but Chouinard's mother disagreed and encouraged her children to get an education. Chouinard went to the University of Moncton and Laval University before going to work for a social development council in Montréal. In 1974, he was finishing up one contract and about to sign another when he met Gilles Thériault through Paul-Eugène LeBlanc. Thériault had gone to Montréal looking for people to help organize the fishermen's union. Chouinard's wife, Monique Gauvin, was an Acadian from Pacquetville, New Brunswick, and she wanted to go home to begin research for her masters thesis on the co-operative movement. So in the spring of 1975, the two arrived in Moncton.

Réginald Comeau became the MFU organizer in northeast New Brunswick. (COURTESY REGINALD COMEAU)

Initially, Chouinard was nervous about working with Acadian fishermen. Being from Québec, he knew that he would be viewed as an outsider. But he was sympathetic to the cause. He saw inshore fishermen as one of the most exploited groups of workers in the country. Like Thériault, he considered himself a socialist. "Omer was seen as being more hard-lined than Gilles," one Richibucto fisherman recalls. "He was so radical that a lot of people were scared of him at first."

Yet by the time he returned to Montréal in 1983, Chouinard had endeared himself to fishermen throughout the Maritimes. They appreciated his analytical abilities and had learned to live with his radicalism. He was a hard, hard worker who often forgot to eat. He was the classic union organizer—a persistent, single-minded workaholic. "Omer was a special guy," says Valmond Johnson from Richibucto Village. "He would never give up. Even if you were against the union, he would sit with you for 24 hours. He wouldn't win you over maybe, but he'd get you on his side."

But Chouinard also had a comical, absent-minded streak. When the going was rough, fishermen often told Chouinard stories to make them laugh and to ease the stress. One time, during a membership drive on Prince Edward Island, going door to door from dawn to dusk, he took off his shoes at one house on entering and put on one of the fisherman's shoes on leaving. Chouinard was so preoccupied that he didn't notice as he limped back to his hotel wearing one brown shoe and one black shoe and wondering why his foot hurt. There are many such stories, and they have been told over and over again.

Over the years, many people would work for the MFU, but most would burn out quickly and stay only a short time. Gilles Thériault, Réginald Comeau, and Omer Chouinard, on the other hand, would be in it for the long haul. "For us, it was an incredible *formation*," says a Richibucto Village fisherman. "The respect we had for Gilles and Omer and Réginald—for us, they were like our professors."

*   *   *   *   *

In a sense, the presence of Thériault, Comeau, and Chouinard foreshadowed the coming together of fishermen in the southeast and fishermen in the northeast. By this time, Comeau, in the northeast, was beginning to question the value of organizing several small associations. To him, the associations seemed too localized, leaving fishermen still too divided. He believed that if fishermen's organizations were to have any real power, they had to go beyond single villages. There had to be some way of bringing all these little groups together. Comeau, along with Jean-Marie Nadeau, en-

With the hiring of Omer Chouinard in 1975, a strong triad of non-fishermen leadership was now in place. (CEA COLLECTION L'EVANGELINE E36,272)

Val Comeau fisherman Herménégilde
Robichaud became an MFU leader in
northeast New Brunswick.
(COURTESY MFU)

couraged fishermen to form one large association. In January 1975, the Regroupement of Inshore Fishermen of Northeast New Brunswick brought together five associations from 20 communities. The president was Jean-Claude Robichaud of Val Comeau.

Robichaud's involvement in the association was relatively short-lived; in fact, his younger brother Herménégilde would emerge as a major MFU leader in the northeast. "The most important guy in the northeast was Herménégilde," Neguac fisherman Zoël Robichaud recalls. "He was more shy at the beginning, like me. He always had his bottle of 7-UP with him, always put in a little mix before going to a meeting. You always knew when his face got red, there was no problem. He could defend us. We always appreciated Herménégilde for things like that." Then in his early thirties, Robichaud was a few years older than Réginald Comeau. "Herménégilde is a very emotional person," Comeau says. "Back then, he operated very much on a gut feeling that fishermen were being mistreated. He was more interested in blasting the bureaucrats than sitting down and doing an analysis, although once he got involved, that didn't take long to come."

Like many fishermen, Robichaud could read and write only with great difficulty. But he could sit through hours and hours of meetings that jumped back and forth between French and English, and remember enough to recount details to fishermen back home. Robichaud was a strong Acadian nationalist. In future, after the number of anglophone fishermen in the union increased, he continually defended the right of Acadian fishermen to participate in meetings in their own language. "If I spoke in English for too long during a meeting," recalls Gilles Thériault, who eventually handled the task of translating, "Herménégilde would jump on me, demanding equal treatment for the Acadians in the room." Robichaud was a hard-liner who would become the conscience of the MFU on linguistic questions and on general matters of principle.

Shortly after the Regroupement was founded, Jack Nichol of the British Columbia fishermen's union came to Caraquet and spent three days with fishermen. Later that spring, Nichol returned, for the southeast association's annual meeting at the Catholic church in Richibucto. Some of the fishermen from the northeast attended. Nichol encouraged the fishermen to organize a union. "It won't be easy," he said, "but it is the only thing that will give you power. We started fighting 35 years ago, and we're still fighting."

Two months after Nichol's visit, with fishermen in the northeast in the midst of lobster season, a major storm swept down the coast, destroying more than 100,000 lobster traps. Because of joint pressure from the northeast and southeast associations, 540 fishermen received government compensation worth half a million dollars.

In 1976, the two groups decided to adopt a new tactic: withholding their lobster catch from the larger companies in an attempt to force them to negotiate price. In late April, as the season was about to begin in the northeast, Jean-Claude Robichaud announced the first boycott. The going price was the same as the previous year's, 90 cents a pound for canners, and $1.10 for markets. Fishermen, Robichaud said, wanted more.

Some Prince Edward Island and Nova Scotia fishermen in the Northumberland Strait decided to join the boycott. The president of the Northumberland Fishermen's Association, Marcel Tremblay, announced that fishermen would withhold their catch from the three major buyers "in an effort to bolster prices and change their status as beggars."

In mid-August 1976, as the season was opening in southeast New Brunswick, fishermen there also announced a boycott. They organized a major publicity campaign—with a flyer that included instructions on how to boil lobster—and sold most of their catch to tourists on the wharf at prices higher than those the companies had offered. "The lobster boycotts really scared the shit out of the companies," recalls Richibucto Village fisherman Jean-Guy Maillet. "Lobster was more scarce back then, and I knew one fisherman in

Cap-Pelé who sold half a ton the first day to tourists. That was a big cut out of the companies, you know, and it really scared them."

Although none of the companies agreed to sit down and negotiate with the fishermen, they did increase lobster prices the following year. Whether it was a direct consequence of the boycotts or simply of a fluctuation in the market was irrelevant. Fishermen began to believe that through united, militant action, they could influence the price of fish.

The lobster boycotts also helped draw in fishermen from other parts of the Gulf of St Lawrence.

In late 1976, the southeast and northeast associations organized two leadership training sessions—one at Inkerman and one at Richibucto. Forty fishermen, potential leaders, were chosen to take the course, which lasted eight weeks and provided an in-depth grounding in the principles of trade unionism. The leadership courses of the past now seemed superficial in comparison, as people with a wealth of experience and knowledge were invited from around the region.

Charlie Murray, a long-time organizer (now deceased) for the Canadian Seamen's Union, talked about the first major attempt by fishermen and plant workers to organize a union at Lockeport, Nova Scotia, in 1939. Lawrence Wilneff of the Canadian Seafood Workers Union talked about problems that he had faced in organizing plant workers in Nova Scotia. Dalhousie University professors Rick Williams and Sandy Siegel presented research that they had done on the growing monopolization in Atlantic Canada's fishing industry.

For the fishermen, unused to the discipline of a classroom and the rigours of intellectual debate, it was an intensive, stimulating time. For fishermen in the northeast in particular, it was a turning point. By the end of the course, they decided that what they wanted—what they needed—was also a union of fishermen.

CONNECTIONS: A FIGHTING MARITIME UNION IS BORN

The Maritime Fishermen's Union has taken the road of a fighting union. This means that the MFU, contrary to the old associations, was taking an orientation that would strongly defend the survival of the inshore fishermen, counting on our own energy and in conjunction with the labour movement.
—MFU convention, December 1977—

FOR FISHERMEN in southeast and northeast New Brunswick who wanted a union, getting a majority of fishermen to support the concept was the first major challenge. By the end of 1976, fishermen began to feel that they were making progress, though it wasn't easy. Given the number of fishing villages and the distances between them, much of the time was still consumed by knocking on doors or visiting wharves, trying to convince other fishermen of the validity of the idea.

The effort was made more difficult by the fact that fishermen didn't have the legal right to unionize. The province's Industrial Relations Act covered only workers in a traditional employer-employee relationship; boat-owning inshore fishermen were not. While fishermen were following the usual union-organizing proce-dure—getting fishermen to sign union cards and pay a two-dollar fee—they were, in effect, asking them to sign up for something that was, at the time, little more than a promise.

The companies flaunted the situation to their advantage. "Our company always obeys the law in regard to unions when certified by a majority of a unit," Jim Bateman, manager of National Sea's Paturel plant in Shédiac, wrote to the Professional Fishermen's Association of Southeast New Brunswick. But the fishermen were *not* certified, and Bateman knew it. They didn't have legislation that "enabled" them to be. Obtaining such enabling legislation would be their next major challenge.

Soon after they had returned from Vancouver, fishermen had

begun the process. In June 1974, they met with Deputy Minister of Labour Ray Campbell to discuss what the government could do to make a union of fishermen possible. Campbell promised to investigate. They also asked for a meeting with Labour Minister Rodman Logan, but Logan didn't agree to see them until more than a year later. The meeting, held in Fredericton in August 1975, was also attended by Agriculture Minister Malcolm MacLeod and Fisheries Minister Omer Léger. The reception was similar to the one the fishermen had received from Jack Davis in Ottawa. "Logan was very arrogant," Gilles Thériault recalls. "He acted like we didn't know what we were talking about and we didn't know what we wanted." Adds Réginald Comeau, "He treated us like children."

Thériault and Comeau came out of the meeting expressing disappointment. "Provincial government officials say publicly that fishermen should organize, but they're not very enthusiastic about the idea of a union," Thériault told the media. A month later, Fisheries Minister Léger told the Moncton *Times-Transcript*, "We are of the opinion that fishermen should have a respected body which can make its position heard, but a fisherman is an independent businessman. You don't negotiate a price for a product as you would negotiate a salary."

Despite his apparent disinterest, Labour Minister Logan set up an interdepartmental committee to study the question. An internal report, never made public, was forwarded a year later to the Policies and Priorities Committee, headed by Premier Richard Hatfield. In April 1976, Hatfield established the province's first Select Committee on Fisheries, to hold public hearings the following February on the question of collective bargaining for fishermen.

In the meantime, fishermen continued to meet with government officials, who alternated between expressing confusion about procedure and suggesting that the proposed union did not have majority support from fishermen, anyway. "We lost a lot of time talking to politicians," fisherman Jean-Guy Maillet recalls. "But it was part of our *formation*—we had to go through that stage. I remember guys like Gilles and Omer saying, 'What the hell do you want to meet with the minister for?' But again, that's the way fishermen were brought up, to depend on the local politician."

By early 1977, fishermen began to feel that they were getting nowhere. "The fishermen were getting worn down thinking that they'd never have an organization," says Gilles Thériault. So they decided to found their union and fight for enabling legislation later. In February, fishermen from Baie-Ste-Anne south to the Nova Scotia border formed a dozen locals in as many villages in preparation for the founding meeting in March.

When the Maritime Fishermen's Union was officially established in Baie-Ste-Anne, it was almost anti-climactic. "It was like a sigh of relief," recalls Thériault. "Fishermen had been working on the idea for three years." Nevertheless, besides allowing fishermen to adopt a constitution and elect leadership, the founding meeting renewed their determination to fight for an effective organization.

They came out of the meeting and went on the offensive. In April, they stormed the offices of Associated Fisheries of Canada Limited, the main lobster buyer in the northeast. Plant manager Eric Robichaud had agreed to negotiate lobster prices, then changed his mind, saying that the company would negotiate only when the union was certified. "It was the first time we had ever occupied company offices," recalls Val Comeau fisherman Herménégilde Robichaud. "There was about 150 fishermen. Jean-Marie Nadeau [MFU staff] was with us. It lasted about one day. The company guy phoned the police to come and get us, but the officer said we weren't breaking anything, so there was nothing he could do. In the end, the company didn't negotiate prices, anyway."

In early August, on the eve of lobster season in the southeast, nearly 100 fishermen marched on the E.P. Melanson plant in Cocagne and the National Sea plant in Shédiac, the two major lobster buyers in that region. National Sea's Jim Bateman came out to speak to them. Bateman agreed that his company's price was low, but he argued that its profit margin could not allow for the increases that the fishermen were demanding. (The company was paying $1.10 for canners and $1.25 for markets; the fishermen wanted $1.30 and $1.65 respectively.) "Shareholders have not received dividends for several years," Bateman told the crowd, "and the company's profit is one percent of its sales. Would you stay in business if you were making a profit like that?" E.P. Melanson and National Sea, like Associated Fisheries, also refused to negotiate with the MFU until it was legally certified.

Fishermen continued their protest and later, when the season began, launched another boycott. This one, however, was less

Richard Hatfield refused to move on collective bargaining legislation, even though his Select Committee on Fisheries had recommended in favour.
(CEA COLLECTION L'EVANGELINGE E37,872)

successful than the one the year before. Faced with record landings, fishermen were not able to withhold enough lobster to make even a dent in the companies' purchases. At the same time, they began to realize that until they could convince the provincial government to change the legislation, they would not be able to get the companies to take them seriously.

In June, MFU fishermen met with Richard Hatfield in Caraquet. Again, they emerged expressing disappointment. "The first thing the premier asked us was how we felt about a marketing board," Jean-Claude Robichaud told the press. Hatfield agreed to think about legislation, however, and to make a decision within two months.

Later that month, the report of Hatfield's Select Committee on Fisheries was released. It said that fishermen should "increase their participation in the marketing of their products" and should develop a better understanding of the marketplace so that their negotiations would be realistic. "The province," the report concluded, "should … foster mechanisms whereby fishermen can collectively bargain prices." The 1977 report would be the first in a long series of reports in all three Maritime provinces that would recommend inshore fishermen be given collective bargaining rights.

Within months, however, Hatfield informed fishermen that he would not proceed with legislation. "The premier said his main reasons were that he doesn't believe the MFU is fully representative of the fishermen," Baie-Ste-Anne fisherman Harold Manuel told the media, "and he isn't convinced that a union is the organization fishermen want." Manuel vowed that the MFU would continue its fight.

At the same time that the MFU was confronting the companies

In August 1977, MFU fishermen in New Brunswick demonstrated outside the E.P. Melanson plant in Cocagne (above) and the National Sea plant in Shédiac, demanding that the companies negotiate lobster prices.

(CEA COLLECTION L'EVANGELINE E9183/E9184)

and the government, it was also facing internal problems. Within weeks of the founding meeting, some fishermen began to feel uncomfortable with their president's approach towards company and government officials. To some, Rodrigue Brideau seemed too friendly, too accommodating. "Brideau tried to work both sides of the fence," recalls Manuel, "and the fishermen didn't like it. They wanted militancy."

When the MFU's Provincial Council finally removed Brideau, it gave several reasons: Brideau had met privately with the management of one of the companies (union fishermen had agreed that no one should ever meet alone with company or government officials); he had given information to a member of the Legislative Assembly that was supposed to be divulged later; and he had met alone with government members. The union's newsletter noted:

> The basic problem then is the following: our ex-president Rodrigue Brideau still believed that the best way to settle the problems of the fishermen was to collaborate politely with the companies and the government.... He had not understood that when we fishermen had got rid of our old associations in order to found our union, it was a way of saying no to collaboration with the companies and the government.

Manuel, the secretary-treasurer, took over as president. "Harold wasn't near as good a fisherman as he was working with the MFU," recalls Prince Edward Island fisherman Ivan Shaw, who became a good friend of Manuel's. "He had the experience by fishing, he was quick with the mind, he knew what he was talking about."

Almost 50, Manuel was an NDP supporter, a rarity in New Brunswick at the time, and he had a trade-union rhetoric that he had learned as a member of the United Auto Workers during a stint at General Motors in Ontario. "I had it in the back of my mind that in order to have something, you had to have the backing of a group. Not a small group, a large one," he says.

Manuel's first wife had deserted him in the early 1960s, leaving him to cope with half a dozen children, three of them still in diapers. When he remarried, his second wife rarely left his side. She came to the MFU office in Richibucto every day, travelled everywhere with Manuel, sat by his side at press conferences and conventions. Her constant presence eventually created problems and unneeded tension in the MFU. But for the time being, Manuel came into the president's job committed to the idea of a union for inshore fishermen and confident in his ability to make it work.

*   *   *   *   *

In the spring of 1977, not long after the Maritime Fishermen's Union was officially founded in New Brunswick, MFU locals were also established in Nova Scotia. Both the Guysborough County Fishermen's Association and the Northumberland Fishermen's Association voted to join the MFU after Gilles Thériault spoke at their annual meetings.

Some Nova Scotia fishermen, in fact, had been talking about a union for close to a decade. In the late 1960s, British Columbia fishermen's union representatives Jack Nichol and Homer Stevens had come east on a mission to organize the unorganized. They found a group of interested fishermen in the Canso area and decided to focus their energies there. By 1970, they had signed up inshore fishermen and trawler workers in the Canso, Mulgrave, and Petit-de-Grat area.

At the time, neither fishermen nor trawler workers had the right to unionize under the Nova Scotia Trade Union Act, and what followed was a 15-month strike for recognition. The situation was complicated by the fact that the United Fishermen and Allied Workers' Union (UFAWU) had been expelled in the early 1950s from the Trades and Labor Congress, the forerunner to the Canadian Labour Congress, for communist leanings. As the strike progressed, other unions got involved in what amounted to a raid. The dispute turned bitter, and the UFAWU—facing violent opposition not only from government and companies but also from organized labour itself—eventually lost and went home. The trawler workers were absorbed by the Canadian Brotherhood of Railway, Transport and General Workers—after Gerald Regan's Liberal government amended the Trade Union Act to allow them to join a union—but inshore fishermen remained as they had always been, unorganized and without collective bargaining rights.

Although the dispute left fishermen in a foul mood for a few years, it was formative for several who would later play key roles in the MFU: Con Mills of Louisbourg, who worked for the UFAWU in

Canso, as well as out west after the strike failed, but who returned to the province in 1979 and became an inshore fisherman; Edison Lumsden, president of the UFAWU local in Canso, who later became president of the MFU local in Guysborough County and vice president of the union; Jamie MacKenzie, a Canso fisherman in his early fifties who was considered by many to be the intellectual in the group; and Everett Richardson, whose name was made famous by Silver Donald Cameron's account of the 1970-71 strike.

Nova Scotia's fishery is the largest in Atlantic Canada. In 1979, for example, when the total landed value of fish and seafood was $53 million in New Brunswick, it was $215 million in Nova Scotia, $156 million in Newfoundland, $39 million in Québec, and $29 million in Prince Edward Island. On Canada's east coast, Nova Scotia has historically led the way, both in landings and value, while New Brunswick and Prince Edward Island have generally trailed a distant third and fifth respectively, though the fishery is important to the economy of both provinces.

In Nova Scotia, the inshore fishery is the backbone of hundreds of villages along the coast. During the 1970s, there were an estimated 10,000 inshore fishermen in the province.

Nova Scotia's fishery is also the most diversified in the region. Inshore fishermen in eastern New Brunswick, on Prince Edward Island, and along the Northumberland shore in Nova Scotia all fish in the Gulf of St Lawrence, and their multipurpose fishery is relatively homogeneous. They fish five to six months a year, depending on ice conditions, and share basically the same fish stocks, seasons, gear, and markets. But such uniformity was and is not the case in Nova Scotia as a whole. Fishermen in Cape Breton, Canso, and along the Eastern Shore depend heavily on groundfish, as well as on lobster and herring, and face constant competition from the offshore fleets.

In southwest Nova Scotia, fishermen fish 10 to 12 months a year, with close proximity to rich groundfish, lobster, and scallop grounds and direct access to the Boston market. In 1979, the catch of fishermen in Yarmouth, Digby, Shelburne, and Lunenburg counties—the four counties making up the southwest region—accounted for 70 percent of the total landed value of fish and seafood in the province. Southwest Nova Scotia was the area provincial politicians talked about when they talked about the fishery.

In southwest Nova Scotia, inshore fishermen work most of the year, with close proximity to rich scallop grounds. (COURTESY DFO HALIFAX)

Throughout the 1970s, scallops rivalled groundfish as the number-one species in Nova Scotia in landed value, though the fishery across the Maritimes remained overwhelmingly dominated by groundfish—by cod in particular. By 1974, the groundfish fishery was in crisis, and inshore fishermen in Nova Scotia were feeling the effects. They, like fishermen elsewhere in the region, were facing problems with government regulation and industry concentration.

More than any other fishery, Nova Scotia's has been dominated by the large companies. By the middle of the 1970s, the two industry giants had emerged: H.B. Nickerson and Sons Ltd of North Sydney and National Sea Products Ltd of Halifax. In April 1977, the *Globe and Mail* called National Sea "Canada's largest groundfish company," with seven major plants in the four Atlantic provinces, a variety of smaller ones, a fleet of deep-sea trawlers, and extensive fishery operations in Rockland, Maine, and Tampa, Florida. Nickerson, meanwhile, had a fleet of 40 vessels and seven major plants. The two companies had processing plants or buying stations almost everywhere in the region.

When, in the summer of 1977, Nickerson, the smaller of the two, announced that it had taken over National Sea, creating one giant fish company, the *Globe and Mail* noted, "The merger leaves only about a dozen reasonably-sized independents and fishing co-operatives in Nova Scotia, plus affiliates of several national and multinational companies." (The multinationals included Usen Fisheries of Boston, Massachusetts, with plants in Nova Scotia and Prince Edward Island, and B.C. Packers Ltd and Connors Brothers Ltd, both subsidiaries of George Weston Ltd, with plants in Nova Scotia and New Brunswick.)

Stephen Kimber, in *Net Profits: The Story of National Sea,* writes that the takeover of National Sea by Nickerson "rocked the province's political and business establishment." It also sent shock waves throughout inshore-fishing communities. Although fishermen would later be proved wrong—the major companies would be on the verge of bankruptcy by the turn of the decade—at the time they thought that concentration was a trend that was likely to continue.

As early as 1974, organizing efforts had begun among inshore fishermen in Nova Scotia to combat the growing power of the large companies. That year, the Company of Young Canadians (CYC) hired a young Newfoundlander as a community organizer. Fred Winsor had worked with fishermen's co-ops on the Northern Peninsula in his home province. When he came to Nova Scotia, Canso seemed a likely place to start. Winsor found, however, that Canso fishermen were not that interested in organizing: many of them were still smarting from the strike.

Over the years, inshore fishermen in Nova Scotia, like their counterparts elsewhere, had belonged to co-ops organized under the umbrella of the United Maritime Fishermen. They were also members of associations, though the organizations were different things in different places. Some were based on type of gear, bringing together, for example, herring gillnetters in a particular area; others were simply local groups formed to get work done on a wharf. Most were crisis-oriented. "The Northumberland Fishermen's Association," recalls Antigonish fisherman Stuart Beaton, "would meet once a year and deal with whatever crisis was at hand. But there was no connection outside the immediate area. We didn't even know there were French-speaking people in New Brunswick." There was also no staff, no work done between meetings, and no continuity from one year to the next.

In the spring of 1975, a federal lobster task force, initiated by newly appointed fisheries minister Roméo LeBlanc because of the crisis in the industry, held hearings in Halifax, bringing together for the first time the various fishermen's associations in Nova Scotia. That summer, Fred Winsor, still on the CYC payroll, travelled across the province to talk to fishermen. In the fall, he began to work with an association on the Eastern Shore, on an issue of concern to many fishermen, the 200-mile limit.

The federal government had begun talking about introducing a 200-mile limit as a way of stopping foreign vessels from overexploiting the resource in Canadian waters. (As noted, groundfish landings in the Northwest Atlantic had decreased by about 40 percent between 1965 and 1974, and herring landings had dropped by more than 50 percent between 1969 and 1974. Yet offshore fleets were still fishing as hard as before.) In 1976, the Department of Fisheries unveiled the Atlantic Canada Groundfish Management Plan. It was the first attempt to limit fishing in what, a year later, would become Canadian waters. "All of a sudden," recalls Alphonse Cormier, today the department's director of resource allocation, "we were talking about quotas and seasons. That had been unheard of until then."

Inshore fishermen, however, were facing similar competition from the Canadian offshore fleet. They wanted a 50-mile limit to protect *their* rights—to keep the offshore vessels out of *their* waters. "In the build-up for the declaration of the 200-mile limit," says Fred Winsor, "our analysis was that it wouldn't do anything for inshore fishermen. The government was planning to replace the foreign fleet with a Canadian offshore fleet. The fishermen wanted something to prevent the Canadian offshore fleet from fishing close to shore."

The CYC hired Paul Hansen to work on the same issue with the Northumberland Fishermen's Association. The 50-mile campaign, as it was known, was the springboard Nova Scotia inshore fishermen needed to begin talking about a union. As Dalhousie University professor Rick Williams later wrote, "This campaign was successful in identifying and linking together a new group of fishermen leaders from different areas who saw the need for a strong fishermen's organization."

In the spring of 1976, a meeting billed as "the first of its kind in the history of the organized fisheries" was held in Halifax. Sponsored by the provincial Department of Fisheries, it brought together fishermen from associations in Cape Breton, the Northumberland Strait, Guysborough County, the Eastern Shore, and southwest Nova Scotia. "The province wanted to find out what the hell was going on with fishermen," says Fred Winsor. At the meeting, a steering committee of fishermen was set up. Over the next six months, they explored the possibility of forming a province-wide association financed by government.

Through his CYC connections, Fred Winsor knew that fishermen in New Brunswick were talking unionization. In 1974, he had met Gilles Thériault, Réginald Comeau, and Jean-Marie Nadeau. In December 1976, Winsor, along with Northumberland Strait fisherman Marcel Tremblay and Guysborough County fisherman Leon Fisher, attended the leadership training course held in Richibucto. "It was in Richibucto," recalls Winsor, "that Gilles Thériault did a presentation that sold Leon on the idea of a union for fishermen."

Soon after, Nova Scotia fisheries minister Dan Reid announced funding for the establishment of a province-wide fishermen's organization. But the $50,000 was given to an existing group, the Atlantic Fishermen's Association, formed in 1974 by herring-seiner fishermen in southwest Nova Scotia. The association had already tried to bring the roughly 15 associations in the province under one umbrella. But by 1977, seiner fishermen had broken away, and the organization was calling itself the Nova Scotia Fishermen's Association (NSFA). The name was a misnomer, however, because the NSFA didn't include fishermen from outside the southwest of the province.

The NSFA was no more successful than any other association in the province in uniting fishermen. But it was based in southwest Nova Scotia—which most politicians considered to be the only "real" fishery in the province—and that, together with the fact that it wasn't calling itself a union, probably explains why the fisheries minister gave the funding to this group.

In February 1977, the Northumberland Fishermen's Association organized a meeting in Tatamagouche, attended by representatives of seven inshore fishermen's associations in Nova Scotia. The need for some kind of large organization was on the agenda, and Gilles Thériault of New Brunswick and Bill Short of the Newfoundland fishermen's union had been invited to speak. In the end, the fishermen voted in favour of unionization.

"There was a lot of fear expressed about strikes," recalls Fred Winsor, "but when the vote was taken, it was unanimous." The fishermen agreed, however, to keep the idea quiet for the time being because they believed that many other fishermen in the province weren't ready for it. They also wanted government funding. At that point, no plans were made to connect with unions in New Brunswick or in Newfoundland, though events would unfold more quickly than expected.

Two fishermen who had voted in favour of a union were Edison Lumsden and Jamie MacKenzie of Canso. They subsequently invited Gilles Thériault to speak to their organization, the Guysborough County Fishermen's Association. The association had been set up after the Canso strike had failed, though its members believed that it wasn't accomplishing much because it couldn't convince the companies to negotiate prices. That April, a majority of members voted to join the MFU. The Guysborough County Fishermen's Association continued to exist but with a much smaller membership.

A week later, Thériault spoke again to the Northumberland Fishermen's Association, headed at the time by Marcel Tremblay, who had been a leader during the lobster boycotts of 1976. In April 1977, the association voted to become Nova Scotia's second MFU local.

In February 1978, a third Nova Scotia local was formed, in Sydney, Cape Breton. "When the union caught on here," recalls Big Bras d'Or fisherman Stuart Squires, whose brother Kevin also became involved in the union, "it caught on really quick and really hard. In the first year, all of a sudden everyone was a member of the union. People saw it as a good idea, not so much to gain in prices but as a way of drawing fishermen together. The appeal of the MFU was that it had the potential to encompass everyone on the island as opposed to having small little associations."

Gradually, MFU organizers were hired: Charlie Arbuckle, Hasse Lindblad, and Ron Crawley in Northumberland; Fred Winsor in Cape Breton; and Ron Stockton in Guysborough. Of these, only Lindblad became a fisherman. He had grown up on a dairy farm in Pictou County and had fished as a helper in the mid-1960s before moving to Toronto and taking a job with the police force. After six years, he returned home and worked at the H.B. Nickerson plant in Lismore until he was hired by the MFU and then started fishing.

Why did Northumberland Strait fishermen want a union? "To a large degree," says Lindblad, "Nickersons ran the whole show on the shore here at the time ... them and National Sea. There was a lot of suspicion that they acted together to set prices, and the prices were low. Basically, fishermen felt they needed some say in the market price." In 1986, Lindblad became president of the MFU for two years. In the meantime, however, one of his first tasks was to recruit a president for the Northumberland local whom he knew fishermen would respect. Lindblad wisely asked Percy Hayne, Jr, of Pictou Landing to run for the job.

In his mid-twenties, Hayne had started fishing at the age of 14. He had also worked in construction during the off-season, which had given him experience in trade unions. Although shy, Hayne was a highliner, a leader among fishermen in his community. Even today, fishermen have great respect for the best among them. Hayne was a strong, principled fisherman who, as a result of his union involvement, became widely respected throughout the province by buyers and government officials alike.

*　　*　　*　　*　　*

At the same time that the Maritime Fishermen's Union was taking root in Nova Scotia, the idea of a union was also gaining ground in Prince Edward Island.

The fishery there was almost completely an inshore fishery. Lobster was the most important species, accounting in 1978 for about 75 percent of the total landed value ($22.5 million) of fish and seafood in the province. In 1978, roughly 5,000 people worked in the industry: 2,000 as inshore fishermen and 3,000 as plant workers.

During the 1970s, Prince Edward Island had nearly two dozen small, independent processors who operated several months a year, though the bigger companies were becoming more prevalent. Usen Fisheries of Boston operated a fleet of small trawlers out of Souris, catching mainly redfish in the Gulf of St Lawrence. H.B. Nickerson owned a plant in Georgetown (which would close in 1982), and National Sea had plants in Morell and Summerside. Both companies had buying stations along the shore.

Fred Winsor (left), a native of Newfoundland, became an MFU organizer in Cape Breton in the late 1970s; Kevin Squires, brother of Big Bras d'Or fisherman Stuart Squires, also got involved in the union.
(COURTESY FRED WINSOR; COURTESY MFU)

When organizer Hasse Lindblad (left) went looking for a president for the Northumberland local, he chose Percy Hayne, Jr, of Pictou Landing. Lindblad became president of the MFU in 1986. (COURTESY MFU)

In July 1974, mackerel fishermen in the Alberton area, on the northwest shore of the island, went on strike against National Sea. The company's price, they said, was simply not enough to make it worthwhile putting to sea. The men began to kick around the idea of a union. With the help of labour contacts, they organized a meeting in Charlottetown with guest speakers Father Des McGrath and Richard Cashin of the Newfoundland fishermen's union and Gilles Thériault. Nearly 500 fishermen attended. "The place was packed," recalls Thériault. "There seemed to be a genuine interest in doing something."

The fishermen set up a steering committee to examine the feasibility of a union. "It was a poor committee," recalls Oliver Smith of Mount Stewart, who ended up as chairperson. "There were four or five guys that were completely intimidated by the buyers. There were also a few association guys who would never say anything detrimental about the government." As well, there were a couple of members whom Smith considered "fanatics," very pro-union fishermen who were unwilling to consider anything else. Thériault had noticed the divisions at the Charlottetown meeting. "It was evident that people were coming from different angles," he says. "Some wanted to try and strengthen the associations; others wanted to look at a marketing-board concept."

After several months, the disparate group finally hammered out a constitution for an organization called the United Fishermen of P.E.I. Information was mailed out to fishermen all over the island. The feedback, however, was negative. "There was a high percentage of fishermen who wanted a new organization but not a union," says Smith. "They were scared of a union because they thought it would call a strike in the middle of lobster season." With that, most of the steering-committee members lost interest and drifted away. The remaining ones continued to work, with support from a regional development council in Charlottetown, but on the idea of a marketing board. When government funding for the council was cut, the effort died.

But the idea that fishermen needed some kind of new organization was not completely abandoned. On the island, as elsewhere in the region, there were fishermen's co-ops and associations in many harbours. In the late 1960s, in response to government regulations, several had come together to form the P.E.I. Fishermen's Association (PEIFA), supposedly to give fishermen a united voice. But not everyone felt represented by it.

"The PEIFA seemed to be an organization of a few old harbour bosses," recalls Terrence MacDonald, a young fisherman from Savage Harbour. "In a lot of harbours, there's always one or more fellas who think they own the place. They would be association members, and they'd have their little meetings with the DFO and provincial fisheries. Things that worked in their favour was what they were after. The younger fellas, we weren't involved at all. We weren't even allowed into the meetings. I remember one time, we were trying to get some work done on the wharf. There was a couple of old fellas here. They were dead against it. They lobbied politicians not to do the work. They thought if the facility was fixed up, it would be an invitation for more fellas to come in and fish out of here. I remember groups of those old-timers getting together and buying up licences that were for sale and letting them die so younger guys couldn't get in and be competition for them."

Breaking that system of control was one of the reasons why MacDonald was interested in a union. The other was price. At the time, National Sea was the only lobster buyer in Savage Harbour. In 1977, for whatever reason, the company decided to forgo its usual practice of paying rebates after lobster season. That got fishermen talking again about the need for a union. The idea, in fact, had never really been forgotten. Two key fishermen, Junior Coffin, who had travelled the province with Oliver Smith seeking support for a union, and Louis Campbell of Covehead, one of the so-called fanatics on the steering committee, had continued to push for a union even after the committee had died.

At the same time, interest in a union had been growing at the western end of the island. For years, fishermen there had participated in the spring herring fishery off Escuminac. Fishermen like Ivan Shaw of Howards Cove and Jamie Ellsworth of Miminegash made the three-hour trip across the Northumberland Strait and stayed all week, living on their boats tied to the wharf. As a result, they had got to know New Brunswick fishermen and their attempts to organize a union.

In February, about 40 P.E.I. fishermen gathered in Alberton to hear Harold Manuel and Gilles Thériault talk about unionization. A newspaper report noted: "Much of the discussion at the meeting centered on the possibility of strike action if the union failed to reach an agreement on a minimum price. There were obvious doubts and fears about an unwise strike." Nonetheless, more than 30 of the men present voted in favour of the MFU's setting up a local on the island.

Manuel and Thériault promised that the fledgling MFU would move into Prince Edward Island if enough interest was demonstrated. Fishermen like Ivan Shaw and Jamie Ellsworth spent the following year on the road, travelling from wharf to wharf, and asking fishermen to sign union cards. In March 1978, a local of the union was finally founded in Miminegash, bringing together fishermen in the western end of the island. Then Ed Frenette was hired. A young New Brunswicker, he had studied the co-operative movement at the University of Prince Edward Island and Memorial University of Newfoundland. Despite limited resources, he began travelling the island, meeting with fishermen and recruiting new members. A few months later, a second local of the MFU was established, in the Savage Harbour-Rustico area.

*   *   *   *   *

With the lobster boycotts of 1976, the demonstrations against the companies throughout 1977, and the pressure on government to pass collective bargaining legislation, the Maritime Fishermen's Union began to build an image as a militant organization whose members were prepared to take radical action to achieve their goals. This radicalism distinguished the MFU from the two types of fishermen's organizations that had come before: co-operatives and associations.

The MFU also had a different analysis of fishermen. While co-operatives and associations regarded fishermen as independent businessmen, the MFU viewed them as ordinary working people. True, the union said, fishermen did invest capital in equipment, unlike other workers, who have only their labour to sell. But in reality, the MFU argued, fishermen in the Maritimes were very poor. The money they invested—together with the limited amount of fish they could catch—gave them little leverage with the companies. A union, therefore, would help fishermen improve their wages and working conditions.

It was an analysis that would prove, over the years, to be neither as black and white nor as simple as first thought. But it was a starting point. And it was the rationale for fighting for legislation that would give fishermen the right to negotiate for their labour—for the price of their fish. The MFU was prepared to fight for the inshore fishery on the basis that it was the most important fishery on the East Coast, the lifeblood of many communities. The MFU believed that the offshore was secondary and should be permitted only to supplement the inshore, only when the inshore could not catch enough fish to supply the plants.

Soon after it was founded, the MFU began to establish links with organized labour. In June 1977, several representatives attended the New Brunswick Federation of Labour's annual meeting, where a resolution was passed backing the fishermen in their struggle for collective bargaining legislation. Once locals were formed in Nova Scotia and Prince Edward Island, fishermen in those provinces began to attend labour conventions as well.

At the same time, the MFU asked the Canadian Labour Congress (CLC) to allow it to affiliate. In March 1978, the CLC granted jurisdiction for inshore fishermen in the Maritimes to the MFU. A month later, MFU president Harold Manuel and executive secretary Gilles Thériault travelled to the CLC's annual convention in Québec City, where they made a plea for support, and returned with hundreds of dollars in donations. Organized labour would be a major supporter of the MFU in the years to come.

Prince Edward Island fisherman Ivan Shaw spent a year on the road, encouraging island fishermen to sign cards. In March 1978, an MFU local was formed in Miminegash.
(COURTESY MFU)

At the union's convention in Shippegan in December 1977, where Harold Manuel was officially elected president, Edison Lumsden from Canso, Nova Scotia, became vice president, and Louis Godin from Maisonnette, in northeast New Brunswick, became secretary-treasurer. A wiry fisherman who had worked in the mines in northern Ontario, Godin, then age 50, had belonged to an earlier co-op in his village and was an original member of the Association Professionnelle des Pêcheurs du Nord-est. He had taken the leadership training course at Inkerman in late 1976.

Manuel, Lumsden, and Godin were surrounded by a solid core

In December 1977, Edison Lumsden (left) of Canso, Nova Scotia, and Louis Godin of Maisonnette, New Brunswick, joined the MFU executive as vice president and secretary-treasurer respectively. (CEA COLLECTION L'EVANGELINE E9094)

of fishermen from the three provinces, as well as competent staff, who shared their class analysis, their sometimes black-and-white vision of right and wrong, and their willingness to defend, at all costs, the rights of inshore fishermen. In future, mass actions— occupations, demonstrations, even a hostage-taking—would bring in the broad participation of fishermen that had always been missing with the old associations. As one federal fisheries official later remarked, the MFU "could always call up the troops when and where required." Needless to say, this militancy had not been seen among inshore fishermen before, and it frightened a lot of people.

At the same time, it appealed to others. The MFU became the darling of the left in the Maritimes, attracting the support and assistance of intellectuals throughout the region who saw the attempt to organize inshore fishermen more as a social movement than anything else.

For a lot of fishermen, the MFU represented new hope and a new approach to dealing with problems in their industry.

WHEREFORE
ART THOU, ROMEO

"There was always something behind that program that was fishy."
—Richibucto Village fisherman Antoine Daigle—

I F ALL THE ACTIVITY between 1974 and 1978 proved one thing, it was that inshore fishermen in the Maritimes wanted a union. Normally, workers who want to organize a union sign up members. Then they take their case to a labour relations board, which certifies the union as the bargaining agent if a majority of employees have signed cards. Fishermen had taken the first step, but they could not proceed to the next. Without legislation that enabled them to be certified, that option was not available to them.

Fishermen were not trying to force anyone to join a union. They were merely asking for a right enjoyed by workers in almost every other industry in Canada—the right to form a union if a majority in a given area were in favour.

But in the world of real politics, things aren't so simple. The struggle for collective bargaining legislation was most advanced in New Brunswick, but the provincial government, from the premier on down, still insisted that legislation would be considered only after the Maritime Fishermen's Union had proved that it had a majority of fishermen on-side. Richard Hatfield maintained his position even after his Select Committee on Fisheries had recommended in June 1977 that the province "foster mechanisms whereby fishermen can collectively bargain prices" and even after the same committee under a new chairperson reiterated that recommendation a year later.

Shortly after locals were founded in Nova Scotia and Prince Edward Island, fishermen there also began to demand legislative changes, but both governments echoed New Brunswick.

The problem for the MFU, of course, was money. Organizing is an expensive proposition. Most unions support themselves through the collection of dues deducted by employers from paychecks, a process known as automatic check-off. Today, it is a standard part of collective agreements. Again, the MFU didn't have that option because it didn't have legislation allowing it to negotiate collective agreements. Organizers had to knock on doors every year and ask members to pay their dues. It was an inadequate system. Dues were only $72 a year, or $6 a month. Staff had even calculated how much they were per day to show fishermen that it was not a lot of money.

But many fishermen refused to pay because they believed that there was nothing to be gained by it. As Nova Scotia fisherman Graeme Gawn says, "I've had people tell me, 'I don't have to pay. You guys are doing a good job. I'm going to get the benefits anyway.'" The sentiment was widespread—and based in reality. When the MFU won a greater herring quota for the inshore, all inshore fishermen benefited, not just those who had paid dues. When the union convinced government to close the Northumberland Strait to boats of more than 50 feet, all inshore fishermen benefited, not just those who had paid dues.

It was a classic catch-22. Many fishermen promised to join the union and pay their dues once the MFU won collective bargaining legislation. But the MFU couldn't convince government to pass such legislation until it could prove that a majority of fishermen were members.

As a result, the MFU was chronically short of money. In the mid-1970s, the situation had become worse as sources of funding began to dry up. The Trudeau government disbanded the Company of Young Canadians, cut positions, and began to phase out the Local Initiatives Program and Opportunities for Youth. The future of regional development councils like CRASE and CRAN also became uncertain.

Meanwhile, as all three Maritime provinces were refusing to pass enabling legislation—legislation that would have given the MFU a solid financial base—they began to fund fishermen's associations. In 1976, for example, the New Brunswick government established a five-year "aid to associations" program, immediately giving $50,000 to various fishermen's groups, including the Regroupement of Inshore Fishermen of Northeast New Brunswick. A year later, when that association became part of the MFU, it was no longer eligible for funding.

"The government will subsidize associations, it will not financially aid a union," Fisheries Deputy Minister Léonce Chenard explained to the media. "To oblige all fishermen to join or subscribe to a union would be anti-democratic, make a political body out of the union and the fishermen serial numbers of an organism [*sic*]." *L'Evangéline* editorial writer Paul-Emile Richard, who supported the MFU, called the funding a form of blackmail to dissuade fishermen from joining a union. "It must be noted that these subsidies are granted ever since there is talk of a union," he wrote.

In Nova Scotia, as noted earlier, the provincial government announced $50,000 for the Atlantic Fishermen's Association at a time when fishermen elsewhere in the province were trying to organize a union. In Prince Edward Island, the provincial government had been paying the office expenses of the P.E.I. Fishermen's Association (PEIFA) since its founding in the late 1960s. In 1976, the Province funded the hiring of a full-time employee for the PEIFA. (In 1990, the government was still financing the association to the tune of $30,000 a year.)

Two federal programs also hindered the efforts of the MFU, and both were initiatives of Fisheries Minister Roméo LeBlanc.

*   *   *   *   *

LeBlanc grew up in Cormier Cove, an Acadian village not far from Moncton. The son of a railway worker and sometime farmer, LeBlanc was the youngest of seven children and the only one to get an education. Stephen Kimber, in his book on National Sea Products, quotes LeBlanc's former wife as saying, "I know it sounds corny, but if you're going to understand Roméo, you have to understand his background. He's the only person in a thousand from his area who made it, and he feels he owes a debt for that. He doesn't want anything more than to help the fishermen and the Acadians. That's what drives him."

"It's true that I have certainly never been able to forget the conditions in which I grew up," LeBlanc says today. "I was able to get an education only because my sisters worked as maids in Boston and sent money home." After graduating from St Joseph's College in Memramcook, LeBlanc became a journalist, working as a Radio-Canada correspondent in Washington and London. In the late 1960s, he was executive assistant and press secretary to Prime

After taking over the fisheries portfolio in 1974, Roméo LeBlanc (second from right) quickly developed a reputation for favouring the inshore sector. Here, he is flanked by the DFO's Art May, Edmond Haché of APPNE, and inshore fisherman Frank McLaughlin. (CEA COLLECTION L'EVANGELINE E9077)

Minister Lester Pearson and, later, Pierre Trudeau. In 1972, LeBlanc was elected to Parliament. Shortly after he was re-elected in 1974, he was named to the fisheries portfolio.

LeBlanc came into the job just as the Maritime Fishermen's Union was getting under way. "I saw the organization at first as an agitating organization," he recalls. "In those days, meetings consisted of getting a bunch of angry fishermen together, angry for half a dozen reasons, calling in a certain number of necktie-wearing MPs, bureaucrats, et cetera, and then kicking them. Better-read guys like Gilles Thériault and Paul-Eugène LeBlanc would eloquently insult them, and then fishermen would applaud, and the meeting would break up until the next one. I always thought it was a bit of a mug's exercise because it didn't solve problems."

LeBlanc says that he went into the fisheries portfolio with a guarantee from Pierre Trudeau that he would be the Eugene Whelan of the fishery, that he would be a friend of the fishermen in the same way that the Liberal agriculture minister was a friend to farmers. "The reality struck me very quickly when I became minister," LeBlanc says, "that bureaucrats in the department tended to consult the companies, be it B.C. Packers or National Sea, and assume that that was the voice of the fishery." He decided that it was time the fishermen had their turn at the table, but to do so, they needed to speak with one voice. "I always told them to organize," he says. "Be a union, be a co-op, be an association. Be whatever you want but hang together, because if you don't, you'll hang separately."

LeBlanc soon developed a reputation for favouring the inshore sector. In one of his first speeches after the 1974 election, he held up British Columbia as a model for fishermen in Atlantic Canada. "As you know," he told a meeting of the Atlantic Provinces Economic Council in Halifax, "the fishermen in British Columbia play an active role in determining the price they receive. The fishermen and the processors know they are married, and they also know that in 1974 women's liberation has arrived. In the matter of prices and of what happens to the fish, the Atlantic coast fishermen also should have a bargaining voice." Six months later, he told reporters, "How would you feel when you leave home in the morning if your income depended on whether you get a good story or five good stories? You negotiate a wage. Fishermen can't do that. Fishermen leave in the morning darkness, and they have no idea if they'll have anything in their nets at the end of the day. What other segment of our society is living that way?"

As Dalhousie University professor Rick Williams writes of LeBlanc:

> ... during his tenure there was a genuine opening up of opportunities for fishermen to participate in policy and management processes. For the first time, fishermen's organizations began to make some real gains for their members through this route. Under LeBlanc, the bias of fisheries policy shifted away from the preoccupation with expansion of the corporate sector, and there was greater emphasis on community stabilization, effective conservation, and a more balanced distribution of quotas among the offshore, near-shore and inshore fleets.

LeBlanc's approach was readily apparent in the 1976 report *A Policy for Canada's Commercial Fisheries*, the result of what the federal Fisheries Department called "the most thorough inquiry yet made into Canada's post-war fishing industry," initiated in response to the crisis of 1974. The report announced help for the industry, mainly to prop up markets, to the tune of $130 million over three years. It admitted that fisheries policies of the past had "tended to be simplistic in the approach to resource management and relatively non-interventionist and uncoordinated in regard to industrial and trade development."

The report also announced a new direction for fisheries policies. In the past, it said, fishing had been regulated in the interests of the fish. In future, it would be regulated in the interests of the people who depended on the fishing industry, something that would require "more direct participation by the people affected in the formulation and implementation of fishery policy"—an apparent reversal from past consultative committees, which had involved only the large companies.

LeBlanc, the architect of this new direction, wanted inshore fishermen to participate in the management of the industry. But fishermen, given the government's historical tendency to respond only to the offshore sector, were understandably suspicious. The report pointed out that the small-boat share of groundfish landings had been decreasing steadily in recent years and that 70 percent of groundfish were now landed by the mid- and offshore. At the same time, however, it identified overcapacity—particularly in the inshore sector—as the major problem. There were just too many vessels and too many fishermen, the report said, for the amount of fish available. As inshore fishermen read between the lines of the report, they had good reason to wonder what this new minister had in mind.

Still, LeBlanc's period in office would be marked by major changes that would help, if not outright favour, the inshore fishery. In 1976, he banned vessels of more than 100 feet from fishing in the Gulf of St Lawrence, promising that they would have greater opportunities offshore once Canada's 200-mile limit was introduced a year later. At the end of 1978, under pressure from the MFU's Northumberland local, LeBlanc banned vessels of more than 50 feet from fishing in the Northumberland Strait (and they remain banned today).

LeBlanc also reorganized Department of Fisheries and Oceans (DFO) management regions. Historically, the Atlantic fishery had been divided into three regions—Québec, the Maritimes, and

Newfoundland. For fishermen in the Gulf of St Lawrence, that meant that their sector had been lumped in with the offshore and foreign fisheries operating off Nova Scotia. As a result, the concerns of inshore fishermen in the gulf had often come second to harried bureaucrats in Halifax who were more preoccupied with the other sectors. In April 1981, LeBlanc made the Gulf of St Lawrence a separate fisheries region with an office in Moncton. The Nova Scotia fishery, from the tip of Cape Breton to the southwest of the province, then became the Scotia-Fundy Region.

LeBlanc, furthermore, was the first fisheries minister to allow joint ventures with foreign vessels, the so-called over-the-side sales that often gave inshore fishermen a market and a better price. And it was his decision, also in 1981, to make the Gulf of St Lawrence herring fishery once again an inshore fishery.

Before long, the industry, not without a certain amount of enmity, was calling LeBlanc "the minister of fishermen."

Despite his reputation, however, LeBlanc initiated two programs that directly undercut the MFU's efforts to gain membership. In 1976, he announced a pilot program to hire nine people to work with fishermen in designated areas of New Brunswick and Nova Scotia. "Just when the union was getting strong, they put these community-service officers in place," recalls Richibucto Village fisherman Antoine Daigle. "If you had a problem with income tax, you went to see this guy. He could do just as well as the union would, and you didn't have to pay him. Why pay the union when you could have the same service for nothing? There was always something behind that program that was fishy."

Canso fisherman Jamie MacKenzie says the same thing about the person hired in his area. "He really screwed the union around," MacKenzie recalls. "He was always up the shore in Queensport, encouraging fishermen to start an association." The program also drew away union supporters who had provided leadership. Adrice Doiron, by then in his mid-fifties and suffering a bad back, which made fishing increasingly difficult, was one of the people hired in New Brunswick.

Later, in one of his last acts before the Trudeau Liberals went down to defeat in 1979, LeBlanc offered financing if the multitude of fishermen's groups throughout the Maritimes formed one large organization. In June, representatives of eight fishermen's associations met in Charlottetown "to band together in a major effort to overcome years of bickering," according to one newspaper report. Don Landry, president of the PEIFA, was elected president of the newly formed Eastern Fishermen's Federation (EFF). "The new group will not replace any existing groups," Landry told the media, "but it will give them added financial and political clout."

Whether the organization would, indeed, give fishermen political clout is questionable. But there's no doubt that forming the EFF meant an influx of money. LeBlanc had offered an allocation of 2,000 metric tonnes of squid. The allocation turned out to be worth $1 million when it was sold to the Japanese.

Invested, the money provided a healthy annual income for the EFF. And, unlike the MFU, the EFF didn't require its members to pay dues.

* * * * *

Maritime Fishermen's Union president Harold Manuel, along with executive secretary Gilles Thériault, had attended the founding meeting of the Eastern Fishermen's Federation. In a surprise move—a move that was against the wishes of the MFU executive and directly contrary to what Thériault had just told the EFF in a brief speech—Manuel accepted a position on the federation's executive. A month later, in a vaguely worded press release, Manuel announced the MFU's withdrawal from the organization. The fact was, the MFU had never intended to join.

For one thing, the MFU was leery about another organization formed with government money. Many members had had experience with associations that were considered "tainted" once governments began funding them. "We thought that fishermen should pay for their own organization," says MFU organizer Réginald Comeau. The MFU also felt uneasy about the haste with which the EFF had been created. Perhaps most important, MFU members didn't understand how an organization bringing together inshore, midshore, and offshore fishermen, as well as the co-operative movement, could possibly represent the interests of all groups. At the time, the union was involved in a major battle with the midshore herring seiners. It also faced ongoing conflict with the United Maritime Fishermen (UMF). How could the union, then, become part of an organization that would include both?

When the MFU decided not to get involved, it didn't realize that the EFF would go on to become one of the union's biggest adversaries.

Why did Roméo LeBlanc—the supposed champion of inshore fishermen—decide to set up an organization that would stymie the efforts of an already-existing organization?

It wasn't intended to happen that way, LeBlanc maintains. There was no one organization that included a majority of fishermen in the Maritimes, he says, so for fishermen to have a united voice, they had to have an umbrella organization. He wanted to do something quickly, before the 1979 election, and all of a sudden, there was an unprecedented run of squid offshore. If some of that squid were allocated to an umbrella group that, in turn, sold it, the profits could be used as seed money.

"Deep in my heart," says LeBlanc, "I thought that of all the groups that would get involved in the EFF, the MFU would end up on top of the pile because they had the best leadership. A) They had credibility with the fishermen. They were not guys who fought for licences on the condition that they get an additional one for themselves. They were principled. And B) they knew how to fight. They did not give up the fight easily. I remember talking once to Gilles and saying, 'For God's sake, why did you pull out?' If they could have just forgotten their rhetoric and been involved for two years, they would have emerged as the strongest force in the EFF. They would have ended up by taking it over, by dominating it, because they had the best leadership and the best organizational discipline."

When the MFU, to LeBlanc's surprise, refused to participate, things changed. The EFF's leadership lacked vision, he says today, and "were more interested in giving interviews to the media than solving the problems of fishermen." In the early 1980s, the EFF leadership was still in a "kick-the-department" phase, LeBlanc notes. "Gilles and those guys had gone beyond that. When they attended an advisory-committee meeting, they were credible, they were prepared, they had done their homework."

"The EFF was always a more diffuse voice than the MFU," says Jean-Eûdes Haché, today the DFO's assistant deputy minister for the Atlantic Region, "because it had to represent too many interests. Because of the fact that you had the midshore association from northeast New Brunswick, the seiners, the co-op movement, rather than having an advocate who comes to the table and has a very clear constituency and fights for a specific issue, what you had was a diplomat who wanted to cover all bases, be everything to everybody. In that sense, it certainly dampened the message, the effectiveness of the organization."

By February 1981, LeBlanc was telling the Halifax *Chronicle-Herald* that the decision to establish the EFF had been made in haste and, on reflection, may not have been the best way to go. "If I had the decision to make over again," he said, "I likely would do it differently. I wish I could redress the situation."

That year, LeBlanc did try to redress the situation by offering the same squid allocation to the MFU, as well as to other groups. The MFU, wary of government funding yet desperate for cash, agreed to accept the allocation on the condition that the money be used to establish a pension and health-insurance fund for its members. But there was no squid that year.

By 1982, MFU predictions that the EFF wouldn't be able to represent the varied interests of its members seemed to be coming true. Two seiner groups from the Bay of Fundy withdrew over EFF involvement in over-the-side-sales programs. A year later, the United Maritime Fishermen pulled out, also over the EFF's involvement in what the UMF considered to be the marketing arena. In 1984, the association representing midshore fishermen in northeast New Brunswick withdrew as well.

Intentionally or not, LeBlanc created an organization that caused major problems for the Maritime Fishermen's Union. Secure in its government financing, the EFF became a visible and vocal opponent of the union at every turn, particularly in Nova Scotia and Prince Edward Island and particularly over collective bargaining rights for inshore fishermen. EFF executive secretary Alan Billard, for example, told a CBC Radio Noon host in April 1982 that EFF fishermen opposed legislation because they were afraid of a "big union" imposing itself on fishermen. "We are concerned," said Billard, "about things we see all over North America, where the Teamsters are organizing fishermen in the United States, where the Marxist-Leninists are organizing fishermen in other parts. This is of great concern because not only is this big union, this is big trouble. It is of some concern to look across the country and across the continent and see big unions trying to get a foot into the fisherman's door because they see that as *numbership* and we see organization as *membership,* to quote a commercial that's on TV these days."

It was ironic for Billard to suggest that the MFU was a "big union" when it was the EFF that was sitting comfortably with a million dollars in its bank account. It was also ironic for him to talk about organizing members when that wasn't something the EFF did. Any fishermen's association could join by a vote of its executive, and membership was free. In contrast, each fisherman wanting to belong to the MFU had to sign a card and pay a fee.

Billard continually promoted the view of fishermen as independent businesspeople and encouraged their fragmentation as a group. In the same interview, in response to a question about whether he was worried about the Newfoundland fishermen's union coming into Nova Scotia, he replied, "I hate to say this to you, but most Newfoundlanders don't have a particularly great rapport with the fishermen in Nova Scotia. Fishermen in Nova Scotia are different, and fishermen in southwestern Nova Scotia are different than fishermen in Cape Breton, and they're different than fishermen in the Northumberland Strait. And Cashin is, and always will be, a Newfoundlander, and he's not going to be able to relate that closely to fishermen in Nova Scotia."

From the beginning, the EFF claimed a membership of 10,000, a figure rarely questioned by the media. In the mid-1980s, a CBC fisheries broadcaster was finally challenged to count the membership of groups claiming to belong to the EFF. The figure he came up with was about 3,000, roughly equivalent to the number of fishermen who had signed cards with the MFU.

For their part, some MFU fishermen believed that the creation of the EFF was a deliberate attempt by LeBlanc to thwart their efforts to unionize. Others were less sure. "Fishermen in the northeast found it bizarre," says Réginald Comeau. "We didn't know if it was naïveté or what. We just didn't understand. We still don't understand today."

"My analysis," says Gilles Thériault, "is that the idea may have been well intentioned, but it was too rushed and not well thought out. The end result was that it created an organization that had not many members but a lot of money, and that stood against everything that the MFU was fighting for."

In effect, LeBlanc created an artificial organization whose leadership was never really able to achieve unity among fishermen from the different sectors. If there ever was a common ground—and even this is questionable—it was the EFF's opposition to those fishermen who wanted a union. In years to come, fishermen's groups would expend a lot of energy fighting—not the companies, not the governments—but each other.

A COMMITMENT
TO CHANGE

"The province will recognize the right of fishermen to unionize."
—Fisheries Minister Jean Gauvin, December 1979—

WEDNESDAY, MARCH 15, 1978. The morning after the Legislative Assembly had opened in New Brunswick, 19 yellow school buses and dozens of cars arrived at the Royal Canadian Legion building on Upper Queen Street in Fredericton. They came from all parts of eastern New Brunswick and from Nova Scotia, carrying fishermen, their families, and representatives of the labour movement. It was a year, almost to the day, after the Maritime Fishermen's Union had been founded—a year in which the campaign for collective bargaining legislation had gone nowhere. The government continued to insist that fishermen didn't want a union. Today, the fishermen and their families, some 700 strong, were going to prove, once and for all, that the government was wrong.

The women had organized the event. They had sponsored amateur nights in several communities to pay for the buses, and they had telephoned families, often more than once, to make sure that they showed up. Women like Thérèse Landry from Anse-Bleue, Odette Maillet from Richibucto Village, Bernice Robichaud from Val Comeau, and Alfreda Cormier from Cap-Pelé actively supported the union because they knew that fishing wasn't only their husband's occupation but also a way of life for them and their families. Today, the women took charge, passing out placards and directing the crowd as it began to march, chanting, towards the legislative building a mile away. There, they set up a sound system, using a portable generator for power, and began what one newspaper report later called "a lively show that lasted from 2pm until the House set at 3."

For Acadian fishermen in particular, this was a new experience.

Although they had picketed outside company offices and plants during the past year, they had never before demonstrated, en masse, in front of their politicians. "That was part of our political education," recalls Richibucto Village fisherman Jean-Guy Maillet. Some fishermen had never even been to Fredericton, a quiet government and university town with its stately Victorian homes overlooking the banks of the Saint John River. Although a third of the province's population was French-speaking, the capital was English. Its street signs, its business signs, and the language in the stores and on the street were all unilingual. For the fishermen, it felt like alien territory in more ways than one.

A quick succession of speakers were on the rostrum: Gilles Thériault, MFU executive secretary; Harold Manuel, MFU president; Mathilda Blanchard, representing fish-plant workers in the north; and Tim McCarthy, vice president of the New Brunswick Federation of Labour. McCarthy was in the process of announcing financial support for the union when Richard Hatfield emerged from the legislative building. Amid a roar, the premier took the microphone in his hands, waited a moment, then began to speak.

He assured the crowd that he was concerned about the problems of fishermen. "I understand where you're coming from," he told the demonstrators, "but farmers and fishermen are in a different position than plant employees who can join the union of their choice. Action must be taken in the best interests of all fishermen, and I still feel that is in the marketing area." His message, brief and to the point, surprised no one. He had said the same thing on several previous occasions. Hatfield quickly slipped inside the building again. (Later, during question period, he told the House he wasn't convinced that a simple amendment to the Industrial Relations Act was the solution. His words were echoed by Fisheries Minister Omer Léger, who said that he saw the presence of co-ops in New Brunswick as a major stumbling block for a union and that Newfoundland was the only province where fishermen could achieve what New Brunswick fishermen wanted. "That's because there are no co-operatives in Newfoundland, and most boats are owned by the companies," he said. "The converse is true in New Brunswick." This, in fact, wasn't true. In Newfoundland, many boat-owning inshore fishermen belonged to the union.)

After Hatfield left, the demonstration was, for all intents and

In March 1978, 700 fishermen and their families marched on the Legislative Assembly in Fredericton, demanding collective bargaining legislation.
(CEA COLLECTION L'EVANGELINE E19,602)

purposes, over. The fishermen got back onto the buses or into their cars with mixed emotions. They felt elated and excited that so many had come out, yet they felt disappointed and discouraged that the provincial government still refused to budge on the question of collective bargaining legislation. Later, Cap-Pelé fisherman Guy Cormier told the press that the demonstration was a failure. "The actions of the fishermen should have been firmer," he said. "They should have entered the Legislative Assembly and staged a sit-in." But Cormier vowed that fishermen would not give up. "The union is preparing for massive action in the coming weeks on a number of fronts," he warned.

In July, after federal fisheries minister Roméo LeBlanc told an audience at St Francis Xavier University that provinces should "remove the impediments to fisheries organizations in the way that Newfoundland has done," New Brunswick's minister of fisheries sounded another note of caution. Such an organization would have to be extremely careful to maintain competitive prices, Omer Léger said. "There has to be some very good co-ordination if New

Brunswick fishermen are to have unions. Let's not price ourselves out of the market. Some fishermen's union could easily do that."

Born in Waltham, Massachusetts, Léger had won a by-election in Kent South in 1971 when former premier Louis Robichaud stepped down to go to the Senate. Léger was given the fisheries portfolio in 1974, but many considered him weak, as a cabinet minister in general and as a fisheries minister in particular. Léger had, for example, constantly flip-flopped on the question of collective bargaining for fishermen. One day, he told the press that he supported a fishermen's union; the next, that he didn't understand how fishermen, as independent businesspeople, could be unionized.

On September 16, 1978, Richard Hatfield called a provincial election. The MFU promised to shadow all candidates, especially those in fishing ridings along the eastern shore, to force them to take a stand on unionization for fishermen. A few days before the election, Omer Léger again said he didn't believe that fishermen wanted a union. "The fact is that fishermen are quite happy," he told the press. "They've done well these past few years. No one is talking about unionization."

On October 23, Hatfield's Conservative government was returned to office, but the member from Kent South went down to defeat.

*   *   *   *   *

Acadians in New Brunswick had historically voted Liberal. Throughout the 1970s, with a Conservative government in Fredericton, the ridings where the Maritime Fishermen's Union was strong were all in Liberal territory. That partly explains why the MFU made little headway with government during the early years. There was no one in government, and particularly in cabinet, to push for the union.

In 1978, however, there was a breakthrough—for both the Tories and the MFU—with the election of Jean Gauvin in Shippegan-les-Isles. (An even bigger breakthrough for the Hatfield Tories came in 1982 when Acadians voted overwhelmingly Conservative for the first time.) The short, stocky 32-year-old schoolteacher and father of three was the first Conservative to hold the riding since 1912. It was a fishing riding—those who didn't fish worked in the fish plants—and Gauvin had promised during his campaign to support the right of fishermen to unionize. When he took over the fisheries portfolio a few months later, he outlined two priorities: more money for the department, and collective bargaining legislation for fishermen.

In early May 1979, Gauvin announced a task force on unionization (its official name was the Task Force to Study the Commercial Relationships between Fishermen and Fish Buyers in New Brunswick). Headed by Moncton lawyer Roger Savoie, the task force also included Lorne Grant of Fredericton, a former bureaucrat with the federal Department of Fisheries and an expert in marketing, and Aurèle Young, an economist at the University of Moncton.

During the summer, the task force held hearings around the province. In August, it stopped in Caraquet, where Louis Godin of Maisonnette and Frank McLaughlin of Val Comeau presented an eight-page brief calling, once again, for collective bargaining legislation for fishermen. Following their presentation, Herménégilde Robichaud, by now vice president of the MFU in the northeast, got up to speak. "Committees like yours are bullshit," he said bluntly. "You already know what we want." Robichaud also denounced the committee for having a member who did not speak French, Lorne Grant. "How can you be serious sending a unilingual English to meet with francophones?" Robichaud asked rhetorically.

Later, in Moncton, the New Brunswick Fish Packers' Association made a presentation to the task force opposing collective bargaining. "Fishermen are not employees," said association president William Moffatt, who worked for Connors Brothers in Blacks Harbour. "We don't think a labour relations framework is appropriate or applicable for self-employed fishermen. The present system for arriving at prices is the most efficient and workable system available."

Moffatt also maintained that of fishermen in the three regions in New Brunswick, only those in the southeast were unhappy. "MFU organizers are constantly speaking in the press, on radio and to federal and provincial fisheries departments," he said, "but have shown little understanding or concern for either the interests of fishermen, processors or the industry as a whole." (Moffatt may have been reacting to an incident two weeks earlier, when 150 MFU fishermen from the southeast, along with their wives, marched on his association's offices in downtown Moncton, denouncing what they called "unfair price manipulation" by the companies.)

Jean Gauvin entered the fisheries
portfolio with a promise to pass
collective bargaining legislation.
(CEA COLLECTION L'EVANGELINE E37,533)

The task-force report was submitted to government in October, and just before Christmas, Gauvin held a press conference to release its contents. The report recommended that the province "provide the necessary legislation to permit fishermen's unions and associations to be certified and to bargain collectively with buyers." It also recommended that members of co-ops not be bound by this law. "The province will recognize the right of fishermen to unionize," Gauvin told the media. At first, Gauvin wanted to set up another committee to hold more hearings, but the MFU objected to any more delays. Gauvin conceded and set up the Joint Committee on Primary Marketing and Commercial Relationships in the Fishing Industry in New Brunswick. Headed by Fisheries Deputy Minister Léonce Chenard, the committee, made up of fishermen and processors, would draft collective bargaining legislation. Such legislation, Gauvin promised, would be ready by 1981.

*   *   *   *   *

It is clear that Fisheries Minister Jean Gauvin was the driving force behind collective bargaining legislation for inshore fishermen. There are several reasons why. He was on the left of his party—"more progressive than conservative," as Réginald Comeau puts it—and he was not philosophically opposed to, or afraid of, unions. The same wasn't the case with many of his cabinet colleagues, including Labour Minister Mabel DeWare, whose responsibility it would be to introduce the legislation.

"Not only Mabel but the civil servants were very nervous about it," recalls Gauvin. "Civil servants are the most conservative, with a small 'c,' people in the whole system. Everything they've been

Omer Chouinard directed the crowd when 150 fishermen and their wives protested in front of the New Brunswick Fish Packers' Association offices in Moncton in August 1978. (CEA COLLECTION L'EVANGELINE E9185)

sitting on for years is the best. When it comes to new perspectives, new changes, they're very nervous about that, because they always feel that changes jeopardize their way of thinking and deep down their jobs."

Today, Gauvin won't say it out loud, but he believed at the time that one of the most conservative forces was his own deputy minister. Léonce Chenard, now deceased, was considered one of the great experts on New Brunswick's fishery. He had been credited, for example, with bringing herring seiners from the West Coast to develop the province's herring-reduction industry. But he had already gone on record opposing a union for fishermen. When Gauvin appointed Chenard to head the joint committee, it was a way of removing him from the department. Chenard was replaced by Tim Andrew, a former deputy minister of agriculture.

But it wasn't only the civil servants who were nervous. The politicians were, too. They were being pressured by company representatives like William Moffatt of Connors Brothers, who Gauvin describes as "anti-union in principle," and to a lesser extent by Jim Bateman of National Sea Products. Bateman was the vice president of the province's Conservative party and, for many years, chairman of the New Brunswick Fisheries Loan Board. "I had many chats with Jim," Gauvin recalls. "You would be able to convince Jim of the good of the union. With him, it wasn't necessarily the end of the world."

National Sea, in fact, was the least of the Maritime Fishermen's Union's worries, even though the company refused to negotiate with the union until it was certified. From the beginning, vice president Jim Morrow, who handled industrial relations from the company's head office in Halifax, had said that he would accept collective bargaining for fishermen. "I think that kind of shocked Gilles when I took the attitude that, yeah, I'd like to see these fishermen get organized," Morrow says today. "But it was strictly for selfish reasons. What we had going along that shore was just unbelievable, a bribery type of situation." The co-ops were paying rebates after the season, and if the companies wanted to keep their fishermen, they had to go along with the practice. There were also numerous independent buyers competing against each other and forcing prices to rise.

"I said, 'I'm interested in getting contracts,'" recalls Morrow, "'negotiated contracts with fishermen where the price is set with none of these paybacks. I'm interested in seeing the fishermen get their heads together, collective bargaining if you want, but with one negotiation instead of a thousand.' From a clear, common-sense point of view, it made sense."

National Sea had been dealing with unions for years, in its plants and on its trawlers. But Morrow agrees that other companies didn't share National Sea's attitude. B.C. Packers and Connors Brothers, both owned by George Weston, were always anti-union, he says, because of their experience on the West Coast with the United Fishermen and Allied Workers' Union. "As for the smaller buyers or the independent processors, they like to do their own thing," says Morrow, "they didn't like to be regimented. They're totally independent. They didn't want to get into joint negotiations with National Sea. They thought they'd get swept up into this crazy world of industrial relations."

Despite Hatfield's public opposition to unionization for fishermen, Jean Gauvin maintains that he had the support of the premier going into the 1978 election. (This contradiction remains unresolved. When asked, Hatfield maintained that he couldn't remember the details.) Hatfield's promise of support, says Gauvin, was the "green light" that he needed to resist pressure from the companies and to do battle with his more conservative colleagues in cabinet. (Gauvin was irreverent when it came to functioning within government. He quickly earned the nickname Vroom-vroom when, after being appointed to the fisheries portfolio, he bought a flashy $16,500 Trans-am as his government car. Gauvin often came second to the premier in expenditures. In 1982-83, his expenses topped $100,000, including $7,500 for Christmas cards for his constituents.)

Gauvin was also a strong Acadian nationalist. He believed that Acadians had been treated as second-class citizens for too long, and he entered the fisheries portfolio with the conviction that the fishery was the only sector of the economy in which Acadians were a force. He was determined to get more money for the department. "What we had in Acadian regions, in particular, were floating caskets," Gauvin recalls. "The boats the inshore fishermen were using were between 30- to 40-footers that lasted 7 to 10 years. Most of them were in very bad shape. So in order to replace the fleet, we had to put more money into the sector."

During his tenure, Gauvin took part in a number of initiatives that benefited fishermen and plant workers in his riding. As minister, he was involved (some say overly) in the Fisheries Loan Board, and more loans, particularly for larger vessels, were dispensed than ever before. Gauvin was also responsible for licensing many new fish plants on the Acadian Peninsula, especially crab plants, which, some later said, led to the serious overcapacity problem that exists today.

In the early 1980s, he spearheaded a regulation requiring that 60 percent of all crab be processed into cans, a move designed to create jobs on the peninsula. (A few years later, the amount was reduced to 30 percent because the market favoured crab in sections.)

In the same way, Gauvin was prepared to allow fishermen to unionize. If a union was what inshore Acadian fishermen wanted—if it would help improve their standard of living—then Gauvin was all for it. "The problem with the inshore fishery," he says, "was that, because of the nature of the industry, there were so many elements out of the control of the fishermen. The catch might be good, but then there'd be no market. The market might be there, but then the fish wouldn't come or the price would be low. It wasn't the fisherman's fault, but it had a direct impact on the money he was bringing in. So I thought, 'Let them be unionized.' At least it would give them the opportunity of working together."

But more than anything else, Gauvin was the consummate politician. His former deputy minister Tim Andrew likes to tell the story of how Gauvin, a month before the 1982 election, was able to tally his support, poll by poll, in his riding. When the results finally came in, Gauvin was out by 16 votes. "He knew everybody in his riding. He knew how they would vote," says Andrew.

During 1978-82, Gauvin maintains that he didn't calculate the votes he would win by passing legislation for fishermen. "It was more of a gut feeling," he says. "During this time, the union was really working. There were a lot of fishermen in my riding, and a lot of fish-plant workers married to fishermen. I knew I was taking a political risk, but deep down I believed that the vast majority of fishermen were for that bill."

As Gauvin's task force held hearings across the province in the summer of 1979, a series of events began to unfold on the Acadian Peninsula that convinced everyone—not only the provincial minister of fisheries—that the MFU was becoming a force to be reckoned with.

THE HERRING
MAKERS

*"If the union was able to move into southwest Nova Scotia, it was because
of battles like we had on the wharf at Caraquet."*
—Val Comeau fisherman Herménégilde Robichaud—

T HE PROTEST BEGAN almost spontaneously. On Wednesday,
September 19, 1979, inshore fishermen in northeast New
Brunswick blocked the wharf at Lamèque so that a herring
seiner, the *Scotia Point,* could not unload its catch. They stayed put
on Thursday, until the vessel, still loaded with herring, finally left for
another port. On Friday, 200 inshore fishermen gathered at the
wharf in Shippegan to stop two Nova Scotia seiners, the *Margaret
Elizabeth I* and the *Lavallée no. 2,* from unloading their catch.
Again, the fishermen stayed all night and into the following day,
until the vessels, again, departed. Early Sunday, on hearing that
some seiners were headed for Caraquet, fishermen, again, began
gathering at that wharf. They were desperate. They wanted the
public to know that the seiners were destroying the inshore herring
fishery.

The herring fishery in the southern Gulf of St Lawrence was a
classic example of the growing conflict between small-boat fishermen and large-boat fleets. Until the mid-1960s, herring had been
exclusively an inshore fishery. The foot-long speckled fish were
caught when they came into shore in schools to lay their eggs. There
were two important spawning grounds in the southern gulf, the Bay
of Chaleur and Point Escuminac, both off the New Brunswick
coast. In the spring, when the herring came closest to shore,
fishermen used gillnets—usually 20 to 30—which were anchored
at both ends and hauled in by hand once a day. In the fall, fishermen
went out at night to deeper waters and let their nets drift behind
their boats.

During this time, roughly 2,000 fishermen in eastern New
Brunswick depended on herring for their livelihood. For some

fishermen, it was as important as lobster. "For us, herring was a principal fishery," says Caraquet fisherman Jean-Jacques Lanteigne. "Almost everyone fished it. If you didn't have that fishery in the spring, you started your year badly." Throughout the 1950s and 1960s, landings had averaged 35,000 metric tonnes a year. Fishermen knew that there were more herring there, but there was no point in catching it. The only markets were the smokehouses in Cap-Pelé. It didn't take long to fill them, and once that happened—because the smoking process took six to eight weeks—the smokers stopped buying.

The 1965 annual report of the New Brunswick Department of Fisheries had noted, "The fact remains that our herring fishery is far from being adequately exploited. It is estimated that over 100 million pounds of herring caught by New Brunswick fishermen was landed outside the province because of the lack of processing facilities."

That year, the provincial government hired a Halifax consulting firm to study the possibility of developing a herring-reduction industry whereby herring is ground into meal for fertilizer and animal feed. Although it was a growing industry elsewhere, there were only two reduction plants operating on the New Brunswick coast—Gorton-Pew Fisheries in Caraquet and Robichaud and Company Limited in Shippegan—and they had restricted capacity. (National Sea Products had also owned a herring-reduction plant, Eagle Fisheries in Shippegan, but it had just burned down. It was rebuilt a year later.) The report recommended that another herring-reduction plant be built and that a new method of catching the fish be tried—purse-seining by large boats. "In addition to making greater landings during spawning season," the report said, "the boats may be able to follow the herring to the summer feeding area off the Magdalen Islands and make profitable catches there, thus extending the season."

About the same time, the herring fishery on the British Columbia coast was in crisis. The seiner fleet there—made up of more than 200 vessels—was having difficulty finding fish. Landings had dropped by about 50 percent between 1965 and 1967. Finally realizing that the stocks were seriously depleted, Ottawa closed the fishery, except to provide local food and bait. Faced with no livelihood and on the invitation of the New Brunswick government, 16 large British

The New Brunswick government began to encourage the development of a herring-seiner fleet in the 1970s. (COURTESY DFO MONCTON)

Columbia seiners moved to the East Coast. Most were owned by B.C. Packers, which opened a herring-reduction plant in Lower Caraquet called ABC Packing Corporation. (This was one of the reasons why British Columbia's United Fishermen and Allied Workers' Union began an organizing drive on the East Coast. As Jack Nichol wrote to Gilles Thériault in October 1973, "In 1967, we undertook an organizational drive on the East Coast, prompted mainly by the number of West Coast fishermen engaged in the Atlantic herring seining industry. B.C. companies were heavily involved in the exploitation of the Atlantic herring resource. However, our activities were confined mainly to N.S.")

About the time that the west-coast seiners began to move east, a major concentration of herring was found off southwest New-foundland. This encouraged the development of an indigenous herring-seiner fleet. The New Brunswick government, for example, began to finance the construction of seiners. By 1975, according to the Department of Fisheries annual report, New Brunswick had 9 herring seiners of more than 100 feet, 34 "of medium size," and 60 others, which were used to transport the fish to the plants. Seiners were also built in Nova Scotia and Newfoundland. At the time, the federal Department of Fisheries issued licences on an Atlantic-wide basis. The vessels could fish anywhere in the region. In 1970, when a freeze was finally placed on licences, there were already more than 60 herring seiners licensed to fish in the Gulf of St Lawrence.

Herring seiners have a much greater capacity than inshore vessels. They catch the fish by encircling the schools with large nets that are then "pursed," or drawn together, at the bottom and hauled on deck by hydraulic rollers. The seiners are also equipped with sonar gear, which allows them to find concentrations of herring. Because the fish tend to school more at night, purse-seining usually takes place then. As a result, seiners frequently overran inshore gear. As the seiner fleet grew, gear conflict became a major problem.

The seiner fleet was a source of irritation for the inshore sector in other ways. Paul-Aimé Mallet of LeGoulet fished herring during the late 1960s. "I can remember when around 40 of us inshore boats were waiting at the wharf in Shippegan when a seiner came in," he recalls. "The company decided to unload the seiner first. We knew the company stole from us all the time. For example, you knew your boat could hold 80 barrels. When the company un-loaded it, they only gave you credit for 65 or 70 barrels. With a seiner, with its greater quantity, the company could steal more. So it'd give preference to the seiner, and the inshore guys would have to wait." As well, inshore and seiner fishermen were always compet-ing for markets.

But the worst conflict was over the effect of the seiner fleet on the stock itself. Once the bigger vessels got into the fishery, inshore fishermen began catching only 10,000-15,000 metric tonnes a year compared with landings that were historically three times that. Inshore fishermen maintained that the seiners intercepted the fish before the schools got to shore. "During those years," Mallet says, "we had to continually search for herring. We couldn't find it anymore. Some fishermen started to abandon the herring, and it had been 50 percent of our revenue." In August 1967, after a stormy meeting with provincial and federal representatives failed to settle the issue, inshore fishermen burned the ABC wharf at Lower Caraquet in protest, causing $300,000 in damage.

By 1970, total herring landings in the southern gulf had in-

In the late 1960s, frustrated by the presence of British Columbia seiners, inshore fishermen burned the ABC Packing Corporation wharf at Lower Caraquet.

(CEA COLLECTION L'EVANGELINE E818)

creased to 300,000 metric tonnes, most of it landed by the seiner fleet. The situation was becoming increasingly unacceptable to inshore fishermen. Rubbing salt into the wound, the Moncton *Times-Transcript* published an article in January 1978 applauding a herring captain, Vincent Doucette of Fredericton, for his successful year. According to the article, Doucette's seiner had caught 11,000 metric tonnes of herring in the Bay of Fundy in 1977, worth more than $1 million. The total New Brunswick catch in the Gulf of St Lawrence that year was 61,000 metric tonnes, worth $6.3 million. "Nobody really stopped to think what that meant," says fisherman Jean-Guy Maillet. "If he had been fishing in the gulf, one boat would have taken an equivalent of 18 percent of the total catch." MFU president Harold Manuel pointed out in a press release that Doucette's catch was more than 50 inshore boats, employing 200 to 250 men, could catch in one season. The seiner's crew consisted of 10 men.

Throughout 1978 and 1979, the MFU wrote letter after letter to the federal Department of Fisheries. They also met with Fisheries Minister Roméo LeBlanc and, later, James McGrath, who took over the portfolio during the short-lived Joe Clark era. The MFU wanted the 1979 seiner season to be pushed back, from mid-September, its usual opening date, to October in order to give inshore fishermen a headstart at the herring.

On August 24, 1979, the Atlantic Herring Management Committee called an emergency meeting in Halifax. The MFU asked to attend but was refused because it didn't have a representative on the committee. Instead, MFU members waited in the corridor as seiner captains and government officials discussed the issue behind closed doors. The committee eventually emerged and announced that the seiner season would start, as usual, on September 15.

The anger over herring had been building for more than a decade. For the union, the committee's decision was the final straw. "The guys were so mad about herring that it wasn't hard to mobilize hundreds of them," says fisherman Jean-Guy Maillet.

*   *   *   *   *

The first day of the protest, at Lamèque, had been tense. "The fishermen were very nervous," recalls MFU organizer Réginald Comeau. "They weren't sure how far they could go with it, how much support they would have." But as several hundred fishermen gathered that Wednesday afternoon and stayed on the wharf throughout the evening and then overnight, they began to feel more confident. "They realized then that a lot of people were prepared to fight with them," says Comeau.

By Thursday, the protest began to attract attention. Other fishermen from around the province, as well as the media, were drawn to the area. Paul-Aimé Mallet, then president of the MFU's northeast local, said that fishermen would continue their protest until federal fisheries minister James McGrath came to New Brunswick to talk to them. MFU organizer Omer Chouinard had shut down the Richibucto office and was heading north. On Friday morning, Dick Crouter, Department of Fisheries and Oceans (DFO) director for the Maritime Region, arrived, and talks were held between representatives of the two groups, though nothing was settled. As the protest continued, Comeau and Chouinard tracked down MFU executive secretary Gilles Thériault, who was in Halifax at the annual convention of the Nova Scotia Federation of Labour. Thériault left Saturday morning for the long drive back to New Brunswick. After spending the late afternoon and evening in the office, preparing information for the press, he left for Caraquet, where the protest was now under way.

(MFU president Harold Manuel had also been in the northeast on Friday but had left because he considered the fishermen's actions too extreme. Manuel didn't understand the issue, nor did he realize the seriousness of the situation. On Monday, he attended a squid conference at Oak Island, Nova Scotia.)

By the time Thériault arrived at 6:00 a.m., Sunday, there were already 50 fishermen gathered in the parking lot of the Fisheries School, next door to the Caraquet wharf. No one was sure when the seiners would arrive. By 9:00, when the first vessel pulled into port, the protesters' ranks had swelled to 200. "There was a real sense that fishermen were doing something that was going to have an impact," Thériault recalls. "For years, they had felt powerless. Now, they had a means to finally force the issue." At 11:00, a DFO official tipped off the fishermen that the RCMP "riot squad" was on its way. The news spread quickly through the town, and several hundred curious residents came down to have a look.

Unknown to the fishermen, the riot squad had actually arrived in Shippegan on Saturday and had spent the early evening practising manoeuvres in a parking lot. At 11:00 p.m., Ted Gaudet, then DFO area manager in the northeast, had been telephoned and asked to come to RCMP headquarters. There, he had been briefed on plans for the following day. "They indicated at the time that their procedures were that they would move onto the wharf and try to clear it peacefully," Gaudet recalls. "They said that they had photographs that had been taken on the wharf, and they knew who these people were. They gave me the names, and asked me if these were the leaders. I indicated yes, those were the leaders. They said if they had to clear the wharf that these people would be picked up. They also indicated that once they began, it was their matter. That once the RCMP gets into an operation, we [the DFO] do not get involved whatsoever."

The "leaders" who had been identified were Gilles Thériault, Omer Chouinard, Réginald Comeau, and Herménégilde Robichaud.

The Belle Baie fish plant is the only plant on the Caraquet wharf, a long structure with a U-shaped hook at the end. The herring pump, used to offload fish into trucks for distribution to plants around the province, was directly in front of it. People had gathered between the pump and the plant, in the pathway that led to the road in one direction, to the water in the other. Nothing could get through. RCMP cars began arriving, lights flashing, but they were halted at roadside.

Two RCMP officers, both English-speaking, got out of their vehicles and made their way cautiously to the front of the crowd. Fishermen Paul-Aimé Mallet and Herménégilde Robichaud were there, along with Réginald Comeau, Omer Chouinard, and Gilles Thériault. "You've got to move," said one officer. "We want everyone out of here."

"We're not going," Thériault told them. "This is important to us. Everybody's staying put."

It was only a momentary exchange, but it was enough of a distraction to enable other RCMP cars to circle through the parking lot and around to the back of the plant. These cars contained the riot squad, officers trained to deal with crowd situations. Herménégilde Robichaud recognized some of them from the occupation of the unemployment insurance office in Bathurst five years earlier.

On the fifth day of the 1979 protest against the herring seiners, inshore fishermen blocked the wharf at Caraquet. Before noon, the riot squad arrived and lobbed tear-gas canisters into the unsuspecting crowd.

The officers quickly got out of their vehicles and formed lines between the crowd and the water. They meant business. Wearing gas masks and helmets, holding shields and clubs, they were an unusual and awesome sight for people in the village. "The only thing that sticks in my mind from that day was the sight of those RCMP. I was nervous as hell," fisherman Jean-Guy Maillet admits today.

"We don't want any trouble," Thériault quickly told the officers beside him. "We're not here for violence. We don't want anyone to get hurt." His words were drowned out by the ominous sound of men beating clubs on shields as they approached the crowd. In seconds, tear-gas canisters came flying through the air. One landed at Thériault's feet, knocking him off balance. He stumbled, smashing his glasses on the concrete. Three RCMP officers grabbed him, hand-cuffed him, and hauled him off to a waiting vehicle. People screamed as more tear gas flew into the crowd. Some began to panic; others, to flee. Herménégilde Robichaud had been near Thériault when the canister landed. An asthmatic, Robichaud began to take an attack as the gas filled his lungs. Just then, some officers grabbed him. Gasping for breath, he tried to tell them that he was having an attack. But none of the officers spoke French, and Robichaud couldn't find the words in English.

All of this had taken only a few seconds. After Thériault and Robichaud had been taken away, and as tear-gas fumes hung in the air, the remaining crowd moved back into the Belle Baie parking lot. People began to regroup as Omer Chouinard jumped onto the back of a truck to calm people and plan the next move. But suddenly, a canister landed at Chouinard's feet, and as the gas again wafted through the crowd, people dispersed for good. An hour later, while RCMP officers stood guard, the trucks began to unload the herring from the seiners that had reached port. On Monday, the RCMP riot squads returned to the Caraquet and Shippegan wharves, but the fishermen did not. "All quiet in herring war," a newspaper headline concluded.

Thériault and Robichaud were taken to the jail at the Caraquet Town Hall. As a nervous Robichaud paced in his narrow cell, worried about what his family would think, Thériault caught up on some much-needed sleep. Several hours later, Chouinard and a local lawyer arrived and bailed them out. Chouinard, Thériault, and

Represented by Moncton lawyer Donald Poirier (left), fisherman Herménégilde Robichaud and MFU executive secretary Gilles Thériault stood trial in Caraquet on charges arising from the protest. (CEA COLLECTION L'EVANGELINE E9085)

Robichaud stopped for supper at Réginald Comeau's home in Sheila, then headed to Moncton. Both Thériault and Robichaud would be convicted of mischief in a much-publicized trial in Caraquet in the New Year.

It would take another week after the protest for the DFO to settle the issue. Seiner fishing was halted in the interim, though the inshore continued to fish. Recognizing that the situation couldn't continue, the seiners and the inshore finally agreed to negotiate with DFO officials. In the end, the DFO placed observer teams on the seiners to see whether spawning herring were being taken, provided funding for inshore fishermen to buy sonar detectors and other equipment, allowed an MFU representative on the Atlantic Herring Management Committee, and moved the opening date of the seiners' season to October (and from then on, the season for the seiners would begin in October). On October 3, the seiner fleet resumed fishing.

Inshore fishermen could live with the settlement, though they didn't consider it a great victory. More important was the support that they had received for their cause, not only from other fishermen but also from the public. Many people were shocked that tear gas had been used, especially on women and children. It was the first time, in fact, that people remembered tear gas ever being used on the Acadian Peninsula. Provincial justice minister Rodman Logan, ultimately responsible for bringing in the riot squad, was called upon, in letters to newspapers, to defend his decision.

A week after the incident, an MFU "day of solidarity" was held at the Caraquet arena. Supporters came from all over the province, including representatives of regional development councils, the New Brunswick Federation of Labour, the National Farmers Union, the Kouchibouguac expropriates, and the Bathurst Labour Council, as well as Nova Scotia fishermen who also fished herring in the southern Gulf of St Lawrence.

The real victory for inshore fishermen would come in 1981, when the total allowable catch was set at 12,000 metric tonnes for the inshore and 3,000 metric tonnes for the seiners, whose quota had been 55,000 metric tonnes a year earlier. Throughout the 1970s, the quota split had been 80 percent for the seiners and 20 percent for the inshore; now, it was reversed. "There was no doubt in our minds that it was a result of 1979, even if it was a year and a half later," says Gilles Thériault.

Ted Gaudet, today DFO director general of the Gulf Region, agrees. "It was at that point that inshore fishermen had sensitized everyone to the fact that there was a major problem in the herring fishery," he says, "that the inshore fishermen were not satisfied with the allocation process, that the seiners were getting too much fish, and that things must change to allow the fish to come back to the inshore fishermen. Basically, it took one and a half, two years for the scientific assessment to take place, to say, 'We have a major problem here.' That's when the cuts were made, and those cuts automatically gave priority to the inshore."

Gaudet maintains that it was Roméo LeBlanc, once again fisheries minister, who decided to give the greater share of the herring to the inshore sector. "He felt that because of the importance of the herring to the inshore fishery, that inshore fishermen should be given priority," Gaudet says.

After 1981, though problems were far from solved, the herring fishery in the southern Gulf of St Lawrence became, once again, primarily an inshore fishery.

The year before, the MFU had started to lobby for the seiners to get out of the gulf altogether, and soon after, that began to happen. With the reduced quota, it was no longer worthwhile for the Bay of Fundy seiner fleet to fish in the gulf. In 1983, the 16-vessel gulf fleet and the 49-vessel Scotia-Fundy fleet agreed to stay in their own region. Later the two sections of the gulf fleet reached a similar agreement: the 8 northern New Brunswick vessels would fish in the southern gulf, and the 8 Newfoundland vessels would fish off western Newfoundland. The number of herring seiners in the southern Gulf of St Lawrence had dropped dramatically, from 64 before 1983 to 8 in 1985. A government-sponsored buy-back program introduced in 1984 reduced the New Brunswick fleet even further. By 1987, there were only 6 herring seiners in the northeast.

* * * * *

In coming years, inshore fishermen would point to the 1979 herring battle on the wharf at Caraquet as a major turning point for the Maritime Fishermen's Union. Of all the battles that the union had fought and would fight, it was the one that strengthened and increased the membership, that won over the public. "The importance?" asks fisherman Jean-Jacques Lanteigne. "It woke the people up. Not just the fishermen but people in general. People didn't really understand the situation of fishermen before. And it made fishermen realize they needed a solid organization to protect their rights. More fishermen became union members, more dues came in."

"If we were able to move into southwest Nova Scotia in 1983, it was because of battles like we had on the wharf at Caraquet," says fisherman Herménégilde Robichaud. "I remember the first time we had a meeting in southwest Nova, fishermen said nothing was possible, there were too many seiners. Then they saw what we accomplished. They had the same problem as us. They were in the process of disappearing."

But all that was still in the future. On Monday, September 24, 1979, after the tear-gassing in Caraquet, Thériault, Chouinard, and Robichaud were back in the Richibucto office, preparing for a press conference that they had called for the following day. They wanted to explain what had happened in the north and to announce that a day of solidarity would be held in a week's time. As they drove to Moncton on Tuesday, after consulting with fishermen all over the province, they felt pretty confident. The fishermen had at least got their point across, and the herring situation could no longer be ignored.

Just before 5:00 p.m., the three men pulled into the parking lot of the Moncton Union Centre. Reporters were milling about. "What's everybody doing outside," Thériault absent-mindedly thought to himself as he parked his car. "The press conference is inside." As Thériault, Chouinard, and Robichaud climbed out of the car, they recognized a lot of faces. All of them seemed excited. "You're not allowed inside," CBC reporter Rudy Amirault told the three men, "because you're all communists."

COMMUNISM:
A HERRING OF
ANOTHER COLOUR

"Union centre management bans 'COMMUNIST MFU.'
'To my knowledge, Harold Manuel is an avowed Communist,'
says manager Harley Harrison."
—Moncton *Times-Transcript*, September 26, 1979—

THE MONCTON UNION CENTRE had been a focal point of labour-movement activity since it was purchased by several unions in the early 1960s, during a strike against Canadian National Railways. A former school, the two-storey brick building housed most union locals in the area, as well as offices of the New Brunswick Federation of Labour (NBFL) and the Canadian Labour Congress (CLC). The Maritime Fishermen's Union had often held its meetings there. But not today.

The media had set up their cameras, put their tape recorders in place, and were waiting for the MFU's five-o'clock press conference when centre manager Harley Harrison entered the room. A former president of the Canadian Union of Public Employees local at the Moncton Hospital, Harrison had been growing privately irritated by the occasional presence of the MFU at the centre. When he spotted a Halifax journalist who wrote for a Marxist-Leninist newspaper, he brusquely ordered her to leave. He left the room himself but returned a minute later to tell everyone to get out. He said that he hadn't realized that the press conference was being held by the MFU, because the room had been booked through the CLC.

The MFU is not allowed to use the building because the union is controlled by communists, Harrison told the stunned group. "At least their executive. To my knowledge, Harold Manuel is an avowed communist." He explained that the centre had a policy, established several years earlier, that communists were not allowed to use the building. (In fact, the policy stated that political parties were not allowed to hold meetings there. The NDP had got into hot water during the 1978 provincial election campaign for doing so.)

As a result, everyone ended up in the parking lot, waiting for MFU members to arrive. A spicy story about tear-gassing on the wharf at Caraquet had become even spicier with the addition of a new element—supposed communist infiltration of the union. Both Thériault and Chouinard, however, were left speechless by the accusations. They had little to say to the waiting crowd. "I knew Harrison from going to federation of labour conventions," Thériault says today. "I knew he was a right-winger. But these accusations seemed to come totally out of the blue."

The next day, NBFL president Paul LePage told the press that the MFU would be expelled from the federation if it were proved that the union was controlled by communists. "The communist philosophy is to destroy unions, not to make them better," he said. That evening, however, LePage met with MFU representatives and the following day withdrew his comments, turning his anger instead against the centre manager. "Mr. Harrison should refrain from making such statements unless he has evidence to support his accusations," LePage said. The federation president offered his support for the union's Day of Solidarity, which was coming up on Sunday.

Until this time, the MFU's relationship with both the NBFL and the CLC had been good. Inshore fishermen were seen as one of the last and largest groups of unorganized workers in the region, and the labour movement was interested in seeing them organized. One of the MFU's first contacts had been Allister MacLeod, a tall, distinguished-looking man who held the CLC's top job in Atlantic Canada. A Cape Bretoner, MacLeod had been active in the labour movement from the time he had started driving a bus and had joined a local of the Canadian Brotherhood of Railway, Transport and General Workers in Sydney after the war. In 1962, the union set up a council of locals and hired MacLeod as executive secretary. In 1970, MacLeod went to work for the CLC as its Nova Scotia representative. Five years later, he moved into the regional director's job, where he stayed until he retired in 1987.

MacLeod worked to have CLC jurisdiction for inshore fishermen in the Maritimes transferred to the MFU. He also got funding for the union. In the spring of 1978, the CLC allocated $40,000

The MFU's relationship with organized labour had more or less been good since the union's founding. The NBFL's Tim McCarthy (left) and the CLC's Allister MacLeod had both supported the union. (COURTESY MFU)

over two years to help the union hire organizers in Nova Scotia and Prince Edward Island. (The amount was later increased.)

Just two weeks before the blow-up at the Moncton Union Centre, MacLeod met with MFU representatives in Truro, Nova Scotia. "He saw the relationship between the MFU and the CLC as being good," the meeting minutes said. Seemingly, the relationship between the MFU and the labour movement was good, though a conflict was brewing beneath the surface.

*　*　*　*　*

There are at least two truisms about the role of communists in the organization of fishermen in Canada. One, communists *have* been involved in most major attempts to organize fishermen on both coasts. Two, the presence of communists in organizing drives has been used by governments or companies to discredit the effort, to deny the need for a union, or to paint all participants with the same brush.

Canadian historians Irving Abella and David Millar, in *The Ca-*

nadian Worker in the Twentieth Century, point out that during the 1930s, communists were largely responsible for organizing the militant unions of the Congress of Industrial Organizations. They had even faced opposition from the old Trades and Labor Congress. Abella and Millar suggest that Canadian workers owed a debt to communists who took on tough organizing jobs at a time when no one else was willing.

Nowhere has this been more apparent than with inshore fishermen. One of the first major attempts to organize fishermen in the Atlantic region was in 1939 at Lockeport, Nova Scotia, where both organizers, Pat Sullivan and Charlie Murray, were known communists. As noted in *Lockeport Lockout,* that didn't seem to matter to the people of Lockeport, but it did matter

> to the companies and government, whose red-baiting tirades turned Communism into the central issue of the dispute. This red-herring allowed government to discount the central role played by such Lockeport men as Ben MacKenzie and Bob Williams, and to deny the legitimacy of the fishermen's struggle. Somehow, the same fishermen that government had portrayed for years as too strong-minded and too independent to join a union had suddenly become, in the eyes of the same government, weak-willed enough to be led by "outsiders" whose interests were supposedly contrary to their own. As in other struggles—then and now—wanting to improve working conditions became synonymous with being a Communist.

Homer Stevens was another example. A long-time member and one-time president of the British Columbia fishermen's union, he is also a communist. This became a major factor in the union's defeat at Canso during the 1970-71 strike. At the same time, a fisherman quoted in Silver Donald Cameron's book on the event described Stevens as "for twenty years, the only man that had guts enough to come to Nova Scotia to try to organize the fishermen."

In the same way, there were communists involved in the MFU— though Harold Manuel was not among them.

The late 1960s was a time of political turmoil, not just in Canada but around the world. Universities were alive with political dissent, and students and faculty who considered themselves left wing were struggling to find a political ideology and, in many cases, a political alliance that made sense in an increasingly alien society. Full of idealism, young people really believed that they could change the world.

The University of Moncton campus, as noted earlier, was one of the "hot spots" in the country. Although Acadian nationalism was the spark, the debate was by no means unilineal: people were also interested in various shades of socialism and communism. Several such people moved on to become key activists in the MFU—Gilles Thériault and Omer Chouinard in particular.

Once he had left the campus, Thériault became one of the leaders of the Party Acadien (PA). From the beginning, the PA was a nationalist party, though some members wanted a blend of nationalism and socialism. Thériault was among them. He became more convinced of his views after spending a year abroad in 1975-76. European ideas of socialism and communism were much more developed, and he came back committed to pursuing his involvement in the PA, but a socialist PA.

Omer Chouinard, too, considered himself a socialist, though he was more of a thinker than an activist. He found himself continually challenged. "During the 1970s," Chouinard recalls, "the big issue was always getting involved. Why do intellectual work if you're not involved with the people at the base? Or as Mao put it, 'If you want to taste the apple, you have to take a bite.'" So in 1975, after he and his wife moved back to New Brunswick, both decided to become politically active.

At the time, several "groups of reflection" had formed to discuss the issues of the day. One was in Moncton and consisted of a dozen or so PA members who had organized a study group to better understand questions of socialism and communism. In 1977, the group split from the PA over orientation, a split comparable to, though more local than, the Waffle break from the NDP in the late 1960s. When that happened, the Moncton group, which included both Thériault and Chouinard, decided to investigate another alliance.

It invited representatives of two Montréal-based sectarian groups to come to New Brunswick to make presentations: In Struggle and the Marxist-Leninist League of Canada. Ideologically, the two groups were similar. They were both pro-China, rather than pro-Soviet Union. Practically, the League had closer links with the working class, and members seemed to be less academic. In the end, the Moncton group decided to join the League, again a decision not unlike those of leftists across the country who joined a variety of sectarian parties during this period.

The decision, however, had not been made lightly. It had taken a lot of discussion and a lot of soul-searching. For Chouinard, it was an about-face from an earlier position. Left-wing sectarian groups had been very evident in Montréal during the early 1970s, but Chouinard and his friends had considered them too extreme. By the mid- to late 1970s, however, those same friends were joining those same groups. "The people we knew, the independent groups, had a tendency to say we had to join larger groups. We had to work together, to have more impact," he says.

Chouinard felt a little uneasy about joining a sectarian party, as did Thériault. "I was very hesitant to join," Thériault admits today. "There was something that attracted me about it, but something also that I was uncomfortable with. It seemed very rigid." Thériault was seen as a key person because he had already established credible links with the working class—with inshore fishermen. He eventually agreed to join, and shortly after, the League sent a staff person to work full time in the Moncton area. Behind his back, the fishermen called the staff person "the Lieutenant."

Meanwhile, both Thériault and Chouinard were becoming public figures because of their work with the Maritime Fishermen's Union. Soon after its founding, the MFU adopted a policy of nonalignment with political parties. Fishermen realized that there was nothing to be gained by publicly supporting any political party. They knew that there *was* something to be lost. Some fishermen were strong Tories, others were Liberals, and the odd one even supported the NDP.

The union's policy of nonalignment, however, did not extend to what people—fishermen and staff—did in their spare time. As Thériault and Chouinard became more involved politically, some fishermen started to worry, though most believed that the men had a right to do whatever they wanted as long as they kept it separate from their union involvement.

Doing so wasn't that simple. The MFU was constantly in the news, and Thériault was frequently seen on television or heard on radio. The distinction between Thériault and Chouinard as MFU staff, and Thériault and Chouinard as left-wing radicals was becoming fuzzy to some fishermen—and even fuzzier to the public. The content of the union's newsletter didn't help. Articles denounced the "capitalists" and the "bourgeoisie," and often they were illustrated by angry crowds with fists raised. Some fishermen and some staff began to see the newsletter as dogmatic.

In the meantime, the Marxist-Leninist League, which had changed its name to the Workers' Communist Party (WCP), put pressure on both Thériault and Chouinard to recruit members. Mistakes were made. Before the MFU's annual convention in December 1977, for example, Thériault and Chouinard hand-delivered copies of the WCP's newspaper, the *Forge*, to the homes of each fisherman delegate. The paper included a list of resolutions to be put forward at the convention, including one that said, in effect, that the MFU opposed the two world superpowers. There were others that were equally "out of proportion," to use the words of one fisherman who bluntly told Thériault and Chouinard to stop being so "out to lunch."

Another time, one week before the Fredericton demonstration in 1978, Chouinard attended a meeting of the union in the northeast and suggested that the WCP banner, wide enough to extend across the street, be carried at the demonstration. Planning for the event had taken two months of hard, meticulous work. MFU staff had visited each community several times to rally support. Now it looked as if the effort could go down the drain because all the fishermen and the public would remember was a gigantic communist banner. Some people at the meeting were outraged that Chouinard would suggest such a thing. The fishermen wisely voted against the motion.

They couldn't, however, stop WCP members, as well as members of In Struggle, from coming to the demonstration and handing out their literature or selling their newspapers. Both parties frequently attended MFU-organized activities. Inshore fishermen, with their new-found consciousness about political rights, were seen as ripe for the picking.

Thériault always tried to be up front about his opinions. "My political beliefs are no secret," he told the press when the issue broke at the Moncton Union Centre. "I believe in the principles of communism, but I have always stated that as a personal belief. It has nothing to do with agreeing with what Russia is doing. There are certainly progressive people on staff, but not a majority of one political belief." To both Thériault's and Chouinard's credit, they always worked within the democratic structures of the union. Resolutions were presented, and fishermen—not staff—had a right to vote on them. Nonetheless, the situation was bound to come to a climax.

* * * * *

Harold Manuel had been growing uncomfortable in his position as president of the Maritime Fishermen's Union. In September 1978, less than a year after officially taking office, he presented a letter of resignation to the MFU's Maritime Council. Manuel felt overwhelmed by the amount and complexity of the work involved in trying to lead a union of fishermen from all three Maritime provinces. "One of my main reasons for resigning," he wrote in a prepared statement, "is my lack of memory which is due to the fact that there is too many activities scheduled at the same time and being burdened with both responsibilities of president and secretarial work. I cannot observe and plan these activities properly, therefore my decisions do not count."

Manuel further believed that he wasn't getting enough support from Maritime Council and that the staff were running the show. He also wrote that there was increasing pressure on him, from outside the MFU, to rid the union of some of the employees, those considered communists. "The CLC at this time would like to see some of the workers out of their way because of their political beliefs," he said. Maritime Council, however, didn't accept Manuel's resignation at this time, believing that it would be a setback for the union, which had already lost one president and had barely got under way in Nova Scotia and Prince Edward Island. Manuel agreed to stay on, but his problems didn't go away.

Exactly where this "outside" pressure was coming from is not clear. Allister MacLeod, then CLC regional director, maintains that he didn't know what Thériault's politics were and that even if he did, he wouldn't have cared. "I dealt with Gilles on matters pertaining to the problems of organizing fishermen," MacLeod says. "Never once did he ever indicate his politics to me, whether he was a socialist, a communist, a Liberal, or whatever. I suppose even if he was a communist, he had a right to be one in the same way that I had a right to be a New Democrat, as long as it didn't interfere with our relationship relative to what we were doing. It didn't bother me one damn bit."

MacLeod was bothered, however, by some of the other staff, in particular by Ed Frenette, whose position on Prince Edward Island was being funded by the CLC. MacLeod recalls being approached by Frenette at a meeting in Charlottetown. "I ran into him outside the bar, and he wanted to meet with me," says MacLeod. "What he wants to do is break away from the MFU completely, and he uses all kinds of arguments with me why he should do this. He tried to tell me Manuel was a commie. He said Gilles was some kind of commie. This was five to six months after he was hired. I knew then that whatever good he was going to do, it wouldn't be worth what we were paying him."

Frenette, for his part, denies the story. "I remember calling him [MacLeod] once because I had had a call from Harold Manuel complaining that communists were running the union," Frenette says.

MacLeod had also become increasingly dissatisfied with the CLC's having no say in who the MFU hired, even though the CLC was providing the money. He questioned whether some of the staff had sufficient background in the fishery and in organizing. And although he considered himself a close friend of Harold Manuel, MacLeod recognized that the MFU president's capabilities were limited. "If I was going to hire someone tomorrow to organize fishermen, and I wanted someone who knew how to do it one on one, I'd have Manuel with me, yes," says MacLeod. "But in terms of leadership abilities?... If it wasn't for Gilles, he wouldn't have gone half as far as he did. Gilles really carried the ball."

MacLeod maintains that it wasn't until after the confrontation at the Moncton Union Centre that he became concerned about the communism issue, and then mainly because the accusations could damage the credibility of the union and of the labour movement in general. Two weeks later, MacLeod met privately with Manuel. The following is part of Manuel's written account of what took place:

He [MacLeod] states that the MFU has fallen and is not controlled by its members but by the workers who are sympathizers to the Communists, and also working for the party. The deal at union center was brought about from many things, firstly the demonstration that was held at the fish packers association, where we assembled at the union centre parking lot without permission, and the league papers were left around the lot. Every public gathering that the MFU had, the papers of the Forge and Struggle were being distributed.... Following all these statements and projections ... he asked me if I made a split, how many would follow me? or would the majority follow Gilles. I told him that I didn't know but one thing was clear. It was either me or all the workers, and start all over again. I had been dragged down to the lowest and I was finished.

Manuel read this aloud to Maritime Council when it gathered on October 21, 1979, for an emergency meeting at the Richibucto office. The atmosphere was tense as 14 fishermen and six staff filed in. The voices heard that day reflected the diversity of opinion that was the MFU.

Canso fisherman Jamie MacKenzie chastised Manuel for meeting alone with MacLeod, and denounced what he considered red-baiting tactics. "It's the old red scare," he said, "I'm fed up with it." Herménégilde Robichaud said that if MFU organizers and members were not free to believe and say what they wanted to, "then we have a poor union. When people work in common, the label 'communist' is always there."

Prince Edward Island organizer Wanson Hemphill wanted the issue resolved. "Being called communist is not the same as being called Liberal, Conservative or NDP," he maintained. "Omer and Gilles must choose between the WCP and the union." Jamie MacKenzie disagreed. "If Omer and Gilles are forced to choose," he warned, "then one day we will all have to choose." Richibucto Village fisherman Jean-Guy Maillet, for his part, said that fishermen were playing into the enemies' hands by spending so much time on the issue. "We should unite on the real issues instead," he argued.

Throughout the discussion, there was one underlying theme: what was the MFU president going to do about the situation? Some fishermen wanted to continue the debate until the issue was resolved. "We are kicked out of the Union Centre and the N.B. Federation of Labour is considering kicking us out," said Percy Hayne, Jr, of Pictou Landing. "We have to do something." Northumberland organizer Ron Crawley thought that the men should take the time necessary to know where they stood and how they wanted to respond.

Others, however, wanted to move on, and in the end, Manuel agreed. The group voted to issue a press release denouncing Harley Harrison's accusations, then turned to other business. The fishermen decided to put up a united front, though they themselves were far from united. For many, the biggest problem—even bigger than the communism issue itself—was the lack of leadership.

For some time, many fishermen had believed that Harold Manuel was in over his head, that he didn't have what it took to be a leader. During the Richibucto meeting, they looked to him for direction, but it was not forthcoming. Manuel was simply overwhelmed.

But Manuel wasn't prepared to admit it. He went into the union's annual convention in Memramcook the following January still uncertain whether to run again. Some fishermen, in fact, had been encouraging him; many others had been lobbying Guy Cormier of Cap-Pelé. On the first day of the convention, Cormier was nominated. Manuel's nomination followed. The order was important because the last candidate nominated had to be the first to say whether he would allow his name to stand.

That put Manuel in a bind. If he said yes and Cormier said yes, Manuel would be certain to lose to the more popular Cormier. On the other hand, if Manuel said yes, and Cormier later said no, then Manuel would be president for at least another year. As much as he was ambivalent about giving up the job—for Manuel, it had been prestigious; he had also sold his fishing gear, so he had no work to return to—he was afraid to face the humiliation of losing in a two-way race.

The following day, as elections began, Manuel announced that he wouldn't allow his name to stand. His health was not good, he told delegates, and he wanted to step down before it got worse.

The day after the convention, however, Manuel told a different story. Rumours of his ill health, said one radio report, had been greatly exaggerated. Manuel had told the reporter that his illness was more of the spirit than of the body. "The organizers of the MFU—the majority of them—are communist supporters," he said. "This first came to my knowledge a year and a half ago, but I had no idea of the impact or extent of their power in the organization.

Now it is to the point where they have control of the MFU.

"I am not a communist," Manuel continued. "I refuse to work with anyone with any communist affiliation whatsoever."

Newly elected president Guy Cormier was quick to challenge Manuel's allegations. "The power of the MFU rests in the hands of the fishermen regardless of the views of the organizers," Cormier told the media. "The organizers are there for organizing purposes. They don't participate directly in meetings, cannot bring in motions, nor do they vote on resolutions." Cormier pointed out that the MFU constitution forbade discrimination on the basis of political beliefs. "I really don't see any problem," he said, "because the fishermen are convinced that the union is what they need, and the workers for their part may be of different political beliefs from us, but they do great work for us, and they have the full support of the fishermen."

*   *   *   *   *

The Maritime Fishermen's Union was still on the Moncton Union Centre's blacklist when the annual convention of the New Brunswick Federation of Labour rolled around in June 1980. The Saint John and District Labour Council and the Canadian Paperworkers Union called for the ban to be lifted, but their resolutions were stalled. Finally, in February 1981, the ban was removed.

The controversy surrounding the Moncton Union Centre, the MFU, and communism was a temporary hiatus in an otherwise good relationship between the union and organized labour. "I don't think it hurt it a bit really," says the Canadian Labour Congress' Allister MacLeod. "I'd be surprised if there was ever a financial appeal that went out on behalf of the MFU that unions didn't make a donation."

More important was the effect on the overall credibility of the MFU. Certainly, for a time, the MFU was considered by some to be a communist union. Among fishermen, those least bothered by it seemed to be those most involved in the MFU. "What changed my mind was when we went to Vancouver," says Baie-Ste-Anne fisherman Bill McIntyre. "Homer Stevens was a communist, ay, and I questioned a lot of fishermen about it. And they said, 'We don't care what the man is, as long as he does the job we want him to do.' So then I kind of changed my mind. I was doubtful at first because you're brainwashed in school, ay, about communism, and I still don't really know today what communism is. But the fact that Gilles and Omer were communists didn't bother me a damn bit. They never tried to influence me on anything. But were fishermen around here bothered? Fella that didn't want to join, that was his excuse. Was it a major issue in the union? I don't think so, no."

The presence of communists in the union did generate a lot of discussion that otherwise might not have happened. "I think Gilles and Omer at one time were going overboard with the whole communism thing," says fisherman Jean-Guy Maillet. "Again, they were doing an extremely good job for the union, and I think if they had kept a lower profile with their beliefs, it would have saved us a lot of tough meetings and accusations. At one time, our role was mostly trying to defend them. I think they realized that, too."

Many people say that anglophone fishermen were the most bothered by the communism debate. "On the Acadian Peninsula, I never heard people talking about it," says Zoël Robichaud of Neguac. "It was more of a friction with the anglophones. I almost never went to a meeting with anglophones that it didn't come up."

In fact, communism was the reason that fishermen in the Cape Tormentine area eventually withdrew from the MFU. There were about 100 fishermen at wharves in Cape Tormentine, Amos Point, and Murray Corner, and some had been involved in the union right from the start. An MFU local had been formed in early 1977, and Amos Point fisherman Rod Pauley had run for president at the founding meeting. At one point, a majority of fishermen from the Cape Tormentine area had signed cards.

But fishermen there were never interested in a union so that they could bargain collectively. They had historically received better prices for their lobster than other fishermen in eastern New Brunswick, because a larger proportion of their catch was market-sized. They believed that collective bargaining could only bring their prices down. Instead, they wanted a union in order to have input into fisheries regulations. From the beginning, Cape Tormentine fishermen felt uneasy in a group dominated by Acadians, whom they saw as being more militant. But in the end, it was the communism issue that led to their withdrawal.

"The major thing that happened here was that the fishermen thought the union was getting too radical," says Rod Pauley. "That's the whole story. The literature got more radical than people here thought it should be. One of the union papers, the one that really did it, was an arm coming out of a coffin. We were being so oppressed or whatever, and that pretty well finished it for guys here." Rod Pauley's older brother Reg, a highline fisherman who never supported the union, agrees: "We saw what was happening in Marxist-Leninist countries, and we knew that it wasn't something we wanted here. We didn't feel comfortable with it." By the early 1980s, only a handful of fishermen in the Cape Tormentine area would still consider themselves MFU members.

The communism issue also made life difficult for federal Department of Fisheries and Oceans bureaucrats. "I was having a helluva time selling the MFU as a credible organization to my superiors because of its radical positions, its Marxist-Leninist tendencies," says Ted Gaudet, area manager for the northeast at the time. "It was frustrating because you were trying to deal with the MFU as a fishermen's organization, yet at the same time, there were all these signals coming out that it was a communist organization." It also put pressure on some staff members. Jean-Marie Nadeau, one of the original organizers in the northeast, left the union because of it. "The only good thing I can say about the whole communism period was that a real effort was made during this time to involve women in the union," he says.

In Nova Scotia and Prince Edward Island, the effect is less clear. "If it hurt anywhere," says the CLC's Allister MacLeod, "it was probably in Prince Edward Island. You have to remember, P.E.I. is a very conservative place." The island's vice president, in fact, resigned over the issue. Ivan Shaw, a close friend of Harold Manuel, didn't agree with the way it was being handled. (Shaw later rejoined the union and still pays his union dues today.) The co-operative movement on the island and the Eastern Fishermen's Federation often resorted to red-baiting to discredit the MFU. In Nova Scotia, former fisheries minister Donald Cameron, during a debate in the Legislative Assembly in 1982, denounced the MFU for being communist-led.

Although most of the accusations of communism focused on New Brunswick, the reality was that throughout the region, many MFU staff and volunteers had affiliations that could be and were construed as "communist." In Prince Edward Island, for example, nuns and priests who had worked in the Third World and supported

Hatfield wants to bury Us !

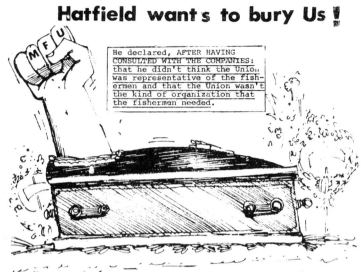

He declared, AFTER HAVING CONSULTED WITH THE COMPANIES: that he didn't think the Union was representative of the fishermen and that the Union wasn't the kind of organization that the fisherman needed.

NOTHING WILL STOP THE UNION FROM CONTINUING THEIR BATTLE

countries like Nicaragua devoted tremendous energy over the years to helping the union. In some people's view, anyone who supported Nicaragua was a communist. In Nova Scotia, the Labour Research and Support Centre, based at Dalhousie University, was thought to condone some brand of Marxist-Leninism. Its members also supported the union in various ways.

Yet at the same time, organizing did continue. Except in the case of Cape Tormentine, the union had problems attracting and keeping members more because it lacked resources and wasn't a legally recognized union than because it was seen as being communist-led. In Prince Edward Island, for example, there was a major membership drive in the fall of 1978, and more than 400 fishermen signed cards. In the following year, however, many of them heard little from, and saw even less of, the MFU because it wasn't able to make regular visits or become involved in every issue that came along. For MFU organizers, just learning to understand the fishery was a challenge in itself. By the time Ed Frenette decided to leave the union in mid-1981, membership on the island had dwindled to a handful of solid members, mainly in the Savage Harbour and Miminegash areas, and a lot of names on paper.

In Nova Scotia, organizing had followed a similar pattern. MFU staff went into an area and got fishermen to sign cards but made few return visits. It was even difficult to say who was a member and who wasn't: a fisherman might sign a card but then not pay his dues. The union was always reluctant to say how many members it had, as the information would inevitably be used against it by its foes, the EFF in particular. By 1978, locals had been established and organizers hired in Guysborough County, the Northumberland Strait, and Cape Breton. But by 1981, the organizers had all left, mainly because the union had no money to pay them. One organizer was hired to cover the whole area, and he began again the time-consuming process of signing up members. No inroads had yet been made into southwest Nova Scotia, still considered the main fishing area in the province.

The other side of the coin on the communism issue—and on this most people agree as well—is that involvement in a sectarian group provided MFU staff with an ideological framework and a discipline to continue to build the union when times got tough. And there were some very tough times. "Sure they made mistakes," says former federal fisheries minister Roméo LeBlanc, "but I think if there had not been some real ideological commitment, they would have gotten discouraged a lot faster."

MFU organizer Réginald Comeau agrees. "Without the communism issue," he says, "the union wouldn't have been as militant as it was. We needed to be militant. We would never have won the battles that we did—the battle over herring, for example—if we hadn't been militant. For me, there was as much positive in the communism period as there was negative."

The bottom line was that both Gilles Thériault and Omer Chouinard were dedicated workers—competent and skilled in organizing—who weren't in it for their own personal gain or, obviously, for the money. They were in it because they believed in the cause of inshore fishermen. And for the fishermen, that was what counted most.

The late 1970s was a critical period for the MFU. By the time the convention of January 1980 was over, Harold Manuel was gone and Guy Cormier was in place as president. Unlike Manuel, Cormier had a clear vision for the union. He was an intelligent, strong leader who had the respect of staff and fishermen everywhere.

For Cormier, the important thing, above all, was that fishermen have a union, that fishermen learn to work together. Although rumblings of communist influence continued to be heard, by the time Cormier was well into his first term as president, they had all but disappeared. The political involvements of both Thériault and Chouinard were much more low profile, and Cormier was happy to keep it that way.

By 1982, the communist affiliations of both men ended when the Workers' Communist Party and In Struggle folded. For the Maritime Fishermen's Union, the 1980s had begun.

LEGISLATION IN NEW BRUNSWICK: "ONE DOWN, TWO TO GO"

Following deliberations over the past year ... my minister of fisheries will be placing before you legislation establishing the rights of collective bargaining in the fishing industry.
—New Brunswick Throne Speech, 1981—

The Fisheries Bargaining Act, which was referred to the Law Amendments Committee at the last session of the legislature, will again be placed before you for approval.
—New Brunswick Throne Speech, 1982—

THE EXTENSION of Canada's jurisdiction from 12 to 200 miles had promised great things for the country's fishing industry. After centuries of exploitation and decimation of fish stocks by foreign vessels, Canada, it seemed, was finally going to take control of its fishery. On the East Coast, there was a mood of optimism and excitement. The number of boats increased, and the number of fishermen jumped; the number of plant workers rose from 14,000 to 25,000. In the Atlantic region alone, fish plants tripled to 600.

But such expansion only compounded problems. By 1981, the fishery was again in crisis. As journalist Ralph Surette wrote in *Atlantic Insight* in November 1981:

The codfish off Newfoundland didn't migrate near the shore. The herring in the Bay of Fundy were small and oily. The Gulf of St. Lawrence herring fishery was closed to seiners because of lack of fish. The price for groundfish collapsed, setting off a three-week strike by Nova Scotia draggermen. And 10 fish plants in the Atlantic region shut down in August, putting nearly 4,000 plant workers out of work. For the east coast fishery, 1981 has been one long disaster. Things are so bad ... that when the fish companies said they were losing money, the fishermen actually believed it.

It was already a well-worn phrase, but it was taken out, dusted off, and put into use again. There were just too many boats, everyone said, chasing too few fish.

The situation grew worse as western economies slipped into a recession. Inventories were high, prices were low, and interest rates were on the rise. Companies that had overextended themselves during the heady days of the late 1970s were now in trouble. By the end of 1981, the major fish companies in Atlantic Canada—National Sea Products Ltd and H.B. Nickerson and Sons Ltd in Nova Scotia, the Lake Group Ltd and Fisheries Products Ltd in Newfoundland—were all on the verge of collapse.

The late 1970s had also been a period of expansion for the Maritime Fishermen's Union. Locals had been established quickly around the region—three in Nova Scotia, two on Prince Edward Island. But by the early 1980s, the union was in financial trouble. It had never managed to put a structure in place to support itself: dues collection was still voluntary and haphazard. As fishermen, too, were hit by the recession, the MFU knew that obtaining the right to negotiate the price of fish was imperative.

In 1981, the union stepped up its campaign for collective bargaining legislation with major demonstrations in all three Maritime capitals. The first one was in Charlottetown in mid-February. Two hundred and fifty angry fishermen and labour leaders climbed five stories to the office of Premier Angus MacLean to demand legislation. Later, Nova Scotia fishermen confronted Fisheries Minister Edmund Morris at the legislative building in Halifax. And in late March, more than 800 fishermen and support-ers picketed on the steps of the legislative building in Fredericton in what one newspaper report called "one of the most forceful and effective in a series of demonstrations the fishermen's union has staged this year."

While the Fredericton demonstration was going on outside, New Brunswick lieutenant governor Hédard Robichaud was read-ing his throne speech inside. It included a promise to introduce collective bargaining legislation for fishermen. But the MFU was leery. Union president Guy Cormier told the press that fishermen would continue to picket the legislature until the bill was actually introduced. The fishermen kept that promise until mid-April, when many left to get ready for the spring lobster season.

Fisheries Minister Jean Gauvin had said at the end of 1979 that collective bargaining legislation would be in place by 1981. But the Joint Committee on Primary Marketing and Commercial Relationships in the Fishing Industry in New Brunswick, whose mandate was to draft the proposed bill, wasn't set up until July 1980. Headed by Fisheries Deputy Minister Léonce Chenard, it included fishermen's representatives Gastien Godin and Clarence Larocque of the Association Professionnelle des Pêcheurs du Nord-est and Gilles Thériault of the MFU and processor representatives Jim Bateman of National Sea Products, Maxime Cormier of Roma Fisheries Limited in Grande-Anse, and William Moffatt of Connors Brothers. (There was no co-op representative on this committee because the co-op movement thought that it had a commitment from Gauvin to exclude co-ops from the legislation. That was what his task force had recommended in 1979.)

Throughout the rest of the year and into 1981, the committee met to draft legislation. But the process was slow-going. Almost all members lacked knowledge of even the most basic trade-union principles, and several, including Chairman Chenard and Connors Brothers' William Moffatt, were already on record as opposing the unionization of fishermen. By March 1981, frustrated that the process was going nowhere, Gilles Thériault withdrew from the committee.

Jean Gauvin was also becoming frustrated. He had promised to introduce legislation, the session was about to begin, but nothing was ready. "It was going in circles, nothing was happening," he recalls. "I'm not saying Chenard was dragging it purposely, but it's one thing to hear everybody out, consult with everybody, but when the process is done, we should have some action. Again, there was a lot of system resistance. I was trying to handle this issue within the mandate, so I talked again with the premier, and we agreed something should be drafted one way or the other."

Following the meeting with Richard Hatfield, Gauvin told his acting deputy, Tim Andrew, to prepare something. Shortly before Easter, 1981, Andrew, along with Deputy Minister of Labour Doug Stanley and others, put together a piece of legislation that would be known as Bill 94. The haste with which it was drafted would become apparent later.

Incredibly, a government that had dragged its feet on the issue for seven years now had two groups drafting collective bargaining legislation for fishermen at the same time.

Shortly afterwards, the joint committee submitted an interim report to government. In June, committee members finally agreed on a bill that had been presented by the MFU and studied line by line. The joint committee's legislation would eventually become the basis of Bill 25.

On July 15, 1981, two days before the House prorogued, Labour Minister Mabel DeWare finally introduced legislation. Despite her initial opposition, as well as her ongoing concerns about how such legislation would work, the minister had, in the end, agreed to do it. "When there's pressure on you long enough," she says today, "I guess you are finally convinced."

What DeWare presented, however, was not the bill that fishermen and processors had debated long and hard, but Bill 94, the document drafted by the bureaucrats. She gave several reasons for her decision. The joint committee's bill was too long, too complex, and too similar to the Industrial Relations Act. DeWare told the House that it was "not particularly suited to buyer-seller relationships anticipated for the Fisheries Bargaining Act."

DeWare also proposed that Bill 94 be referred "to the Law Amendments Committee in order to give further opportunity for those persons most affected to comment and to make recommendations on this legislation which will have far-reaching effects on the fishing industry in the province of New Brunswick."

It was clear that legislation would not be passed this year.

DeWare's motion brought an outburst from the Opposition. Liberal fisheries critic Onil Doiron, who had been badgering the government on the issue for years, denounced the Tories for waiting until almost the last day of the session before introducing the legislation. He accused them of deceiving fishermen. "In our opinion," Doiron told the House, "the government never intended this bill to become law, despite what it said. I do not know what pressures were brought to bear on the government, on the minister of fisheries, in particular, but one fact stands out. He decided long ago that legislation would not be put in place this year. For three years now, this government has been using stalling tactics to postpone the passage of legislation giving fishermen the right to organize."

Premier Hatfield dismissed the accusations. "A number of fishermen have spoken to me about this matter," he said simply, "and they want to see the bill and have time to consider it before it is passed." DeWare had the final say: "Mr. Deputy Speaker, I feel that the government did not break its word. We said that we would introduce the bill and we did do that. I would like to explain that when the committee presented its proposals to us for drafting the bill, it was a very cumbersome document with over 100 sections. We felt it was unworkable at the time and that it would take quite a bit of work to bring it down to a form we could present in the House. This isn't a stalling tactic."

The Opposition, along with the MFU, asked for a fall session so that the legislation could be dealt with that year, but the government refused. "We've been betrayed," Richibucto Village fisherman Jean-Guy Maillet told the press.

*   *   *   *   *

There were several striking differences between the joint committee's proposed legislation, the basis for Bill 25, and the bureaucrats' legislation, or Bill 94, which DeWare had introduced. They became evident as the Law Amendments Committee began hearings later that year. No one—neither fishermen nor processors—made presentations in favour of Bill 94, but everyone, including members of law amendments, questioned the glaring differences between the two.

The MFU's lawyer was Raymond Larkin, a native of Prince Edward Island who practised in Halifax. In a prepared brief, he pointed out that the joint committee's legislation was based on two principles:

1. Collective bargaining rights for fishermen should be equivalent to the rights enjoyed by workers under the Industrial Relations Act; and

2. Viable collective bargaining in the fishing industry requires a small number of bargaining units defined by reference to large geographic areas; certification of a fishermen's union in these units would require that all primary purchasers in the area bargain with the certified union.

He emphasized that both processors and fishermen had agreed on these principles. "In contrast," he told the Law Amendments Committee, "Bill 94 represents a major departure from these principles and from generally recognized structures for free collective bargaining."

There were major problems with Bill 94. First, it did not include fishermen paid on a share basis. This, according to Larkin, ignored the fact that sharesmen had the same interests as boat owners in dealing with processors. It showed, he said, a "lack of sensitivity in the bill to the democratic principles of trade unionism."

Second, Bill 94 allowed a union to be certified for each individual buyer or for several buyers within the same geographic area. A fisherman could conceivably belong to several bargaining units at the same time. This system, Larkin pointed out, would create instability, confu-

Halifax labour lawyer Raymond Larkin represented the MFU during its battle for collective bargaining legislation. (COURTESY MFU)

sion, and fragmentation. The joint committee's bill, on the other hand, recommended one bargaining unit per region (northeast, southeast, and Bay of Fundy) and per species and fishing category (inshore, midshore, and offshore) in each region. For example, all inshore lobster fishermen in southeast New Brunswick would belong to the same bargaining unit, and a contract would be negotiated with all lobster buyers across that region.

Third, Bill 94 required a compulsory vote with every application for certification—a practice that allows companies to influence the membership before the voting takes place. As well, each fisherman would have voting strength proportionate to the size of his annual catch. Fishermen who caught more would have more say. Larkin pointed out that the requirement of a compulsory vote was a significant departure from the Industrial Relations Act, which permitted certification after a majority of employees had signed cards. Furthermore, a weighted vote was "deeply offensive to the principles of equality and democracy in the work place to which the trade union movement is committed. In the fishing industry, the democratic principle of one man-one vote is widely accepted."

Larkin also pointed out that Bill 94 had no provisions to protect fishermen from unfair labour practices or from company discrimination because of union involvement. Nor did Bill 94 provide for a union security clause requiring companies to deduct union dues.

"In conclusion," Larkin said, "Bill 94 is unworkable as a scheme for collective bargaining for fishermen in New Brunswick. It is difficult to see how the interests of either fishermen or processors can be served by such a bargaining structure." He suggested that the legislation be dropped. "It was clear to us," he says today, "that Doug Stanley [labour deputy minister] had taken a look at Bill 25 and found it too complicated, too complex, too cumbersome. There were also some things in Bill 25 that the industry still didn't like. So Bill 94 was a simpler, more manageable document with some of the irritants to the processors removed. I don't think we saw it as a huge conspiracy. It was more of a bureaucratic response."

Processors also opposed Bill 94. In its brief, the New Brunswick Fish Packers' Association reiterated its opposition to any legislation. But if the government was going to go ahead with it, the processors said, Bill 94 should be redrafted based on the principles already agreed to and put forward by the joint committee.

Eventually, the government decided to listen and let Bill 94 die. In the spring of 1982, Labour Minister Mabel DeWare, with no apology, introduced Bill 25 to the House. "This is the successor to Bill 94," she explained. "Bill 94 was referred to Law Amendments and over the course of the winter I sought the input and advice of a number of interested groups and individuals.... The advice has been most helpful to me in formulating this new bill."

Bill 25 was, in fact, almost identical to the bill that had been drafted by the joint committee. Modelled closely on the province's Industrial Relations Act, it included sharesmen in the definition of a fisherman; spelled out bargaining units based on geography, species, and fishing category; removed the section giving fishermen a weighted vote (though it kept the compulsory vote); included protection against discrimination because of union involvement; and provided a union security clause. It also called for the establishment of a fishing industry relations board to administer the legislation. Surprisingly, however—especially for the co-op movement—co-ops were not excluded from the legislation.

Richibucto Village fishermen read the Fisheries Bargaining Act, passed in April 1982. (OMER CHOUINARD/COURTESY MFU)

The theme of the MFU convention in early 1983 was "one down, two to go."
(COURTESY MFU)

On April 30, 1982, Bill 25, the Fisheries Bargaining Act, received Royal Assent.

Although processors favoured Bill 25 over Bill 94, they were not happy about the speed with which it went through the House. They wanted Bill 25 to go back to law amendments. "The feeling is that the bill is being pushed through by a minority of fishermen who do not represent substantial groups of fishermen," said New Brunswick Fish Packers' Association executive director Kim d'Entremont. "The legislation is an opportunity for certain organizations to impose themselves on certain groups of fishermen to negotiate for them."

For the MFU, however, the passage of Bill 25 was a major victory. The union had begun the fight in 1974, and since then, there had been committees, studies, and reports nearly every year that had recommended collective bargaining legislation for fishermen. After eight years, fishermen in New Brunswick finally had the right to negotiate the price of fish. The fishermen were jubilant, and the theme of the MFU convention in early 1983 would be "one down, two to go."

It had been a long battle, but it was clear that the government could no longer hold off. Jean Gauvin had come into office on a promise to provide collective bargaining rights for fishermen. Although Gauvin was considered a progressive—and an Acadian nationalist—and both were elements in the legislation finally being passed, the bottom line was, another election was coming up in the fall of 1982. The consummate politician knew that there was support for the legislation. He wasn't about to risk going into an election without having passed it.

While the events of history are never the responsibility of one person, there is no doubt that in the fight for collective bargaining rights for fishermen in New Brunswick, Jean Gauvin emerged as an important figure. The situation in Nova Scotia, however—where a similar struggle by fishermen had been going on simultaneously and where Labour Minister Ken Streatch had emerged as a key player—would prove to be a study in contrasts.

IN NOVA SCOTIA:
THE RETURN OF THE
MICHELIN MAN

*"The Michelin Bill was the result of a deal hatched under a
slimy rock by a bunch of vipers."*
—J.K. Bell, NSFL, December 1979—

*"If you look at the major changes in labour legislation in Nova Scotia in
the last decade, you'll see that almost all of it has been inspired by
Michelin. Some of the things that have been done for Michelin have had
an effect on organizing efforts in other industries."*
—Raymond Larkin, April 1980—

THE LEGISLATION that the Maritime Fishermen's Union had
presented to the joint committee in New Brunswick had in
fact been drafted in Nova Scotia by lawyer Raymond Larkin.
In early 1977, the MFU had approached Larkin to write a
constitution for the newly forming group. Later, when MFU
fishermen in Nova Scotia began to talk about the need for collective
bargaining legislation, Larkin advised them to go through the Joint
Labour-Management Study Committee.

Set up in 1962, that committee was made up of representatives
of major employers and labour groups in the province. The
government had made a commitment not to change labour legislation without the committee's advice, and over the years, even
though administrations had come and gone, that commitment had
been honoured. The Joint Labour-Management Study Committee
was touted across the country as a progressive force in resolving
conflicts before they even arose.

Nova Scotia's Trade Union Act had two sections: Part I covered
general workers, and Part II, construction workers. Fishermen did
not come under the act because they were not considered employees. The MFU wanted the study committee to set up a sub-
committee to draft a third part that would cover inshore fishermen.
In 1978, Larkin, on behalf of the MFU, approached the committee

As in the rest of the Maritimes, fishermen in Nova Scotia were not covered under the province's labour legislation. (COURTESY MFU)

for support, and a sub-committee on fisheries was established. Its labour representatives included Raymond Larkin, Lismore fisherman Hasse Lindblad, MFU executive secretary Gilles Thériault, and Charlie Moulton of the Canadian Brotherhood of Railway, Transport and General Workers (which included trawler workers). Management representatives included Jim Morrow of National Sea Products, Roger Stirling of the N.S. Fish Packers Association, William Moffatt of Connors Brothers, and Sherman Zwicker, the mayor of Lunenburg. In late 1978, the sub-committee began to meet.

Larkin had drafted a proposal. "The union's position was that the bill should be incorporated into existing legislation," he explains. "That's why we wanted a part three, so that down the road, when the pressure came on, it would be harder to take those rights away." Management representatives, however, didn't agree. They argued that in the fishery, there weren't normal employer-employee relations; the word "strike" didn't have the same meaning. They wanted a separate bill, and they hired a lawyer to draft it.

The issue became a major sticking point between the two sides. Finally, sub-committee members agreed to put the matter to Innes

Christie, a labour-law professor at Dalhousie University Law School who is considered to have one of the finest legal minds in the country. Christie agreed with the management side. "At that point," Larkin says, "the union was in the position of either refusing to go along or agreeing to accept special legislation."

It accepted, and Larkin drafted another bill, a 100-page document modelled on the Nova Scotia Trade Union Act. The bill was, in fact, the basis of the legislation that was eventually passed in New Brunswick.

By the time 1979 drew to a close, the sub-committee had reached agreement on a piece of legislation. Normally, the document would have gone back to the Joint Labour-Management Study Committee for approval. But that never happened. Throughout the year, another drama had been unfolding that would directly affect the efforts of inshore fishermen in Nova Scotia to obtain the right to unionize.

The United Rubber Workers (URW) had been trying to organize employees at the Michelin Tire plant in Granton, 90 minutes north of Halifax.

*   *   *   *   *

Michelin Tire had come to Nova Scotia in the late 1960s and had built two plants, one in Bridgewater, south of Halifax, and another in Granton. At the time, Nova Scotia was actively wooing international companies to invest in the province, and Michelin was seen as a major catch. The government had bent over backwards to provide financial incentives. To the French-owned tire manufacturer, known for being notoriously anti-union, the province offered a stable workforce with little history, at least in some areas, of union involvement.

For Michelin, the combination had paid off. By 1979, its business was booming. Stephen Kimber, in an article in the *Financial Post Magazine,* wrote that Michelin's 3,600 employees accounted for 7 percent of the province's manufacturing sector and that its annual payroll was close to $60 million. Needless to say, in a province lacking in entrepreneurs, Michelin had political clout. Throughout the decade, labour legislation had been modified twice to help stifle organizing attempts at the company's two plants.

In 1977, the Toronto-based URW attempted, without success, to organize the Granton plant. Both Michelin plants had been constructed to safeguard the company's technology: they were highly compartmentalized so that workers in one department sometimes did not even know of the existence of workers in another. This physical structure was also a formidable obstacle to unionization.

In 1979, the URW tried again. Two days before Easter, Labour Minister Ken Streatch asked for a meeting with the Joint Labour-Management Study Committee. A boyish-looking farmer from the Musquodoboit Valley, Streatch, a Conservative, had been elected in the fall of 1978, and Premier John Buchanan had quickly appointed him to the labour portfolio. Streatch wanted the committee to review a draft of what he called "broad-based collective bargaining legislation."

The legislation said, in essence, that when a company had more than one plant in the province and that when one plant depended on the other for its operation, a union must sign up a majority of the workers at all the plants before it could be certified as bargaining agent. Given that there is a 90-day time limit in Nova Scotia for a signing-up campaign, labour leaders on the committee agreed that the bill would make organizing Michelin virtually impossible.

But not only labour representatives were opposed. "I was one who did not see the point of having the Michelin Bill," recalls National Sea's Jim Morrow. "Michelin treated its employees so well, at least in terms of pay, that I couldn't see that the union would get in." Other management representatives argued that the bill was written so loosely that it could apply to a lot of companies that had branch plants. It could, for example, force workers in a small fish plant to belong to a union because their counterparts at a larger plant in the province had voted in favour.

In effect, Streatch's bill represented a major departure from accepted labour legislation across the country.

But perhaps more important than the bill itself was the question of procedure. The government usually gave the study committee six months to assess proposed changes. Streatch, however, was presenting his bill as a *fait accompli*. Some committee members were outraged.

The bill was eventually reworked so that it applied only to Michelin. Nevertheless, it was passed in late December 1979—a month after the URW vote had been taken at Michelin's Granton plant. A day later, provincial development minister Roland Thornhill announced Michelin's intentions to build a third plant in Nova Scotia and to expand its two existing facilities to create 2,000 jobs. The timing of the announcement, Thornhill assured skeptical reporters, was strictly coincidental.

Passage of the bill nullified the URW vote. The ballots had been sealed in ballot boxes and, as a result, were never counted. It also brought a major outcry from labour leaders across the country. "The Michelin Bill was the result of a deal hatched under a slimy rock by a bunch of vipers," the Nova Scotia Federation of Labour's J.K. Bell told a reporter. With that, the federation pulled its representatives off the Joint Labour-Management Study Committee. The sub-committee on fisheries folded.

It was a historic moment, the end of a procedure that had worked well for nearly 20 years.

In an ominous foreshadowing of events to come, Raymond Larkin, one of the URW's lawyers, told the *Financial Post Magazine:* "If you look at the major changes in labour legislation in Nova Scotia in the last decade, you'll see that almost all of it has been inspired by Michelin. Some of the things that have been done for Michelin have had an effect on organizing efforts in other industries."

*   *   *   *   *

Throughout the late 1970s, there was a growing sentiment in Nova Scotia that inshore fishermen should organize. In February 1978, provincial NDP leader Jeremy Akerman had introduced a private member's bill giving fishermen the right to unionize. Later that year, provincial fisheries minister Donald Cameron told a meeting of fishermen that he might consider some kind of legislation if it were proved that a majority of fishermen were in favour, though he personally considered fishermen to be businesspeople and therefore not able to belong to a union.

In June 1980, Cameron resigned from the portfolio, saying that he needed to spend more time on his dairy farm. In a parting shot at the Maritime Fishermen's Union, he told the *Sou'wester,* "I want to see some legislation to give fishermen the legal right to negotiate, then fishermen can pick the group they want. But I'm not willing to rush in and help an organization which admits that there is a communist presence within their midst. The former MFU president Harold Manuel has admitted this, so has Hasse Lindblad and Kevin Squires. I don't think any government is going to turn its fishermen over to an organization that has been verified as communist." (A fisheries newspaper published in Yarmouth, the *Sou'wester* noted that Cameron had got off on the wrong foot in the portfolio because he had openly favoured the offshore in a province where 80 percent of the fishery was inshore. For example, Cameron had supported federal fisheries minister James McGrath when he announced in 1979 that he wanted to reopen the Gulf of St Lawrence to vessels of more than 100 feet.)

Cameron was replaced by Edmund Morris, a former broadcaster and mayor of Halifax. Morris had been involved in the fishermen's strike at Canso in 1970, participating on a citizen's committee set up to supervise a vote among the fishermen. "Morris saw himself as a liberal in a den of Tories," recalls one observer. Being on the left in John Buchanan's government was a lonely place to be, and Morris would be more open to the unionization of fishermen than his predecessor.

In October 1980, Morris' department issued the *Fisheries General Policy,* which stated:

> The concept that fishermen should associate for their own advancement should be supported. Such an association or associations could represent them in policy and regulatory matters, such as consultation on allocation of resource quotas; encourage fishermen to work out differences among themselves rather than urging government to attempt to resolve all conflicts; allow them to negotiate such matters as fish prices; and provide collective benefits such as group insurance and joint purchasing of equipment and supplies.

With the collapse of the fisheries sub-committee, the MFU had been left with a nearly completed draft of collective bargaining legislation but with nowhere to take it. "After the Michelin Bill, we talked strategy," recalls Raymond Larkin. "We realized that the government would only listen if there were a lot of bodies. We had to go into political mobilization." On a Sunday afternoon in early December, 250 fishermen gathered at a meeting in Port Hawkesbury, on the Cape Breton side of the Canso Causeway. Labour Minister Streatch had been invited but had declined. Fisheries Minister

Edmund Morris, however, did show up. He urged the fishermen to read his newly released government policy paper on the fisheries.

"The government is working with all speed to accommodate the desires of inshore fishermen for legislation," he said. If the Department of Labour wasn't interested, the Department of Fisheries was. Morris said that he was setting up an interdepartmental committee to study the implications of legislation for inshore fishermen.

The committee, headed by Morris' deputy minister, Sandy MacLean, held hearings in January and released its report in April. The 34-page document said:

> Notwithstanding the possible difficulties, it is clear that a number of fishermen, represented by the MFU wish to be able to unionize under legislation similar to the Trade Union Act. Given the commitment in the Fisheries General Policy 1980 to the principle that "it is desirable that fishermen themselves decide what type of association they need" the committee feels that such fishermen cannot be deprived indefinitely of the legislation required to facilitate their goal. The committee therefore recommends that the government endorse the development of collective bargaining legislation for those fishermen who wish to unionize.

(The report pointed out that most of the western world had established "various organizational mechanisms" to protect inshore fishermen from unfair pricing practices, though only British Columbia and Newfoundland had resorted to a traditional trade-union approach. The Maritime region, it seemed, was one of the last places in the world where fishermen were expected to accept, without question, the prices that companies offered.)

On April 30, 1981, Morris rose in the Legislative Assembly and promised legislation for inshore fishermen: "It is appropriate to recognize under law, for independent fishermen who are boat owners and who wish to do so, the right to bargain collectively with fish buyers for fish prices and other conditions of sale. It is therefore the intention of the Government of Nova Scotia to introduce legislation recognizing the right of boat owners to bargain collectively at the next session of the legislature."

On Morris' request, the fisheries sub-committee came together once again to study legislation (though labour representatives would never return to the Joint Labour-Management Study Committee itself). Because the bulk of the work had already been done, it didn't take long to draft a bill that the fisheries minister could present to the Legislative Assembly.

Morris, however, never had the chance.

*   *   *   *   *

Fisheries Minister Edmund Morris was replaced in the fall of 1981 by former labour minister Ken Streatch. Whether Streatch's appointment was a deliberate move on the part of the Buchanan government to head off collective bargaining legislation for fishermen remains buried in the confines of cabinet secrecy. (Streatch refused to be interviewed.) There is no question, however, that the Buchanan administration was anti-union and pro-business, a stance that had characterized the Conservative government since its rise to power.

Streatch came into his new job full of energy, saying that he would not introduce legislation for fishermen immediately. "I'm not going to be stampeded into bringing in legislation that I'd have to debate that I'm not comfortable with," he told a Halifax *Chronicle-Herald* reporter.

By the spring of 1982, however, Streatch had changed his mind and was prepared to move on legislation—but *his* legislation. In May, he introduced "a free enterprise" bill for fishermen. Three paragraphs long, it virtually echoed the *Fisheries General Policy:*

> An independent boat-owner fisherman may join an association of his own choosing for the purpose of advancing the common interests of the members of the association and to promote representation of those interests in the following areas: (a) policy and regulatory matters; (b) consultation on allocation of resource quotas; (c) negotiation of fish prices; (d) obtaining collective benefits such as group insurance and joint purchase of equipment and supplies.

The bill also said that "no one shall discriminate against an independent boat-owner fisherman by reason of his membership in an association."

After all the effort and painstaking consultation that had gone into drafting legislation—and despite Morris' commitment—

Streatch introduced a skimpy document that gave fishermen the "right to associate," something, the MFU pointed out, they had had at least "since the days of William the Conqueror." The bill did not require companies to bargain with fishermen.

The labour movement was outraged. Nova Scotia Federation of Labour (NSFL) vice president Lawrence Wilneff called the bill "nonsense." The NSFL's J.K. Bell said it was "a slap in the face" for organized labour. "Our Federation of Labour broke off relations with the Buchanan government because of the Michelin Bill," he told the press, "but we agreed to co-operate with Edmund Morris in the interests of fishermen in order to develop effective draft legislation. Now you've thrown this back in our faces." NDP leader Alexa McDonough called it a "farce."

Streatch had said that his bill was "an expression of the Progressive Conservative government's policy of support for free enterprise." That was his only statement to go unchallenged by organized labour.

Not everyone, however, agreed with the labour movement's assessment. Stan Purdy, the spokesperson for the Eastern Shore Fishermen's Protective Association and president of the Eastern Fishermen's Federation (EFF), liked the bill. "Fishermen don't want anything stronger than that," Purdy told the press. "I would say 99 percent of the fishermen are against legislation going any deeper than that." Later, EFF executive director Alan Billard told the *Chronicle-Herald*, "We simply made it possible for our associations to meet with Mr. Streatch. They all told him they don't want unions, so Mr. Streatch is very correct in saying the fishermen do not want unions. If the Nova Scotia Federation of Labour says they do, then they're all wet."

The bill sailed through second reading, then went to the Law Amendments Committee. There, Lismore fisherman Hasse Lindblad, representing the MFU, charged that Streatch had consulted groups known to oppose collective bargaining legislation but had refused to meet with organizations known to support it. Lindblad told the committee:

> On March 10, Streatch cancelled an all-important meeting with the Joint Committee and travelled that same evening to Pictou to meet with a recently re-activated association headed up by two fishermen who double as buyers. This particular association centred on the

Caribou wharf is not representative of the fishermen of that wharf let alone the Northumberland Shore, and appears to have been reactivated mainly to lobby against collective bargaining legislation.

When the Minister was invited to meet with up to 200 fishermen of the Northumberland local of the MFU in Antigonish on April 4, he declined. He also declined to meet with 75 delegates representing 400 members of the Cape Breton local in Sydney March 31. At both meetings, unanimous resolutions were passed calling for collective bargaining legislation.

At this time, the MFU still had locals only in Northumberland, Guysborough, and Cape Breton. Of the 10,000 inshore fishermen in the province, the union had at best 1,000 in its membership. It hadn't made inroads into the Eastern Shore or southwest Nova Scotia. A lot of fishermen in the province, especially those in the southwest, opposed unionization.

But, as far as the MFU was concerned, that was beside the point. The union emphasized again, for those who may have missed the point, that the legislation was *enabling* legislation—that a majority of fishermen in a designated area would have to be in favour before the union could be certified there. Said Lindblad:

It is not an historical accident that the drive for collective bargaining is coming from Eastern Nova Scotia and Cape Breton inshore fishermen in the main. The structure of the Nova Scotia fishing industry leaves these fishermen working under conditions of semi-monopoly. It is undeniable, for example, that the shore price for lobster on Northumberland Shore is established by the Nickerson/National Sea interests. After lobster fishermen set traps on May 1 this year, these Nickerson-controlled corporations set a ridiculously low price after all indications had suggested a higher price to fishermen....

Similarly, the same Nickerson controlled corporations were able to set a price for cod this spring in Canso and most ports on Cape Breton. This price ranged from two to ten cents lower per pound of cod than what a few smaller operations were offering. I want to be clear about this: very few fishermen in these ports had the option of switching buyers. For one thing, the smaller buyers were few in number and have limited capacity and markets. For another, many fishermen are locked in by debt to the Nickerson interests.

In contrast, fishermen in southwest Nova Scotia were much more competitive. Maybe they didn't believe that they needed a union, the MFU argued, but they shouldn't stop fishermen in other parts of the province from having one.

The union's arguments were to no avail. On June 26, 1982, Ken Streatch's "Act to provide for associations of independent boat-owner fishermen" became law. "People were disgusted," recalls Cribbons Point fisherman John Andrew Boyd. "I think most people realized that this was the most anti-labour government that was ever elected in Nova Scotia."

OTHER THINGS:
LOBSTER POACHERS
AND LICENSING POLICY

*"There are people today who say they will pay their union dues
forever because of that licensing policy."*
—Antigonish fisherman Stuart Beaton—

IT WAS A CRISP SPRING DAY, and Omer Chouinard was racing through the bushes of Kouchibouguac National Park. Beside him, on the seat of his car, were two sacks crammed with $35,000 in cash. The herring had been running like crazy off Escuminac, and as usually happened in such circumstances, the price had dropped dramatically. The Maritime Fishermen's Union had decided to take the matter in hand and had organized fishermen to sell their herring together.

The union had found a company willing to pay the price that fishermen wanted, though the company would only buy through the union, not from hundreds of fishermen. The company's check, however, was much too large to cash at the *caisse populaire* in Baie-Ste-Anne. The fishermen wanted to be paid in cash—under the table, so to speak. So Chouinard had set off for the Royal Bank in Richibucto, some 45 minutes away, cashed the check, and was on his way back as fishermen milled about the Escuminac wharf, waiting for their money.

At the time, the Kouchibouguac expropriation was very much in the public eye. Buildings had been burned, and threats had been made. The RCMP was on alert. When two officers spotted a vehicle speeding through the park, a bearded character behind the wheel, they immediately pulled it over. They were doubly suspicious when they saw the sacks of money. The officers searched the car and radioed headquarters, looking for an excuse to arrest the MFU organizer. Finally, after 45 minutes, they let him go. Chouinard sped on to the wharf, where he doled out the money. Then he borrowed a truck—his car was having mechanical problems—hurriedly backed up, and smashed into a wharf pole. It was the first brand-new truck that Ste-Anne-de-Kent fisherman Paul Nowlan had ever owned, but he took the incident in stride. "Omer was always in a hurry in those days," Nowlan recalls nonchalantly.

From the beginning, the MFU had devoted much of its time to trying to influence the price of fish—from lobster boycotts and demonstrations to organized sales. The union was also involved in issues of resource management, which many fishermen considered equally if not more important. For fishermen, there was no point in getting a good price if there were no fish to catch. More and more, MFU fishermen had become involved in federal Department of Fisheries and Oceans (DFO) advisory committees. Such involvement gave them input into the way quotas were divided between the inshore and offshore sectors—MFU representatives were often able to win an increased share of quotas for inshore fishermen—and gave them a say in how seasons were established or what gear was allowed. It also gave the union a forum for initiating new ideas. The most significant, perhaps, was the MFU's licensing-policy proposal, implemented in the early 1980s.

Throughout the 1970s, the federal government had increasingly restricted access to the fishery. In 1976, Fisheries Minister Roméo LeBlanc decided to categorize lobster fishermen: Class A applied to fishermen who had no other means of making a living; Class B, fishermen who had part-time jobs outside the fishery; and Class C, doctors, teachers, and other professionals whose licences would be terminated within two years. In 1979, the DFO also introduced full- and part-time categories for other fisheries.

The intent of all this categorization was to limit the fishery to those whose livelihood depended on it. But by the end of the decade—aside from the fact that fishermen were totally confused—there were major problems with the licensing system.

One was that licences applied to the vessel, not to the fisherman. A fisherman may have had licences for herring, mackerel, groundfish, and lobster, but if he wanted to sell one, in most instances, he had to sell all of them—along with his boat. There was little flexibility.

Another was the participation clause. For example, a fisherman had to fish herring each year or lose his licence. This forced fishermen to fish whether or not it was the best thing for the stocks. "It was always a worry when I started fishing," says Pictou Landing fisherman Percy Hayne, Jr, "that they were going to take away your licence."

In the mid-1970s, federal fisheries minister Roméo LeBlanc classified lobster fishermen. (COURTESY DFO MONCTON)

Fishermen also complained of patronage. "If there were going to be any crab licences issued," recalls fisherman John Andrew Boyd, "it was normally people in the area who were tied in with the government that knew about them first and got them. I remember in 1980, in district 26, they were going to reissue six crab licences. When the guys got to the meeting, the DFO guy said, 'Well, actually there's not six licences, there's only five. [A prominent Liberal], he was promised one.' And the guys said this couldn't go on."

Roméo LeBlanc appointed Cliff Levelton, a former fisheries assistant deputy minister, to study the problems with the licensing policy. Levelton's report, released in 1979, confirmed what fishermen had been saying. "The current licensing system ... is not easily understood by those in the fishing industry or even by those administering the system," it said. "It has become overburdened, cumbersome, inconsistent in application and unresponsive."

In particular, Levelton wrote, there was too much red tape in getting a licence, licence transactions were not publicized, "inappropriate decisions" were made on the allocation of licences, and changes were implemented to licensing policy without adequate

Antigonish fisherman Cameron
MacKenzie travelled the region to
convince fishermen of the validity of
the bonafide fisherman's permit
policy. (COURTESY MFU)

consultation. In preparing his report, Levelton had held hearings around the Maritimes. One of the presentations eventually became the basis of a new licensing policy for the southern Gulf of St Lawrence. The proposal came from the Northumberland local of the MFU. "Percy was really the brains behind the idea," says Gilles Thériault, "although Cameron MacKenzie took the ball and ran with it."

The intent of the proposal was to give priority to fishermen who depended on lobster for their livelihood. Originally called a "one licence" policy, the name was eventually changed to the "bonafide fisherman's permit" policy. Much of the legwork to refine and sell the idea was done by the MFU's Northumberland local. Antigonish fisherman Cameron MacKenzie, in particular, travelled the region to convince other fishermen of the policy's value.

A "bonafide" fisherman was one who had a Class A lobster licence or made 75 percent of his income or $15,000 from fishing in the year before the policy was implemented. Those who qualified received bonafide fisherman's permits that allowed them to transfer individual licences (the licences were now on the fisherman, not on the boat), hold licences without having to use them, and receive priority for new licences and government programs. "The bonafide permit was really a gold card," explains the DFO's Alphonse Cormier. "With that gold card, you could get other fishing licences, either new ones, which were offered first to bonafide fishermen, or by transfer from other fishermen."

All other fishermen were classified as part time (later, as commercial). These fishermen had to work as helpers for two years before becoming eligible for a bonafide permit, but they could only get

Antigonish fisherman Stuart Beaton belongs to the Northumberland local, which originated the idea of the bonafide fisherman's permit. (COURTESY STUART BEATON)

one from a bonafide fisherman. The number of bonafide permits was frozen at the number issued in 1983, when the program was tested on Prince Edward Island, the Northumberland Strait, and the gulf side of Cape Breton.

A year later, the policy was extended to the whole southern Gulf of St Lawrence. Of 12,000 fishermen in boats of less than 50 feet, roughly 3,400 were classed as bonafide. On average, each fisherman held four licences.

The policy recognized that the fishery in the southern gulf was multipurpose. A fisherman could sell a licence or not and could participate in a particular fishery or not, depending on what he thought best for himself and for the resource. "It really protected the stocks," says Percy Hayne, Jr. "When scallops were down here a few years ago, fishermen just didn't bother going fishing." They no longer had to in order to keep their licence.

The bonafide fisherman's permit policy, however, didn't accomplish everything that the MFU and the DFO had hoped that it would. Originally, it was thought that the number of part-time fishermen would decrease as more and more licences were transferred to bonafide fishermen. In that way, the fishery would become even more profitable for full-time fishermen. But the number of part-timers has decreased only to a limited extent: people have kept up their licences so that they can go fishing as helpers when they need to supplement their income.

Nonetheless, the policy has simplified, streamlined, and depoliticized the licensing system, and it has given fishermen a say in how the resource is managed. It is one of the rare examples of policy being designed by fishermen and presented to the DFO, not the other way around.

"The MFU fought long and hard to get the lobster fishery back on track," says the DFO's Ted Gaudet. "They were deeply involved in the establishment of licensing policy. Their role in developing the bonafide policy was a major one. It's a policy that has now been modelled throughout the Atlantic region."

For the MFU, the policy paid off in other ways. Says Antigonish fisherman Stuart Beaton, "There are people today who say they will pay their union dues forever because of that licensing policy."

*   *   *   *   *

Another big issue for fishermen in the Gulf of St Lawrence was lobster poaching. Shortly after Roméo LeBlanc had announced his plan to categorize lobster fishermen, he tried to increase the size limit for lobster. But fishermen turned thumbs down on the idea, because the present size limit was not being respected by a lot of fishermen or being enforced by the Department of Fisheries and Oceans. What was the point in increasing it?

In some Maritime communities, lobster poaching has never been tolerated, but in others, it has been rampant. Baie-Ste-Anne, Escuminac, and Pointe-Sapin, in New Brunswick, are among the worst examples, because these communities are on the line that separates the spring and fall lobster seasons. Fishermen there can participate in one season or the other, though not in both. But that regulation, in force since the late 1800s, did not stop many from doing so.

Regulations also did not stop fishermen from setting more than the legal number of traps, from brushing the eggs off "berried" females, or from bringing in undersized lobsters. In 1928, the MacLean Royal Commission underscored the Escuminac line as a heavy poaching area. It noted that in 1926 a fisheries officer had been killed, presumably by poachers, though they had never been brought to court. The report suggested that education, along with improved patrol boats and more fisheries officers, would help solve the problem.

But a half-century later, lobster poaching was worse than ever, and many fishermen blamed the DFO for lack of action. "I had never poached before," says a Baie-Ste-Anne fisherman who was a strong union supporter, "but when everybody else was doing it, I said, 'What the hell.' And I told the fisheries officers, 'When you're serious about stopping it, let me know.'" (When the same fisherman was later involved in the lobster co-management program, he lost a lot of traps on the wharf at the hands of angry poachers.)

There is no doubt that over the years, many fishermen poached to feed their families. It was also common among cottagers who, for some reason, were able to rationalize that taking lobsters out of a fisherman's trap wasn't really stealing.

But for others, poaching was big business. At one point during the 1970s, an RCMP officer estimated that trafficking in illegal lobster between Montréal and Escuminac was a multimillion-dollar business. To some, the poacher was a local hero; to most, he was a person not to be crossed. To criticize a poacher openly was to risk having your house set on fire or your boat sabotaged. "Lobster poachers were like today's Colombian drug runners," recalls Gastien Godin, executive director of the midshore fishermen's association in northeast New Brunswick. "The MFU had the courage to try to deal with them."

In 1977, the Prince County Fishermen's Association in Prince Edward Island submitted to the DFO a proposal for a lobster co-management program. Fishermen in some areas of the island were facing similar problems with poaching, and government funding would allow them to hire "guardians" to patrol their waters during the next fall lobster season. The program worked well, and the following year, when it was expanded, the MFU agreed to manage it on the New Brunswick side of the Northumberland Strait.

In the first year, the Escuminac area was not patrolled. Fishermen there were not convinced that it would work, so powerful were the lobster poachers. Many fishermen were too intimidated to report violations, even though it could be done secretly. The program was implemented farther south, between Loggiecroft and Cape Tormentine. The MFU organized meetings in each community to talk to fishermen about poaching. It also established secret protection teams—decided by draw in the union office and changed every few weeks—to keep an eye on things, and it hired patrols trained by the DFO.

The DFO actually caught and charged poachers, but the success of the program lay in the fact that fishermen were more confident reporting violations to the MFU than they were to the DFO. On seeing that the program worked, fishermen in the Escuminac area agreed to implement it there the following year. But it wasn't without problems. As Gilles Thériault noted in a report: "We are confident that the presence of guardians slowed down the activities and I back this statement with the following facts. On October 19, between 12:30am and 1:00am, I received two threatening phone calls. According to what they told me, I was a dead man and the second call was to tell me that they were going to blow up my house. I was not happy with the call but it was a good thing because it proved that what we are doing must be working if poachers were reacting this way."

Overall, the MFU's involvement in the lobster co-management program was sporadic. The union withdrew from the program in 1983 but picked it up again in 1985 and continued to participate for two more years. MFU fishermen felt uncomfortable about the union being thrust into the role of police officer, though few people questioned the program's effectiveness.

"I think the program had a marked impact," says the DFO's Alphonse Cormier, "perhaps more on communications than on hard-core enforcement. It got fisheries officers and fishermen working together for the first time, and developed a network of information exchange that still exists today, despite the fact that the program has been terminated. On an educational level, it really drove home the need for lobster conservation.

"It brought a lot of credibility to the MFU," Cormier continues, "in the sense that law-abiding fishermen and non-fishermen saw the group as wanting to do something about the problem."

A lot of attention was paid to the lobster fishery in the Gulf of St Lawrence during this period. It started in 1976 with Roméo LeBlanc's classification of fishermen, aimed at phasing out moonlighters. In 1978, after fishermen rejected his plan to increase the lobster size limit, LeBlanc announced a multimillion-dollar program under which government would buy back more than 1,500 Class A lobster licences in New Brunswick and Nova Scotia, and reduce the number of licences by 25 percent. Lobster co-management programs to crack down on poaching began at the same time and continued throughout the 1980s.

"I remember in the mid-1970s," says Barachois fisherman Adrice Doiron, "the biologists were telling us to find another way to make a living. The lobster was gone. By the mid-1980s, fishermen were experiencing landings like they'd never experienced for a hundred years."

Many fishermen were convinced that it was thanks to Roméo LeBlanc and the work of the MFU.

ON THE ISLAND: A PLEBISCITE ON HUMAN RIGHTS

"I consider these rights to be God given, because they flow from the dignity of the human person.... You can understand then, why I find it difficult to accept that the exercise of these universally accepted rights should have to find their determination in our Province by means of a plebiscite."
—Charlottetown Bishop James H. MacDonald, 1983—

ALMOST FROM THE TIME it became active on Prince Edward Island, the Maritime Fishermen's Union had taken up the issue of collective bargaining for inshore fishermen. The only legislation on the island that applied to inshore fishermen was the Natural Products Marketing Act, which allowed them to organize a marketing board. But MFU fishermen were convinced that they wanted a union. So right from the start, they began to lobby the government to change the province's Labour Act.

In March 1978, Fisheries Minister George Henderson told MFU representatives that 60 percent of the fishermen on the island had to sign union cards before the government would consider changing the legislation. The fishermen left the meeting feeling fairly confident. It was, at least, an indication that the government might be open to helping them.

That fall, Liberal premier Bennett Campbell set up a committee to review and recommend revisions to the Labour Act. The MFU asked the Labour Act Review Committee also to consider collective bargaining for fishermen. In a one-page memo to Labour Minister George Proud early the next year, the committee recommended that legislation for fishermen be implemented. "We were asked to rule strictly on the principle of whether or not fishermen should have collective bargaining rights," the committee's chairman Roger Kennedy says today. "I believe everyone should have collective bargaining rights if they want them."

In late March 1979, after a meeting with the premier, the labour minister, and the fisheries minister, MFU organizer Ed Frenette

Mackerel was an underfished species on P.E.I. because inshore fishermen often couldn't find buyers. (COURTESY P.E.I. DEPARTMENT OF FISHERIES AND AQUACULTURE)

confidently told the press that the government had promised to make a decision within the month. The next day, however, an election was called, and Bennett Campbell's government went down to defeat to Angus MacLean's Conservatives. The MFU had to start all over again.

A series of events, however, placed pressure on MacLean's government to consider legislation for fishermen. In July 1979, PLURA, an umbrella group of five churches, donated money to the MFU to hire a second organizer on the island, Wanson Hemphill. Later, federal labour minister Lincoln Alexander said that his department was considering legislation for inshore fishermen. In December, New Brunswick fisheries minister Jean Gauvin announced his plans. Meanwhile, the fisheries sub-committee in Nova Scotia was drafting legislation.

In the spring of 1980, the MFU and the P.E.I. Fishermen's Association (PEIFA) were locked in a battle over the first over-the-side-sales program on the island. The federal government had signed agreements with two Bulgarian vessels, which wanted to buy 120,000 metric tonnes of mackerel from inshore fishermen. The boats were scheduled to anchor off Rustico and Alberton. Fishermen were eager to participate—mackerel was an underfished species because fishermen often couldn't find buyers—but the two groups couldn't agree on who would administer the sales. (The government ended up doing it.) "Fish wars continuing between organizations," said a headline in a local newspaper.

On the other end of the island, fishermen in Souris had tied up their boats over the price of cod. Fisheries Minister Leo Rossiter met with them, though nothing was resolved. Government can't tell companies how much to pay for fish, Rossiter told the media, adding almost as an afterthought, "Unity will mean strength. Island fishermen need to organize to have more clout with processors."

Then Rossiter, on urging from the MFU, announced that he would set up a committee to draft legislation. By the fall, however, he had changed his mind and decided to launch what he called "a full-scale investigation of the fishery," the first on the island in 30 years. E.P. Weeks was appointed to head the inquiry. A native of Mount Stewart, Weeks had worked for decades in the federal Department of Fisheries. His report was to be in the government's hands by January 1981.

But both the MFU and the PEIFA were leery. The union's Wanson Hemphill said that a one-person commission was a watered-down fulfilment of Rossiter's promise to study the industry. The PEIFA's executive director, Wayne Harris, complained that Weeks had lived off the island for most of his life. Both groups maintained that three months was too short a time to investigate the fishery and make a proper report.

Fishermen became even more suspicious once public hearings began. Groups had been given the option to meet privately with Weeks, and that was the option chosen by processors, none of whom attended the public hearings. As Weeks noted in his report, "The absence of the processors was a matter of considerable comment on the part of fishermen and others who felt that while the fishermen's various positions were discussed in the open, there was no corresponding discussion of the approaches of the processors."

The PEIFA had always openly opposed collective bargaining for fishermen. Now, however, it presented a brief in favour, though it didn't want the right to strike. "There was always a minority of people within the association who supported collective bargaining," MFU organizer Michael LeClair would later say. "I think they realized that a system of dues would help them, too. Despite their government funding, they were having financial problems as well." The PEIFA, the brief said,

> proposes that fishermen in this province want legislation that will bring producer and processor together to negotiate fair and equitable prices for all species.... A provincial act, including the legal recognition for a fishermen's group as bargaining agent will bring order to an unworkable situation.... A formal recognition of bargaining units would streamline the system, encourage fishermen to have faith in meaningful negotiations and to take a more active role in this most crucial aspect of the fishery.

Early in 1981, rumours began to circulate that Weeks' report had been submitted but that the government was reluctant to release it because it endorsed collective bargaining legislation. In February, MFU fishermen stormed the offices of Premier Angus MacLean. "I remember old Louis Campbell," recalls fisherman Robbie Paynter, then president of the Savage Harbour-Rustico local. "He had been overseas with [former premier] Alex Campbell. He had lost three brothers in the Second World War. And he said to Angus, 'Geez, we fought a war together. Why do I have to come here and fight for something that would help island fishermen and help the economy?' Angus MacLean couldn't answer him."

The premier, in fact, didn't have much to say at all. "Collective bargaining legislation is a complicated issue," he told the group. Shortly after, however, MacLean released Weeks' report. As expected, it recommended that legislation be implemented but that such legislation should not include the right to strike, should exclude co-operatives, and should provide for a province-wide bargaining unit.

Overall, the report was the endorsement the MFU had been looking for, even though the union didn't agree with denying fishermen the right to strike or with excluding co-ops. It should have been regarded as a victory and used to rally the troops to push for the legislation itself. But the MFU was going through internal upheaval in Prince Edward Island. One of the organizers had just been fired by the Savage Harbour-Rustico local, and the other, Ed Frenette, approaching burn-out, was about to resign.

In a letter of resignation, Frenette wrote that lack of income had forced him to look for employment elsewhere. But mainly, he said,

Michael LeClair took over from P.E.I. organizer Ed Frenette. (COURTESY MFU)

he was dissatisfied with the way the union was being run: "Non-leadership has led to an uninformed membership, a frustrated staff and no finances with which to operate...."

Michael LeClair replaced him. Born in Charlottetown, LeClair had studied political science at the University of Prince Edward Island, had graduated in 1973, and had worked at odd jobs ever since. LeClair was clever but hadn't yet found his niche. "When I started with the union," he says, "there were a few harbours where there were sympathetic fishermen, but that was about it. There didn't seem to be any history of fishermen financially supporting the union, although there was a history of fishermen signing cards." LeClair began again the process of signing up members and collecting dues. "I remember the first year," he says, "I collected about 70 or 80 dues, and that was considered a remarkable feat."

Despite the union's internal problems, the debate over the need for a fishermen's organization—and what kind of organization that should be—continued. In late 1982, the PEIFA called on the government to hold a plebiscite to settle the issue once and for all because it felt that the issue had been "a major dividing line" between island fishermen for many years. For the association, said managing director Rory MacLellan, the question was whether fishermen considered themselves labourers or businesspeople. If they considered themselves labourers, then they should vote for a union.

The PEIFA, MacLellan pointed out, had always considered fishermen to be businesspeople. "In calling fishermen businessmen rather than labourers," he told the press, "the association is saying that fishermen should be informed about the marketplace, be able to make their own sales and be in a position to sell their fish for the best possible prices."

MFU fishermen were also talking to the government. "I remember we had a meeting with [Fisheries Minister] Pat Binns up in West Prince," LeClair says. "A lot of fishermen came out. Binns made a commitment that if we signed up a certain number of members in a certain area, he would grant collective bargaining legislation. But when he went back to Charlottetown, the association had come out with the idea of a plebiscite, and that was Binns' way around his commitment."

After Binns announced the plebiscite, both MFU locals on the island scrambled to hold a meeting in Miminegash. From the beginning, the union had asked for enabling legislation. Instead, MFU members were being asked to prove that they had majority support first in a plebiscite, before legislation would even be considered.

The MFU knew that it didn't have a majority of fishermen on the island signed up. It also knew that it didn't have time to sign them up. In a normal certification campaign, the union would have three months to recruit new members. "We had signed a lot of cards in Egmont Bay that winter," recalls LeClair. "We were just starting to break into that part of the island. The support was coming, but you had to go harbour to harbour. There just wasn't enough time."

But beyond that, there was a principle at stake. The fishermen at the Miminegash meeting argued that almost all workers in Canada had enabling legislation that gave them the right to unionize and that other provinces didn't hold plebiscites on such basic issues. "These are our rights," Savage Harbour fisherman Fred Pigott told the group. "We shouldn't have to fight for them." By the time the meeting was over, the group had decided to boycott the plebiscite altogether.

The union received a lot of public support for its position. For many Islanders, the plebiscite was a national embarrassment. Letters to the editor flooded the offices of local newspapers, denouncing the government for denying basic human rights. One of the most vocal opponents was the Roman Catholic Church. The Bishop of Charlottetown, James H. MacDonald, wrote a letter to Fisheries Minister Pat Binns: "The two questions [of the plebiscite] invite a third and logical question: 'Do you wish to suppress the God-given rights of some fishermen?' It is truly incomprehensible that a vote should determine the availability or non-availability of such God-given rights in Prince Edward Island."

Earlier, MacDonald had told a local Rotary Club luncheon, "I consider these rights to be God given, because they flow from the dignity of the human person. In fact, these rights are recognized by such esteemed bodies as the United Nations, and the International Court of the Hague. They are also enshrined in the Constitutions of most countries. You can understand then, why I find it difficult to accept that the exercise of these universally accepted rights should have to find their determination in our province by means of a plebiscite."

Despite the public opposition, the government went ahead with the plebiscite. In March 1983, newspapers around the island carried advertisements. Fishermen had to clip them out, fill them in, and send them to the government in order to get their names on the voting list. Ballots were mailed out on April 25, just as many fishermen were gearing up for lobster season. The first question was, "Do you want union-type legislation for collective bargaining rights?" As if to remind fishermen of the possible consequences of saying yes to the first question, Binns had added a second: "Do you want the right to strike in any fishermen's legislation?"

As lobster fishermen set their traps, they had to ponder these two weighty issues and mail in their ballots by May 5. For many fishermen, there was apparently no doubt in their minds. Of 855 who replied, 554 said no to collective bargaining; 719 said no to the right to strike.

*   *   *   *   *

Journalist Kennedy Wells, in *The Fishery of Prince Edward Island,* dismisses the efforts of the Maritime Fishermen's Union in a page and a half. The MFU always claimed that the law hampered its drive for membership, he writes, "but a host of other factors have combined to prevent the Union from signing up more than a small minority of P.E.I. fishermen. The most important of these is the fisherman's image of himself as an independent operator, dependent on his own skills and resources, answering only to himself. This view may be a romantic one, but it is strongly held."

Wells also points out that the fear of strikes was strong—perhaps a little less simplistic and closer to the truth. Many fishermen throughout the Maritimes equated unions with strikes, but none more so than fishermen on Prince Edward Island, where they depended heavily on an eight-week lobster season. "There was always that fear," says Michael LeClair, "that some union guy would pull up in a big car sometime, somewhere, and say, 'You guys over there, tie up your boats!'"

But there is a lot more to be said about why the MFU has had limited success on the island. One reason, obviously, was money. In his letter of resignation, Ed Frenette maintained that it had been a mistake for the union to move into P.E.I. without having the proper finances in place. It's a position that he takes today. "The money just wasn't there," he says.

"Maybe he's right," says former MFU executive secretary Gilles Thériault. "We were organizing in New Brunswick with no money because people were willing to work for nothing. Maybe we were naïve in thinking that we would find people willing to do the same, over a long period, on P.E.I. On the other hand, we were being asked by the fishermen to move into the province. Guys like Jamie Ellsworth really wanted to belong to the MFU. And we didn't feel we could call ourselves a Maritime union without having a presence in the other provinces."

Except for very short periods, there was only ever one organizer at a time on the island, but there were roughly the same number of fishermen as in New Brunswick, where there were usually three. As well, there were few leadership training courses, for staff or for fishermen.

Another hindrance was the opposition of other groups. In New Brunswick, fishermen's associations in the northeast and southeast had ceased to exist once the union was founded, but on the island both the MFU and the PEIFA operated simultaneously. "The two groups always seemed to be in conflict," Michael LeClair says. "Some fishermen tended to not want to get involved in the fight." Both competed actively for the loyalty of fishermen, but only one, the PEIFA, received funding from the province. "I think the overwhelming factor on the island," says Thériault, "was the presence of the fishermen's association. There was always stronger opposition on P.E.I. than anywhere else in the region. The association had a full-time person paid by the government, and it opposed everything the MFU did."

The Eastern Fishermen's Federation (EFF) also had a strong presence on the island, because that was where it had been founded and where its first president was based. The first executive director of the EFF had been a popular island broadcaster, and his connections with the media served the organization well. For a time, MFU fishermen boycotted a CBC fisheries broadcaster because they perceived a bias against the union.

Also in contrast to New Brunswick, the MFU on P.E.I. never succeeded in attracting co-op members, who numbered around 600. Howards Cove fisherman Ivan Shaw believes that P.E.I. co-ops were always heavily in debt to the United Maritime Fishermen, whereas those in New Brunswick were more financially solvent and thus able to be more independent and more critical.

Not least of all was the nature of Prince Edward Island society and politics. "In New Brunswick, the Acadian identity was a strong factor in getting collective bargaining rights," says Maureen Larkin, a former P.E.I. nun who worked for the union on and off throughout the 1980s. "It wasn't the only factor, of course, but that kind of struggle linked to the preservation of a language and culture was something we didn't have on P.E.I.

"My own observations from talking to fishers," Larkin continues, "is that they do not have any confidence in organization. I have never sensed any real hostility to the MFU in the work I've done, but it was more a lack of confidence that organization would accomplish anything."

Ed Frenette believes that the most important factor—and one that the union was never really able to deal with—was patronage. "The patronage system is so entrenched on P.E.I.," he says. "It determines everything—who gets jobs, who gets grants for boats. Patronage is so much a part of island life. The union talked about fish prices or independence from the fish buyers, but those issues were really secondary to the way people lived. We didn't talk about patronage."

There was, no doubt, a failure on the part of the union to see itself as a political force. On the island, as in the early days in New Brunswick, the MFU's strength was in opposition ridings. Fisheries Minister Pat Binns, for example, was from a Conservative riding in the southeast of the province, which had never been penetrated by the MFU. It tended to be the most prosperous fishing area—fishermen there had always received, on average, 40 cents more per pound for their lobster than fishermen in the Savage Harbour area—and the PEIFA had a strong presence. For this reason, perhaps, the MFU made little progress in dispelling Binns' belief that a union was not what fishermen wanted.

Nor did island fishermen, unlike those in New Brunswick, ever really badger individual politicians for collective bargaining legislation. "It's true that we failed to see the union as a political organization," says Michael LeClair. "But what we had was a provincial government that was anti-union and anti-human. We felt there was nothing we could do, except wait for the government to change."

Even during the plebiscite, the MFU refused to participate. The issue—to boycott or not—had been hotly debated in the organization. Not everyone agreed with the fishermen's decision. Bernie Conway was one. Conway had graduated from the University of Prince Edward Island with a degree in economics in 1974 and had fished lobster for several years before going to work for a furnace company in 1978. He had just started working alongside LeClair when the meeting in Miminegash was called. "It was my first meeting for the union," he recalls. "I didn't know much about what was going on. I didn't even know much about the fishery. But it seemed to me to be a negative position. That somehow, this was a right and that we didn't have to fight for it. To me, I just kind of look at that now and laugh. What have you ever won that you didn't have to fight for?"

Gilles Thériault also disagreed with the fishermen's decision to boycott. "I agree the plebiscite is wrong," he told a Maritime Council meeting, "but it's the political reality. If we boycott it, there's a good chance it will be all over for the union." Both Thériault and Réginald Comeau encouraged island fishermen to get involved in a signing-up campaign to prove to the government that fishermen really did support a union.

At the time, the MFU claimed 450 members on the island. In the end, 301 fishermen, ostensibly non-members, since the union was boycotting the plebiscite, said yes to collective bargaining in the plebiscite. If MFU members hadn't boycotted, the plebiscite could have been close, if not actually won. "I believed that whether we won or lost, the union would have been strengthened on the island if we had participated," Thériault says. Yet island fishermen and staff decided against it. That decision, however, still haunts some fishermen today.

Jamie Ellsworth became the first MFU
president from outside New Brunswick
when he was elected in 1983.
(COURTESY MFU)

The MFU president at the time was Jamie Ellsworth of Miminegash. He was one of the original union supporters on Prince Edward Island, and he became the first MFU president from outside New Brunswick when he was elected in 1983. Both he and his wife, Alberta, are community activists. She is a former Irish-mosser who, along with her sister, Aldona Jones, started an organization for shore workers that was instrumental in effecting many changes in the moss industry.

Jamie Ellsworth is the kind of union member—sincere, honest, concerned about the future of the inshore fishery—on which the MFU has developed its reputation as a principled organization. Today, he still carries a certain amount of guilt about the decision to boycott the plebiscite. Was it a mistake? "We probably didn't have enough members, so in retrospect it wasn't an error," he says.

Could the union have signed up enough members? That is the unanswered, perhaps unanswerable, question. Even Savage Harbour fisherman Fred Pigott wonders. "If we had turned around, forgot about our rights, and decided to fight," he says, "we might have won. We probably had a lot more support for a union than we thought we had. It certainly did us no good at all to boycott it."

Maybe, in the end, there weren't enough fishermen on the island ready to support a union. Maybe the independent self-image or perhaps the fear of a strike was too strong. But it is something that should have been tested in a certification campaign—as it would be in New Brunswick—not in a plebiscite on an issue of such basic human rights.

*   *   *   *   *

By the time the results of the plebiscite were in, union fishermen on Prince Edward Island were feeling pretty low. "Without accreditation you can't do what you want to do in terms of being able to finance an organization. The government knew it was only a matter of time," says Jamie Ellsworth. Michael LeClair was about to leave the MFU, after applying for a job in Latin America. Bernie Conway would take over as organizer and stay with the MFU for the next six years, joined occasionally by Maureen Larkin.

Since 1983, a small core of island fishermen have continued to support the union. They have paid their dues each year, attended Maritime Council meetings, and participated on government advisory committees. "It's worth paying my dues just to have a voice," says Leonard Aylward, a cod fisherman from Tignish who has been the union's island representative on the Atlantic Groundfish Advisory Committee. "I want to see it continue in New Brunswick and Nova Scotia," says Ivan Shaw. "Anything they get over there tends to reverberate on us here." The role of island fishermen in the union continues to be a puzzle for MFU fishermen and staff elsewhere. "Just when you think things are completely dead on the island, they start up again," says one staff member.

In 1978, Newfoundland fishermen's union president Richard Cashin had predicted that Prince Edward Island would be the next province where fishermen would unionize. "The opportunity exists here," he told the annual meeting of the province's federation of labour, "probably more than any other Maritime province because the Island's economy is so dependent on the fishery." That was true. Ten percent of the labour force was involved in the fishery compared with five percent across the Maritimes generally. But what didn't Cashin take into consideration? That Islanders are more conservative than people across the region generally? That they are more parochial and more likely to join an organization with P.E.I. in its title?

It remains an open question today.

JUSTICE DELAYED, JUSTICE DENIED

"The results are so overwhelmingly in favour of the union that
the Board does not feel it necessary to take any further steps
to determine the wishes of [co-op] members."
—New Brunswick Fishing Industry Relations Board, March 1984—

W ITH THE PASSAGE of the Fisheries Bargaining Act in
New Brunswick in April 1982, the Maritime Fishermen's
Union geared up for a major membership drive in the
southeast and the northeast of the province. MFU members went
into the fall season full of energy and confident that certification was
just around the corner. "Just having the legislation was really a shot
in the arm for the fishermen," recalls Gilles Thériault. "They really
put on an all-out campaign."

That summer, the Fishing Industry Relations Board had been
established to monitor the act. Of the seven board members, three
were selected to hear the MFU's requests for certification: Chairman Weldon Graser, also chairman of the Industrial Relations
Board and one of the province's labour-relations experts; Kim
d'Entremont, executive director of the New Brunswick Fish Packers' Association; and Gastien Godin of the midshore fishermen's
association in the northeast.

The act required that 40 percent of members in a geographic area
(northeast, southeast, or Bay of Fundy) and for each species had to
be signed up in a three-month period before a vote could be held.
Then 60 percent of eligible fishermen had to vote, with a majority
in favour, for the MFU to become the official bargaining agent.

In the northeast, there were seven card-signing campaigns for
seven species: lobster, scallops, smelts and tomcod, gaspereau,
mackerel, herring, and groundfish. Seven applications for certification
were submitted to the board in early November. Another nine
applications for certification—representing nine species—were
submitted for the southeast a week later. Once certified, the union
would then choose a bargaining team to negotiate prices for each
species with a buyers' bargaining team.

Fishermen in northeast New Brunswick cast their ballots on certification in December 1982, nine months after the Fisheries Bargaining Act had been passed. (COURTESY MFU)

Certification votes were held in late December 1982 throughout the northeast and in early January 1983 throughout the southeast. When the results were eventually tallied, it would be revealed that more than 80 percent of all fishermen in the northeast who had voted said yes to the MFU becoming their bargaining agent. In the southeast, about 75 percent had voted in favour. It would be a long time yet, however, before the votes would be counted.

Determining whose vote was legitimate was a major challenge in itself. In the northeast, for example, 43 companies had submitted lists of which species they bought and from whom. The MFU had also submitted lists of fishermen. But of course these lists did not match. The companies' had names of fishermen whom the union had never heard of before. There was even a problem sorting out who was who. In one village, for instance, four fishermen had the same name. Pending the resolution of these problems—as well as the issue of certification—the ballots were placed in double envelopes and stored in sealed boxes in the Fishing Industry Relations Board office.

Meanwhile, a much bigger problem was looming in the northeast.

*   *   *   *   *

Now that legislation had been passed, the companies seemed to accept that collective bargaining with fishermen was inevitable. But the same was not true for the co-operative movement. In early January 1983, the Association Coopérative des Pêcheurs de l'Ile Ltée (the Lamèque co-op) filed an application to have its members excluded from the bargaining unit.

The conflict between the union and the co-op movement had been simmering for a long time. From the beginning, the United Maritime Fishermen (UMF) seemed to resent the MFU. UMF leadership didn't like the union's choice of a name, because its acronym caused confusion between UMF and MFU in the media. The UMF also feared a potential loss of membership, and felt criticized by co-op members who also belonged to the union. During lobster season in 1977, for example, one fisherman told the press that the companies, including a UMF co-op, were "stealing fishermen blind." In retaliation, UMF head Arthur LeBlanc wrote the fisherman's co-op threatening to expel him unless he stopped making such statements publicly. On another occasion, LeBlanc complained that the MFU was demanding prices higher than the market could bear. The UMF also engaged in red-baiting of the union, though not in an organized or widespread way.

The bottom line was that the UMF didn't believe that its members needed to belong to the union. UMF management was often quoted as saying that a co-op was already an "advanced form" of a union. At the UMF's annual convention in early 1978, for example, president Richard Savoie told delegates:

> We are not against fishermen who wish to organize themselves under the banner of fishermen's unions and we do not wish to deny them the right to do so if they feel they need these mechanisms to negotiate the sale and price of their product. But I say, and I repeat, that the fishermen members of our co-operatives do not need another union to negotiate the sale and price of their products since their respective co-operative, a union itself, in which they have social and financial responsibilities, performs that function for them.
>
> When our Central states that there is nothing to negotiate and that it will not negotiate with fishermen's unions because it would be a

waste of time to do so, it speaks on behalf of the fishermen, who together with his fellow fishermen who own and control their Co-operative, cannot negotiate with himself. To proceed otherwise would be contrary to co-operative philosophy and practice and would serve to weaken the structural base on which co-operatives rest.

The UMF saw a fundamental conflict of interest: co-op members could not be part of collective bargaining because they would only be negotiating with themselves.

The Maritime Fishermen's Union, on the other hand, maintained that co-op members should be included in any bargaining unit: there was no point in negotiating contracts with companies if co-ops could pay whatever price they wished. The MFU didn't believe that inshore co-op members felt they had enough clout to influence the price of fish. Some of the strongest union members, after all, were also co-op members who *were* interested in collective bargaining.

Furthermore, the union maintained, co-op members wouldn't be negotiating with themselves because the Fisheries Bargaining Act provided for a buyers' bargaining association, which would negotiate on behalf of all companies in a geographic area. The UMF, as a processor, would be represented. (The N.B. Fish Buyers Bargaining Association was certified in December 1984.)

The conflict between the MFU and the UMF grew worse as time wore on, and it was characterized by a lot of nastiness and name-calling through the media, between the "conservative" UMF on the one hand and the "radical" MFU on the other. Long-time co-operator Réal Chiasson maintains that much of it was fuelled not by the UMF management in general but by one individual, a senior manager who was anti-union in principle and "spoke loudly at the time." Be that as it may, the verbal warfare created an impression that a major battle was brewing between the two groups, a battle that was about to play itself out as the union prepared to go through the certification process.

Réal Chiasson was and still is executive director of the Lamèque co-op. An amalgamation of a handful of co-ops on Lamèque Island, it was founded in 1943 to market fishermen's salt cod. In 1950, as saltfish gave way to the fresh and frozen trade, the co-op built its first freezer. A decade later, after the facilities burned to the ground, it moved half a mile away, taking over the old buildings of the Robin company. In 1961, it built a groundfish plant and, in 1974, a crab-processing plant. More expansions followed, and by the mid-1980s, the Lamèque co-op was a sprawling complex with 1,200 employees and about 300 fishermen members. It was one of the largest and most prosperous fishermen's co-ops in Canada.

Chiasson had been hired by the co-op in 1971, after he had helped organize the fishermen's association in the northeast in 1968. A former director of the UMF, he was a strong co-operator. For him, it was simply a question of principle: he couldn't understand how co-op fishermen could be part of a collective bargaining unit. Jean Gauvin's task-force report at the end of 1979 had recommended that co-ops be excluded from any legislation. Chiasson and others had believed that Gauvin had made a commitment to do so.

But when the legislation was finally passed in the spring of 1982, co-ops were not excluded. Lamèque officials and MFU representatives tried to find a solution to the problem but without success. The MFU wasn't so concerned about the Lamèque co-op—it was the only co-op in the northeast, and most of its members were midshore fishermen—but it didn't want to establish a precedent that would affect the southeast, where a lot of MFU fishermen were also co-op members. The union was convinced that if co-op members were not part of a bargaining unit, then collective bargaining for fishermen would not work.

The Lamèque co-op had recently left the umbrella of the UMF after it had started its own marketing consortium with a handful of companies. But it still considered itself a co-op. And as the applications for certification in the northeast went before the Fishing Industry Relations Board in January 1983, the Lamèque co-op prepared to do battle on behalf of co-ops everywhere.

*   *   *   *   *

The challenge for the Lamèque co-op was to convince the board that co-op fishermen were sufficiently different from other fishermen to warrant excluding them from collective bargaining legislation. The co-op's lawyer, Fernand Landry, cited several differences between a co-op and a company: The first was the structure of the co-op, in which every member had one vote no matter how many shares he held. The second was the mode of operation, whereby the co-op paid a price throughout the season, and if there was a profit

The Lamèque co-op was founded in 1943 to market salt cod.
(CEA COLLECTION L'ÉVANGÉLINE E8508)

at the end, it was returned to the fishermen. The third was the co-op's relationship with its members, in which the board of directors was composed solely of fishermen. If a union tried to negotiate on behalf of co-op fishermen, Landry argued, the function—the *raison d'être*—of the co-op would be usurped.

The board held five days of hearings throughout January and February 1983, then adjourned to consider the evidence. It was well into the process when rumours began to circulate throughout the northeast that Kim d'Entremont, who represented processors on the board, had been offered a job by the Lamèque co-op. Réal Chiasson, in fact, had made the approach. "We had already discussed with Kim years before about the possibility of coming with us," Chiasson explains today. "At one stage of the game, we needed to hire someone. So I went to Kim and said, 'Are you free to come?'"

That it was in the midst of the hearings didn't bother Chiasson. "I had an opening," Chiasson says. "I couldn't wait six months. The time was now." (In fact, the position, director of marketing, had just been created. D'Entremont eventually accepted.) Chiasson knew that it would look bad for the Lamèque co-op, but he also knew that he was on safe legal grounds as long as d'Entremont resigned from the board.

D'Entremont, for his part, finally mentioned the job offer to the board's chairman, Weldon Graser. Not surprisingly, Graser found the news distressing, called a special meeting of the Fishing Industry Relations Board, and issued a statement:

> It was my opinion as the Chairman of the Board and a practicing lawyer that this situation could neither be ignored nor tolerated in any way. I could not and will not allow the credibility and integrity of this Board to be suspect or compromised in any way, or that there be even an impression or appearance of indiscretion, conflict of interest, bias or anything other than objectivity. In my view the making of the offer was improper, indiscreet and untimely and the consideration of the offer was also improper and bereft of good judgment in these circumstances.

Graser said that he had accepted the resignation of d'Entremont from the board, and that he had no choice but to dissolve the panel, set up another, and begin the hearings again. "In the circumstances," he told the press, "I do not feel this board can properly function any further in the matter."

So the process began again—with a new panel including Chairman Thomas Kuttner, an associate professor at the University of New Brunswick and an adjudicator with the Public Service Labour Relations Board; Jean-Paul Morel and J. Ward Stewart, representing buyers; and Paul LePage and Klaus Sonnenburg, representing fishermen.

On August 2, the hearings resumed. The Lamèque co-op's lawyer, however, objected to the panel's composition because only two of the five members, LePage and Morel, were bilingual. The board, as in the original proceedings, planned to have simultaneous translation, but Fernand Landry argued that that wasn't good enough. He said that inadequate translation placed his client at a disadvantage and that under the Official Languages of New Brunswick Act, as well as under the Canadian Charter of Rights and Freedoms, his client had the right to be heard and understood in the language of his choice—in this case, French.

The MFU had already asked that the hearings proceed in English because its lawyer, Raymond Larkin, was a unilingual anglophone. Larkin pointed out that the co-op had not objected to the composition of the previous panel, even though its chairman, Weldon Graser, was unilingual. Thomas Kuttner also asked why the matter hadn't been raised during the previous hearings. Landry explained that a majority of the earlier panel members—two out of three—could understand French. Kuttner, however, couldn't follow Landry's logic.

Larkin went on to argue that this was just another in a long series of delaying tactics to prevent certification of the MFU. The MFU, he told board members, had already lost a year of collective bargaining. "You know by looking at the Act that we would have had the right, for example, to submit check-off forms to buyers after certification had been issued," he said. "So the financial cost of this delay of a year has been extraordinary to the Maritime Fishermen's Union. In industrial relations matters, there is no principle that is more universally subscribed to than 'justice delayed is justice denied.' And that, indeed, lengthy delay is destructive of the ability of fishermen or of employees in another context to exercise their rights under the Act."

The co-op's lawyer asked for a postponement in order to get a ruling from the courts. Chairman Kuttner refused, and the panel took a break to consider the issue. When it returned a couple of hours later, Kuttner announced that the question of the right to be heard in the language of one's choice was outside the jurisdiction of the Fishing Industry Relations Board. Because other labour boards in the province used simultaneous translation, the panel decided to proceed with the hearings. (Fernand Landry had also tried to have Raymond Larkin barred from appearing before the board because Larkin was not licensed to practise law in New Brunswick. Larkin pointed out, however, that he had obtained permission from the previous chairman, as long as he was accompanied by a New Brunswick lawyer. The panel decided that this question, too, was outside its jurisdiction. Unless the province's bar society ruled otherwise, Larkin could continue to represent the MFU.)

Finally, the hearings continued. The co-op's lawyer had argued that the MFU wasn't a fishermen's organization under the terms of the act. Gilles Thériault was in the process of being grilled the following day when everything came to a sudden halt. Fernand Landry announced that the Lamèque co-op had won an injunction to stop the proceedings and allow the language issue to be dealt with by the courts.

* * * * *

The Lamèque co-op's challenge to the linguistic composition of the board put the Maritime Fishermen's Union in a difficult position. Of all the grass-roots organizations in Acadia, the MFU was probably the most sensitive and most strident on the question of language. It had used simultaneous translation at its founding meeting in 1977, even though there were few anglophone fishermen present. Gilles Thériault had typically spent hours and hours translating Maritime Council meetings word for word. The MFU had been the driving force, at annual conventions of the New Brunswick Federation of Labour, in getting the federation to adopt a more bilingual stance.

Now, the MFU was faced with a court challenge that could tie up its organizing efforts for years. There's no doubt that the language question was important. Nearly all of the Lamèque co-op's fishermen members were unilingual francophones. The right to be heard and understood in one's own language in judicial and quasi-judicial proceedings—as opposed to speaking through a translator—is still an issue in New Brunswick today.

But at that stage—after the series of delays—it was almost beside the point. MFU members were certain that the Lamèque co-op was simply trying to stall proceedings one more time. Nonetheless, the MFU decided to stay out of it. In a press release, it declared the matter an issue between the board and the co-op. The union would sit back and wait for the courts to decide.

In early October, however, an opportune appointment changed the course of events. Fishing Industry Relations Board member Roger Savoie was named a judge of the provincial court. That left a vacancy on the board, and Raymond Guerette, a bilingual lawyer from Saint John, was appointed. It then became possible to strike a fully bilingual panel when both the union and the co-op agreed to drop the two unilingual members, Sonnenburg and Stewart.

On November 30, 1983, the injunction was lifted. Early in the New Year, the board again began hearings. They lasted three days. In late March, it released its decision. It rejected the Lamèque co-op's request to exclude its members from collective bargaining legislation. The board had been unable to find any significant difference between co-op and other fishermen:

They fish the same species of fish, use the same type of boats, the same gear, get paid the same prices as paid by other buyers, and have the same day-to-day experiences as other fishermen. There is really no difference between them and the other fishermen in the region and the Board is convinced that whatever differences do exist, they are not significant enough to support an application for exclusion, at least not on the argument that there is no community of interest.

Another aspect is the importance of the co-op in the fishing industry of the region. Fully 25 percent of all the fish landings in the area are brought in by the co-op. Exclusion from the bargaining unit could give them a competitive advantage over other buyers and would lead to an imbalance in the system of competition. While this would prove to the advantage of the co-op, it would also lead to disharmony in all fishing industry relations.

The Board is inclined to accept the union's submission on these points and believes that one of the objectives of the Act is the promotion of harmonious and orderly industrial relations. Excluding the co-op fishermen from the jurisdiction of the Act is, in our opinion, undesirable and could lead to industrial difficulties in the future.

The co-op's lawyer had urged the board to count the certification votes of co-op fishermen to see what they wanted, and the board had complied with respect to three species (lobster, herring, groundfish). "The results are so overwhelmingly in favour of the union that the board does not feel it necessary to take any further steps to determine the wishes of the members," the board's report said.

On March 22, 1984, the MFU became the bargaining agent for inshore fishermen in northeast New Brunswick. At a press conference in Moncton, a jubilant Gilles Thériault, with Réginald Comeau at his side, called the decision "an end of an era and a new evolution."

"The union has had difficulties," Thériault said, "that's no secret. But by the end of the year, we'll be whistling a different tune."

On April 26, 1984, the MFU was also certified in the southeast, almost two years to the day after it had won collective bargaining legislation.

The story, however, was not over. In the dying days of the Legislative Assembly that spring, Justice Minister Fernand Dubé introduced an amendment to the Cooperative Associations Act excluding co-op members from the Fisheries Bargaining Act. (A co-op member could voluntarily join the union, but he wouldn't automatically become part of the bargaining unit when the union became certified in his area.) In effect, the amendment quietly reversed the decision that the Fishing Industry Relations Board had made after nearly two years of deliberations, delays, and interruptions.

MFU members opposed the bill when it went to the Law Amendments Committee early the following year, arguing that "by adopting Bill 89, [the committee] will be taking the very serious decision of decertifying through legislation a group of fishermen that has been duly certified through proper process set up by this same legislature."

But it was to no avail. The amendment went through. What the Lamèque co-op had lost before the New Brunswick Fishing Industry Relations Board, it won by going cap in hand to the politicians.

*   *   *   *   *

The Maritime Fishermen's Union had expected that excluding co-ops would make collective bargaining next to impossible, but that turned out not to be the case. In 1984, there was a major shake-up at the upper echelons of UMF management. Long-time director and "old-style" leader Arthur LeBlanc was replaced by François Babin, who had managed a consumer co-op in Richibucto for years and had also served as chairman of Co-op Atlantic. Considered progressive, Babin quickly hired Camille Thériault, whose first task as vice president for membership relations was to re-establish the UMF's credibility with inshore fishermen. "Both Babin and Camille realized that all this bickering with the MFU was going nowhere," says Gilles Thériault. (It also didn't hurt that Camille was Gilles' brother.)

In 1985, largely through the work of these three men, the UMF and the MFU reached an agreement, with each side pledging to respect the other's role: the co-op movement's role in marketing and the union's role in representing fishermen on resource-management questions and in collective bargaining. The co-op also promised to respect union contracts signed with the companies.

The agreement, however, was short-lived. By 1988, the UMF was bankrupt. The writing had been on the wall even before Babin took over. In the early 1980s, the UMF, like all fish companies in Atlantic Canada, was operating in the red. Despite federal assistance, the organization's debt continued to grow. "The UMF's biggest mistake was when it moved into production," says fisherman Jean-Guy Maillet, who, in early 1985, became manager of the Richibucto Village fishermen's co-op. "A lot of bad decisions were made. The Alder Point plant, and the trawlers the UMF bought to feed it, lost millions. Building holding stations in the U.S. and trying to compete with the Americans on their own turf was ridiculous. That lost millions, too. If the UMF had kept to its mandate of marketing, I think it would be alive today."

Nonetheless, the agreement signed between the United Maritime Fishermen and the Maritime Fishermen's Union in 1985 was a historic one. After a long and bitter battle, a truce had been finally declared.

TRANSITION:
FROM PROTEST
TO COMPROMISE

*If the fishermen want to participate in management of their industry and
have a word to say in policy, they have to accept the fact that sometimes we
may have to compromise to get the best overall plan for the longer term.*
—MFU policy paper, 1985—

AFTER THE CRISIS in the Atlantic fishing industry in 1968,
and again in 1974, the federal government had financially
bailed out the industry. Both times, the problems went
away for a few years, but they inevitably came back. Following the
crisis of 1981, government decided to take a different approach. In
February 1982, it set up a task force on Atlantic fisheries, headed
by Michael Kirby, a close advisor to Pierre Trudeau. The group's
mandate was to recommend how to achieve and maintain a viable
Atlantic fishing industry in the long term with "due consideration
for the overall economic and social development of the Atlantic
provinces."

The task force held 135 meetings in 43 communities with
fishermen, processors, provincial government representatives, and
others involved in the industry. It also received written briefs from
90 groups. Its report, when it was finally released in early 1983, was
the most intensive study on the Atlantic Canada groundfish fishery
that had ever been produced. It was touted as the study to end all
studies.

Kirby's task force also had a second mandate, to make recommendations on how to help the financially troubled industry. By
now, all major east-coast companies were on the verge of bankruptcy. His report provided the basis for a restructuring that would
take place in 1983, a so-called rationalization that would lead to the
creation of two industry giants: National Sea Products in the
Maritimes and Fisheries Products International in Newfoundland.

The Maritime Fishermen's Union, in its brief to the task force,
had recommended that all the large companies be nationalized, a

recommendation that Kirby did not support. He did, however, support another MFU suggestion. His report recommended that provincial governments that hadn't already done so should pass collective bargaining legislation for inshore fishermen. (Nova Scotia and Prince Edward Island have yet to act on this recommendation.)

Throughout the 1970s and the early 1980s, the MFU developed a reputation as a militant organization that spoke with a loud, clear voice on behalf of inshore fishermen. It cultivated an image as a group that seemed to be more interested in beating down the doors at DFO headquarters than in sitting quietly at the table. Union fishermen were

Cape Breton's Harold Turner and Con Mills (rear) inspired many fishermen to join the MFU. Turner's death in 1982 was a major setback for the Cape Breton local. (COURTESY MFU)

frequently involved in radical actions that drew headlines around the region. In August 1980, for example, faced with an unprecedented run of squid and nowhere to sell it, MFU fishermen in the Canso area dumped their catch on the Canso highway, a move that convinced the companies to at least sit down and talk to the fishermen.

In 1982, 60 union fishermen in Cape Breton occupied DFO offices in Sydney to push for an increase in cod quotas, and won. They were led by Harold Turner of Glace Bay, a highliner who inspired many fishermen to join the union, and whose untimely death by heart attack later that year was a serious setback for the Cape Breton local. Also in 1982, fishermen's wives demonstrated on the wharf in Escuminac to protest what they considered DFO harassment of their husbands during the commercial salmon fishery. The fishery had reopened on the Miramichi River a year earlier after a nine-year closure, but quotas were low and the women felt that fisheries officers were enforcing them too rigidly.

Throughout this period, despite the battle on the Caraquet wharf in 1979, the herring fishery continued to be a bone of contention between the inshore and midshore sectors. In the spring of 1983, when the DFO announced a two-week extension for the seiner fishery without consulting the inshore, fishermen from eastern New Brunswick hurriedly gathered at DFO headquarters in Memramcook on a Friday afternoon. Angry because the extension would eliminate their market (the seiners would have filled the smokehouses before the inshore sector had a chance to start fishing), more than 150 fishermen stormed the building and insisted that the bureaucrats hear them out.

As office staff began to leave for the weekend, the fishermen demanded that Acting Director General for the Gulf Region Jean-Eûdes Haché, along with three others, Alphonse Cormier, Ted Gaudet, and Rhéal Vienneau, stay. "There was never any threat," Haché would tell the press, "but I decided it would be better if we stayed." The media later called the incident a "hostage-taking," though DFO staff downplayed its seriousness, and no charges were ever laid.

Throughout the evening, the fishermen and the bureaucrats argued back and forth. At one point, Haché said that he wanted to telephone the minister. "I went with him to phone," recalls Richibucto Village fisherman Antoine Daigle, "but it wasn't the minister he called at all, it was Joe Bastarache [head of the smokers' association]. So when we got back, I said to the guys, 'Obviously we don't have the same minister. He called Joe Bastarache.' The fishermen weren't impressed, and they started getting mad." (Haché, apparently, had wanted to warn Bastarache that plans for the seiners' extension might have to be changed because of opposition from inshore fishermen.) For the rest of the night, the fishermen talked and played cards while the bureaucrats took turns napping on the couch in Haché's office.

Early Saturday morning, the DFO officials asked to go to the cafeteria in the next building to have breakfast. Some fishermen agreed to accompany them. But as the two groups crossed the courtyard, an RCMP vehicle that had been patrolling during the night came to an abrupt stop beside them. The officers unlocked the doors, and Haché and his group jumped in as the vehicle sped off. Shortly afterwards, an RCMP riot squad, equipped with shields, helmets and riot sticks, descended on the building. The fishermen

The media called the 1983 occupation of DFO offices in Memramcook a "hostage-taking." RCMP officers removed the fishermen from the building, and later that afternoon fishermen demonstrated in Moncton as meetings were held between the DFO, the MFU, and the seiners' association. (COURTESY MFU)

were convinced to leave by a promise that the DFO would meet with them in Moncton. The RCMP would later say that the fishermen had been "very co-operative."

Later that afternoon, 100 MFU fishermen demonstrated in front of Assumption Place in downtown Moncton as meetings went on inside the building between the union, the seiners' group, and DFO officials. The issue was finally settled, though the incident created a rift between the DFO and the MFU that lasted for several years. "I was personally very distraught by what happened in Memramcook," says Ted Gaudet, today DFO director general for the Gulf Region. "If anyone in the department had been supportive of the union over the years, it had been myself, Jean-Eûdes, and Alphonse. And we were the people held against our will in Memramcook. To this day, I've never received any indication from the MFU that it made a mistake."

Says Jean-Eûdes Haché: "Part of the MFU's *raison d'être* at the time was very much government bashing, fed bashing, as much as it was company bashing. Government and the big companies were usually mentioned in the same breath as being the opponents. I remember when Roméo [LeBlanc] created the Gulf Region in 1981, he had told me, almost tongue in cheek, 'I'll know you're doing your job when I see demonstrations in front of your building.' I had an opportunity to remind him about that later."

*　　*　　*　　*　　*

Yet even as the union was involved in militancy, it also began to be drawn into the government consultative process. By the early 1980s, more than two dozen DFO advisory committees had been established around the region, and the union had representatives on all of them. MFU members found that they were often able to negotiate quota increases or season extensions for the inshore sector. They also began to discover that when a task force such as Michael Kirby's was established, it didn't help their cause to ignore it.

Such participation was always a challenge for the union. Often the hardest part was getting its own members to agree on how an issue should be settled. Again, the herring fishery is a good example. Even after 80 percent of the quota was returned to the inshore sector in 1981, there was still a problem for inshore fishermen in

In 1984, Northumberland Strait fishermen blocked the ferry that runs between Caribou, Nova Scotia, and Wood Islands, Prince Edward Island. (COURTESY MFU)

some parts of the southern gulf. Because herring spawn in northeast New Brunswick before they move along the shore to the Northumberland Strait, fishermen in the Pictou area of Nova Scotia rarely had a chance to catch herring before the quota had been taken by their New Brunswick counterparts. It was a frustrating situation, and in 1984, Northumberland Strait fishermen blocked the ferry that runs between Caribou, Nova Scotia, and Wood Islands, Prince Edward Island, to draw public attention to their plight.

Through the union, they also began a major debate about how to solve the problem. At times, it was very bitter. "There was a lot of ill feeling towards the New Brunswick guys," recalls Nova Scotia fisherman Hasse Lindblad. "It was harder than people realize to keep the fishermen together." When more than 50 Northumberland Strait fishermen were arrested for fishing illegally after the quota had been taken in 1986, the MFU went to court to defend them on the grounds that the way the quota was set denied access to Nova Scotia fishermen in the strait. The union won.

After that, quotas were set by region within the southern gulf. "What it meant for us," says Lindblad, "was that we went from having 500 tonnes to having 10,000 tonnes, from a fishery that lasted a few days to a fishery that lasts a month. Now, when people say, 'What has the union done for me?', we say, 'We've given you a fall herring season.'"

Again, it was a solution that came from within the union, though it wasn't reached easily. "To keep together fishermen from southwest Nova Scotia, P.E.I., Pictou, northeast New Brunswick, and southeast New Brunswick is an impossible task," says Jean-Eûdes Haché. "They all have their own interests. You need a very strong magnet to pull all those poles together. That was Gilles' strength, having enough moral authority, moral suasion to take all those regional, sometimes parochial interests, and come up with a position that could be driven through without losing too many players along the way."

Given provincial rivalries, the solution wasn't without repercussions. Gilles Thériault was accused by some bureaucrats of selling out New Brunswick fishermen.

Throughout this period, as the MFU's participation on government committees increased, its image began to change. The union kept a lower profile, with fewer public demonstrations, fewer marches in the streets, fewer occupations of company or DFO offices. One reason was that fishermen began to feel that they were making progress through negotiations with government. Another was the financial state of the union itself. It could no longer afford to organize such events, and increasing discouragement on the part of fishermen made it more and more difficult to "call up the troops" when needed.

The union had never managed to find a way to support itself, and by now, its impoverishment was very apparent. Stories of the union's—and the staff's—lack of money were legend. With seldom more than a couple of dollars in his pocket, Gilles Thériault usually ran his car on empty. One time, he and Léandre Babineau of Richibucto Village were headed to Nova Scotia for a meeting. On the way across the bridge between Halifax and Dartmouth, Thériault's car suddenly began to sputter and cough, obviously out of gas. A few feet short of the point where the bridge peaked, just as the car was about to stall, Babineau calmly got out and gave the vehicle the push it needed. The two men coasted the way down on empty.

Another time, a group of fishermen from New Brunswick had piled into Thériault's car to go to a Maritime Council meeting in

Big Bras d'Or, Cape Breton. In their haste, they hadn't noticed that his tires were so worn that wires were actually protruding from them. Nor did they realize that his spare tire, too, was shot. When they found out, after the meeting wrapped up, the fishermen refused to return home with him. In still another incident, Thériault arrived at the airport in Halifax, took a taxi into town, but had to leave his watch with the driver while he ascended 16 stories to lawyer Raymond Larkin's office to borrow money to pay the fare.

For years, the MFU moved the location of its annual meeting around, from Caraquet to Charlottetown to Memramcook, for one simple reason. It hadn't paid its convention bills from the previous year. "With all the travelling we did in those years," says Réginald Comeau, "it never occurred to us to stay in a hotel. We didn't have any money." Often, the union had only enough money to pay its staff for a few months of the year. The rest of the time, staff worked voluntarily while collecting unemployment insurance benefits. Needless to say, it was an exasperating situation. Organizing fishermen who were spread out in every little village—each of which had its own problems and concerns—was difficult enough. Doing it without pay was doubly disconcerting, something that required an enormous, almost missionary-like commitment.

"I recall one time getting phone calls from Howards Cove and from Tignish," says former Prince Edward Island organizer Bernie Conway. "The boats were filled with herring, but the fishermen couldn't sell it. They wanted me to come up, and do something. I remember thinking, 'Screw those guys, they're crazy if they think I'm going to come up and do something, and I'm not even being paid.' Some of the guys who were asking for help hadn't even paid their dues." Overwork and the lack of pay was the reason the original P.E.I. organizer, Ed Frenette, had left the union.

In Nova Scotia, there had been several organizers—Ron Stockton in Canso, Fred Winsor in Cape Breton, Ron Crawley in Northumberland—but by late 1981, they had all quit as well, mostly because the union didn't have the money to pay them. The situation was understandable from the staff's point of view, yet such turnover did hamper the organizing efforts of the union. Every time a new staff person came on, it seemed that he or she had to start from scratch—learning about the fishery, getting to know members, and signing up new ones.

Michael Belliveau took over as the Nova Scotia organizer for all three locals. He had worked for a development education centre in Halifax and, later, for the National Farmers Union and the United Rubber Workers. He was part-time editor of the Nova Scotia Federation of Labour's newspaper when he began working for the MFU as well.

As the only organizer in Nova Scotia, he had a large terrain to cover, especially given the mountains of Cape Breton and the isolation of places like Canso. In early 1982, Belliveau took a tour through the area to meet with fishermen, identify wharf representatives, and sign up new members. In Canso, he met with the MFU local, which had been feeling alienated from the union for some time. It was the only local not based in the Gulf Region (it was in Scotia-Fundy), and as a result, its interests often conflicted with those of other MFU locals. "The MFU's policy of forcing trawlers over 100 feet out of the gulf has pushed them onto our doorstep, onto our fishing grounds," Canso fisherman Everett Richardson wrote to the union at one point.

By the spring of 1982, the Canso local began to fade away. Dues collection had been difficult, and the fight for collective bargaining legislation in Nova Scotia had ground to a halt. Fishermen in Prince Edward Island were also discouraged about ever winning legislation. In New Brunswick, Omer Chouinard left the union in the summer of 1983 to move back to Montréal. By then, delays in that province, first in winning legislation, then in being certified, had pushed the union to the financial wall. By 1984, it was more than $100,000 in debt. Gilles Thériault expressed the feelings of a lot of fishermen when he addressed the annual convention in late January:

> Since our founding, no other organization has fought for the rights of the fishermen like the MFU, even though we were as poor as church mice and even if we did not negotiate any contracts. But the time has come to face reality.
>
> Some of those who have never given up before are now at the end of their ropes. In the oldest locals, and in the communities that have been with us since the beginning, active participation is harder and harder to achieve. It is harder to draw fishermen out to meetings. It is not yet disastrous because when there is a crisis, we can still quite

easily fill up a meeting room. But this is not enough. A lot of fishermen are asking why should we fight? Why should we pay our dues? Because if we win some things, the fishermen who have stayed at home without bothering and without paying any dues, will gain the same benefits as us.

At that convention, Thériault was elected president, the first non-fisherman to hold the post, because many felt that only he would be able to solve the union's financial problems. (They were solved, at least temporarily, in 1985 when federal fisheries minister John Fraser, in one of his last acts before resigning over the "tainted tuna" scandal, gave the union $300,000. The money was used to clear debts and to set up an insurance plan for union members.)

During this period—along with having an increased say on government committees and the financial state of the union—a third factor contributed to the changing image and changing role of the MFU. And that was the state of the fishery itself.

Beginning in 1983, lobster landings and prices began to rise simultaneously. "Our fishermen have never received such high prices," the union's newsletter noted. For the next several years, lobster fishermen in all three provinces had record years. "I remember doing a workshop in Cape Breton in the winter of 1984," recalls Dalhousie University professor Rick Williams. "It was at Big Bras d'Or. Stuart Squires was president of the local. There was a bad storm, but we had a good turn-out, anyway, maybe 40 fishermen. So we said, 'Let's spend the morning figuring out what are the biggest problems facing fishermen.' They couldn't come up with any. I was shocked, to meet a group of fishermen in Cape Breton who were basically happy."

Although groundfish landings throughout the region began to decline during this time, fishermen would more than make up for it in record prices. In 1986, the Atlantic Provinces Economic Council reported that National Sea Products had made a profit of $28.5 million over the first three quarters of the year, compared with $6.9 million in the same period a year earlier.

By 1987, the *Sou'wester* was reporting that both National Sea Products and Fisheries Products International were making "gobs of money.... The past twelve months have been a period that if you had fish, especially fresh fish, the American market was waiting to gobble it up." The companies, the newspaper noted, were even making huge profits on marginal items such as frozen cod blocks.

*   *   *   *   *

The Maritime Fishermen's Union had started out as a protest movement to save the inshore fishery, and by the mid-1980s, one could say, it had succeeded. Inshore fishermen throughout the region were doing extremely well. "By then, fishermen weren't just fighting to survive," says MFU organizer Réginald Comeau. "They were fighting for economic gains, for ways of benefiting from the system. They were fighting for better management of the re-source."

The union had moved from protest to compromise. The DFO's Ted Gaudet dates the change from the Memramcook hostage-taking. "After that," says Gaudet, "there was a fundamental differ-ence in approach. Gilles Thériault became a statesman. He would go into meetings and seek compromise rather than confrontation. The union had gone from a fighting mode to becoming a facilitator in solving problems.

"Starting in 1985," Gaudet continues, "that was when Gilles began to get a tremendous amount of credibility with both the industry and the department. He could knock on any door in Ottawa or in the department throughout the region."

Thériault has a different analysis. "Throughout the sixties and seventies," he says, "fishermen were radical because they needed to be radical. The inshore sector was disappearing. But it was a radicalism that came from the fishermen. It was fishermen who burned the wharf in Caraquet in 1967. It was fishermen who blocked the herring seiners in 1979. The union leaders were just there to help organize the fight. It was because of those fights that doors started to open.

"By the early 1980s, fishermen began to realize that they were being listened to, especially in the Gulf Region. The bureaucrats, and even sometimes the companies, started to pay attention when fishermen spoke. By 1985, fishermen no longer needed to burn down wharves to get attention. The fishermen and the union had to go through that radical phase in order to gain credibility, in order to work their way into the board rooms."

The MFU began to change, Thériault maintains, because the times began to change.

The irony, of course, is that when times are good, fishermen don't need an organization. (The corollary is that when times are bad, they can't afford one.) The mid-1980s were good times for inshore fishermen in the Maritimes, and membership in the union began to drop. It was a low point for almost every local. Together, they had only several hundred dues-paying members.

The only expansion during this period would be in southwest Nova Scotia. At the end of 1982, organizer Michael Belliveau had drawn up a five-year plan that included putting the fight for legislation on the back burner and going after membership in the southwest. It was meant to be a long-term plan, but Local 9 would be established much more quickly than anyone had predicted.

The local would be something new for the MFU. Although there would be echoes of days past—when battles would be won through demonstrations and occupations—much of the local's energy would go into marketing, something that the union had only flirted with in the past. Local 9's business approach would be a reflection of the area and, again, a product of the times.

SOUTHWEST NOVA SCOTIA: COLLECTIVE MARKETING

"We've always tried to influence the other fishermen in the union that collective bargaining isn't the right way to go, that collective marketing is the right way to go. Whether we're right or wrong, that's always been Local 9's perspective."
—Meteghan fisherman Graeme Gawn—

OVER THE YEARS, the Maritime Fishermen's Union had occasionally put out feelers to southwest Nova Scotia. In 1978, Dalhousie University professors Sandy Siegel and Rick Williams had visited Shelburne County. In 1981, Gilles Thériault and Susan Johnson, editor of the union's newsletter, had visited fishermen along the French Shore, which stretches from Digby to Yarmouth. But for financial reasons, the union was nervous about expanding into the area, and nothing had come of either venture.

With two-thirds of the province's fishermen, southwest Nova Scotia was considered the home of the Cadillac fisherman, an image that was reinforced in the late 1970s when even deck hands on scallop draggers were making so much money that many began to buy red Cadillacs. In reality, however, not everyone was doing so well. Throughout the decade, inshore fishermen in southwest Nova Scotia, like inshore fishermen elsewhere, were feeling the squeeze of government regulation. "When the government put in a freeze on licences," recalls Meteghan fisherman Graeme Gawn, "they said it was for our own good, that it was for the protection of our future. But then it was used against us. We couldn't get licences anymore." A native New Zealander, Gawn grew up in Toronto, then met and fell in love with a Meteghan woman while on vacation in Nova Scotia.

When Gawn moved east and took up fishing, he found a fishermen's association already in place. The Municipality of Clare Fishermen's Association took in about 50 members from Meteghan, Saulnierville, Comeauville, and Cape St Mary. "It was basically a wharf committee," says Gawn. "We didn't have any clout because we were so small and so local. We couldn't get anything done. So we decided that we had to join a stronger, more broadly based organization." At the time, the federal Department of Fisheries and Oceans (DFO) was in the process of setting up lobster advisory committees in the region, and only organizations—not individuals—could be represented on them.

The Nova Scotia Fishermen's Association (NSFA) was still present on the shore. At one point, it had claimed 3,000 members, though mostly from groundfish and scallop draggers and herring seiners. But by early 1983, because fishermen did not support the organization financially, the NSFA was close to collapse. (By 1984, only a small scallop section of the NSFA remained.) Inshore fishermen began to shop around for another organization to represent them. They invited the Maritime Fishermen's Union and the Eastern Fishermen's Federation (EFF) to make presentations.

"Alan Billard of the EFF came down and gave us a talk," recalls Gawn. "When he was finished, we asked him, 'Where do you get your money?' When we found out what kind of organization it was, that they represented a lot of offshore fishermen, including the herring seiners, that they were financed by the government, all the fishermen in Meteghan took one look at it, and said, 'No, we don't want that. We've already got an association that's ineffective.'

"When the MFU came down," Gawn continues, "and we found out that it was an inshore fishermen's organization fighting for the rights of inshore fishermen, fighting for the things that we wanted—flexibility in fishing, protecting our future as fishermen—we jumped at the chance to join."

In mid-March 1983, Local 9 was founded in southwest Nova Scotia with Aurèle Comeau and Normand Comeau of Cape St Mary as president and vice president respectively and Graeme Gawn as secretary-treasurer. The MFU's large Acadian membership had been an obvious attraction for fishermen on the French Shore. So, too, had its reputation for having fought the herring seiners in the Gulf of St Lawrence.

But the biggest selling points were that the MFU represented only inshore fishermen, that it was Maritime-wide, and that it had already established credibility with the DFO. The MFU could have called itself anything. In fact, that it called itself a union was probably more of a hindrance than a help. "I remember going to some of the first meetings," says Alain Meuse, editor of the *Sou'wester*, the fisheries newspaper published in Yarmouth. "Guys would come up to me and say, 'Geez, don't print my picture. I don't want my brother to know that I'm in the union.' It was hard slugging for them at the beginning."

Unlike Cape Breton and the Northumberland Shore, southwest Nova Scotia has no history of industrialization or of unionization. Few fish plants in the area were organized, and even today, the only non-union scallop crews in the province are based in Yarmouth. "We've got guys in southwest Nova Scotia who send us $200 contributions every year," says Graeme Gawn. "But they won't join. They don't want to carry union cards. They're anti-union, but they support us."

Conditions in southwest Nova Scotia also made inshore fishermen there different from their counterparts in the Gulf of St Lawrence. Lobster fishermen in the southwest fish market-sized lobsters, and their season runs from mid-November to June with a break during the worst winter weather. They sell nearly 100 percent of their catch live to the New England market. Historically, even inshore fishermen have been able to work the market to their advantage by selling directly or by holding their lobsters in ponds until the price goes up.

In contrast, fishermen in the Gulf of St Lawrence fish mostly canners, which don't survive being held in the warmer gulf waters and which are sold to processors. Gulf fishermen have historically received lower prices and depended more heavily on buyers.

"We never fished for a company here," says Gawn. "We jumped from one to another. There's so many fish plants around. The only time we were ever at the mercy of a company was when we were selling herring."

When fishermen in southwest Nova Scotia decided to join the MFU in 1983, they knew what they wanted—and what they didn't want. They didn't want the union to get involved in the lobster fishery, and they didn't want to talk about collective bargaining as a way of improving prices.

They wanted the MFU to help them protect the herring stocks, they wanted the union to help inshore fishermen get a share of the herring fishery, and they wanted the union to get involved in marketing. "We've always tried to influence the other fishermen in

Normand Comeau, Graeme Gawn, and Aurèle Comeau helped found Local 9 in southwest Nova Scotia. (COURTESY MFU)

the union that collective bargaining isn't the right way to go, that collective marketing is the right way to go," says Gawn. "Whether we're right or wrong, that's always been Local 9's perspective."

Inshore herring gillnetters in the Bay of Fundy had faced the same problems as their counterparts in the Gulf of St Lawrence. The arrival of British Columbia herring seiners in the mid-1960s and the growth of an indigenous fleet had devastated the stocks. By the mid-1970s, there were more than 60 seiners in the Bay of Fundy, and they were taking 80 percent of the quota. In 1976, they began to sell their catch over the side to Polish vessels, and later to Russian ones, through Fundy Co-ordinator, an organization set up to market purse-seine herring.

Several hundred inshore herring gillnetters depended on the fishery. But because they weren't organized, they couldn't participate in meetings where quotas were set. If they wanted to sell their herring over the side, they had to go through the seiners' group. In 1982, the *Sou'wester* had noted that the gillnetters had again received "the short end of the stick from this fishery" because of their lack of unity.

In New Brunswick, MFU fishermen had mounted a campaign to

Soon after Local 9 was formed, Dalhousie University professor Sandy Siegel became its organizer.
(COURTESY MFU)

drive the seiners out of the Gulf of St Lawrence. In the Bay of Fundy, however, the approach was different. "The seiners were just too big and too powerful," says Pinkneys Point fisherman Henry Surette. "They had their own lawyers and their own lobbyists. They were just too much for us to fight." The gillnetters decided to fight for their own over-the-side-sales program, a reflection not only of the power of the seiners but also of the business mentality of fishermen in southwest Nova Scotia.

In 1983, once the local was established, Sandy Siegel went to work as the organizer. A professor at Dalhousie University since the mid-1970s, Siegel had been a friend of the MFU for as long. He and Rick Williams had frequently given leadership training workshops for fishermen, and Siegel had been hired as the MFU's education co-ordinator the previous fall. "The thing with Sandy," recalls *Sou'wester* editor Alain Meuse, "he could relate with the guy on the wharf and with the bureaucrats. He could talk on anybody's level. And he didn't bull shit. At industry meetings, he could stand up with any of them, and he got respect for it. He kind of belted you with a velvet glove, that sort of thing."

That year, herring gillnetters again participated in the over-the-side-sales program run by Fundy Co-ordinator. But this time, they were better organized. The MFU set up a VHF radio dispatcher who knew when the Russians needed fish and could contact the gillnetters so that they were there to deliver. Forty-five union boats landed 40 percent of the total inshore quota.

That winter, MFU fishermen mounted a major campaign to convince the DFO to do two things: close Trinity Ledge, the main herring spawning area in St Mary's Bay, for two weeks during spawning season, and turn over management of the over-the-side-

Inshore herring gillnetters in the Bay of Fundy faced severe competition from the seiner fleet. (COURTESY DFO HALIFAX)

sales program to the union. "It was a huge political battle," recalls Siegel, "but in the end, we won. We knew that when we [the MFU] went into southwest Nova Scotia that over-the-side sales and closing Trinity Ledge were the key issues. In order for the union to have an effect and to move forward, we couldn't just lobby government. We had to do something concrete. Those two issues provided an opportunity. There was room to move into a vacuum."

In 1984, the union also got a $50,000 federal grant to hire people to make mesh bags to improve quality in handling herring. Local 9 was becoming a bustling affair. "It was a level of competence that the union had never seen before," recalls Rick Williams, "in terms of a business sense, how to organize and plan, and how to make it work. It was all because of Sandy's incredible drive. In a sense, it seemed like Sandy had discovered a side of himself that he didn't know existed. He became an incredible businessman."

The following year, the MFU sold 2,500 metric tonnes of herring over the side to Russian vessels, more than gillnetters had ever sold before. Trinity Ledge was closed again for two weeks. As Carleton University professor Wallace Clement, in *The Struggle to Organize*, writes, "This whole project has been an important demonstration by the union, obviously significant for attracting members (and gaining revenue) but most important, to establish a presence.... The union has shown, for the first time, that it can be effectively keyed into these lucrative sales."

After the success of the herring over-the-side-sales program in 1985, fishermen asked the union to begin marketing other species. In 1986, Local 9 began an experimental program to box fish at sea in plastic containers. The MFU newsletter noted:

> The early results have been exciting. Fishermen have received as much as a dollar [per pound] for haddock and flatfish. Although we are dealing small volumes we have been successful in getting the Boston Board price rather than the usual "over the road price." The Yarmouth local is also coordinating sales of flatfish and even some processing in conjunction with the UMF. As well, MFU Louisbourg is working closely with the Yarmouth office and the UMF to develop new markets for Cape Breton fish and fish products. Yarmouth is also hoping to tie some P.E.I. flatfish into their marketing efforts."

In late 1986, because it was now handling large amounts of money from all its various projects, Local 9 decided to set up a separate corporation—MFU Local 9 Marketing Limited—with a board of directors made up of union fishermen. The next year, the company began to buy lobster along the shore. "I've seen days," recalls fisherman Henry Surette, "where we'd get one dollar a pound more for our lobster than the price on the shore."

* * * * *

The union's first real venture into marketing had, in fact, been in Cape Breton. In 1985, the MFU local there had leased facilities from the Louisbourg Waterfront Development Corporation that included freezer space, bait rooms, and ice-making and unloading facilities. The intent was to reduce the dependence of longline groundfish fishermen on traditional buyers and to drive up the price on the shore. The union was successful in doing both, and the project continued the following year. For a number of reasons, however—including the failure of some fishermen to respect contracts that they had signed with the union—the 1986 experience was a disaster. The union lost $30,000, and the project was shut down.

It was really in southwest Nova Scotia that the union's expertise in marketing was fine-tuned. The local's marketing involvement drew in membership and helped the local pay its staff. It also enhanced the union's reputation and paved the way for the MFU to get involved in other issues. In the winter of 1985, faced with dwindling quotas, inshore groundfish fishermen marched on DFO offices in Yarmouth and succeeded in getting their quota increased. As Rick Williams writes, "It was an orderly but very strong show of unity on the size of groundfish quotas for inshore fishermen. The success in mobilizing these fishermen has led to concessions from government while strengthening the union's credibility in the area."

In 1987, federal fisheries minister Tom Siddon announced four new lobster permits for the offshore companies in the southwest. MFU fishermen opposed the move because three of the companies were known Conservative supporters. To the union, it was blatant patronage. Even more important, inshore fishermen didn't want permits issued to the offshore: they believed that an increase in the offshore catch meant a reduction in their own. "I remember one of the meetings we went to," says fisherman Henry Surette. "Tom Siddon was there, and he wanted me to drink with him. I said, 'No thanks, you can't buy me with a beer.' All of his arguments, that the offshore would only catch 5 percent of the lobster, I said, that's probably 95 percent of our breeding stock, that's where our small lobsters come from."

The MFU local sent out press release after press release and lobbied the DFO. "It was probably one of the biggest issues we ever fought," says Surette, "but we kept it up because we felt we were right." The opposition was so strong that Siddon finally postponed the licences and set up a committee to study the lobster industry in Scotia-Fundy. "The southwest local mounted a tremendous campaign," recalls Gilles Thériault. "There was so much pressure on Siddon that he was forced to back down. In order to save face, he set up this committee." The committee's final report has never been released, and the offshore lobster permits are still on hold.

"Local 9 brought confidence to the fishermen that they can organize, and that they can be effective," says Ellie Smith, president of the local at the time. "More than anything, it brought to them that they can win."

Because of the MFU, inshore fishermen in southwest Nova Scotia began to have a voice with the DFO. "Sandy was an excellent negotiator," says Thériault. "Other groups would take positions and stick with them, leaving no room for negotiations. But Sandy was always looking for a solution. 'What's the compromise here?' That really impressed the DFO. They had never met anyone like that in southwest Nova Scotia before."

Much of Siegel's time, however, was devoted to the local's business ventures. "It was a reflection of what we needed to do," says Siegel, "because it was what the fishermen wanted. Fishermen in southwest Nova Scotia are very market oriented. They weren't necessarily interested in collective bargaining." But how much energy should be spent on marketing prompted a debate in the union.

Rick Williams was one who opposed it. "My argument," he says, "was that the union's strength had always been in negotiating with the DFO over management of the resource. When you get fishermen together, it doesn't matter where they're from, if you put them in the same room together, they'll work out a common view. That was the job of the organizer. You'd never have a strong union in the Maritimes until you had southwest Nova Scotia, because they represented two-thirds of the fishermen. Your historic task was to build that bridge. Over the long term, the ultimate role of the union was to be an integrating force, to overcome parochialism. Devoting so much time to marketing was taking away from where the union's strength had been."

In the spring of 1988, Sandy Siegel left the union, another victim of burn-out, and moved with his family to the West Coast. By then, the over-the-side-sales program for gillnet herring was almost a thing of the past. Faced with the overwhelming power of the seiner fleet, few gillnetters were prepared to go fishing. There was also no one to oversee the local's business affairs on a full-time basis. Local 9 MFU Marketing Limited faced serious financial problems. By 1989, the company existed on paper only.

"It doesn't discourage me from the union being involved in business kinds of things," says John Kearney, who now works for the MFU in southwest Nova Scotia. "First of all, the union has always had an educational, training aspect to it, where fishermen grow personally and as fishermen through the union. You take someone like Graeme, who was involved in the marketing company and now markets lobster himself. Same thing with Aurèle Comeau. People gained skills through the union, providing them the opportunity to do something they would never have done on their own."

But should a union be involved in business ventures?

"I think it's up to the fishermen to define the role of the organization," Kearney replies. "Fishermen have two basic problems: catching fish and selling it. Those are the two things that they're going to look to an organization for. How they approach those problems depends on where they're coming from.

"In southwest Nova Scotia, I've never seen any interest in collective bargaining. This fishery has always been quite different than the Gulf of St Lawrence or the Newfoundland fisheries because of the proximity to the market and the existence of a number of small entrepreneurs. It's the 'fisherman-packer' tradition, the competitive lobster merchant."

One of the MFU's strengths had always been its flexibility in responding to the needs of fishermen. It is clear that the MFU will continue to be involved in marketing. Elsewhere in the region, MFU fishermen have also begun to market their fish. In northeast New Brunswick, for example, fishermen bought a fish plant in Val Comeau in the late 1980s and are now running it together. But, again, the amount of time the union should devote to it remains an issue.

Ironically, MFU fishermen in other parts of Nova Scotia had believed that they needed the southwest in order to win collective bargaining legislation. At an MFU convention in early 1987, the Cape Breton local called on the union to revive the fight for legislation in the province. But the resolution was defeated because fishermen from southwest Nova Scotia opposed it. They simply didn't want collective bargaining.

FIRST CONTRACT: TO RAND OR NOT TO RAND

"In 1986, companies knew it was the union security clause we were after."
—MFU organizer Michael Belliveau—

I T WAS LATE SATURDAY NIGHT, and Gilles Thériault was still at the office. All day he had been tied to the telephone, talking to fishermen who wanted to know if they could pull their traps tomorrow, talking to buyers anxious to know what was going on. Was there or was there not an agreement between the Maritime Fishermen's Union and the N.B. Fish Buyers Bargaining Association for the fall lobster season. It was August 10, 1985, the first day of lobster season in the southeast.

The night before, Thériault had, in fact, signed a tentative agreement with the buyers. It was a first, and one newspaper would later call it "an historic contract that would end the union's financial instability." The rest of the negotiating committee, however, had not been with Thériault. Fishermen members of the committee had gone home early in order to get up before dawn on Saturday to set their traps.

The tentative agreement still had to be ratified by the fishermen. One clause disallowed Sunday fishing: if a majority of fishermen were in favour of the contract, that meant that they shouldn't pull their traps on Sunday. All day Saturday, MFU staff worked to set up ratification meetings in communities throughout the southeast, but by evening, there was mass confusion. Everyone was understandably uptight. To miss the first day of lobster season could mean a loss of thousands of dollars for fishermen and buyers alike.

The union's goal had always been to negotiate prices before the season started, and since its founding, it had occasionally succeeded. In August 1978, for example, the MFU local in the province's northeast had signed contracts with three companies for the fall herring fishery. But such contracts were due more to the good will of individual companies than to anything else. Buyers were under no legal obligation to negotiate.

So not surprisingly, the ink had barely been dry on the union's certification order in late April 1984 when the MFU notified the New Brunswick Fish Packers' Association that it wanted to talk. But it was already too late. The lobster fishery in the northeast began May 1, and the companies were not yet accredited under the Fisheries Bargaining Act. It would be another seven months before the buyers would be legally certified as the N.B. Fish Buyers Bargaining Association.

The union had been certified in the northeast for seven species and in the southeast for nine. But MFU members knew that they had to concentrate on herring and lobster. Together, these two species accounted for the bulk of the income of most inshore fishermen.

The lobster fishery had typically followed a pattern. Prices were low at the beginning of the season, when landings were high, but they increased as landings levelled off. Generally, prices were highest at the end of the season, when there was little lobster left to catch. The wild card was the independent buyer—the small operator who came on the wharf and offered fishermen 25 cents a pound more for their lobster. (At the time, there were close to 100 small operators in New Brunswick.) When and if that happened, the larger processing companies generally followed suit, though they, too, had cards to play. Some, for example, wouldn't buy a fisherman's herring later in the year if they couldn't have his lobster first.

As a result, the lobster fishery was a free-for-all. Bidding wars frequently forced prices up, which, in the short term, obviously worked to the fishermen's advantage. Over the long term, however, the situation was very unpredictable. Prices soared one year and plummeted the next. Fishermen never knew what to expect.

The union hoped that a contract would bring stability to the fishery. The problem—one that the union hadn't anticipated—was that many independent operators wouldn't bother joining the buyers bargaining association or respect contracts that had been negotiated between the union and the larger companies. This would throw a wrench into what the union expected to be a relatively normal collective bargaining relationship.

In early 1985, the attempt to negotiate began again. But again, the union met with little success. As the MFU newsletter noted at the time:

> We commenced bargaining with the Buyers Association in the spring of 1985 for lobster in district 7C [in the northeast]. The buyers refused a minimum price, refused a moving price, refused basic union security provisions, and demanded a fixed price that was lower than what individual buyers were already offering on the wharf; they offered $1.40 for canners when the fishermen were already receiving $1.70. We were quite surprised that the principal buyers were exercising absolutely no leadership....

For years, the MFU had talked about negotiating a "minimum" price, giving buyers the option to pay more if they wanted to do so. But the MFU soon realized that the buyers were not prepared to talk about a minimum price; they were only prepared to talk about a "fixed" price. "We never wanted to negotiate a minimum price," admits National Sea Products' Jim Bateman. "The buyers' position was that it was really quite useless to negotiate a minimum price. I suppose it would have told us that that's the least we're going to pay, but in a sense, it's a lopsided measure. We're protected on the way down, but we're not protected on the way up. It didn't put any teeth into the situation that needed to have some teeth put into it."

That "situation" was the existence of independent buyers who would still be able to come on the wharf and offer a price over and above the "minimum" negotiated in the contract. (The processors didn't realize that a "fixed" price wouldn't stop that, either. The independents who didn't belong to the association wouldn't respect the "fixed" price.)

As hopes for a contract for the 1985 spring lobster season crumbled, prices again began to increase on some wharves. Processors were forced into paying more for lobster than they thought reasonable because of what they perceived as interference by independent buyers. By summer, as the fall lobster season approached in the southeast, some buyers were more convinced of the necessity of negotiating a contract with the MFU.

By then, the union had also softened its position on a fixed price. "The buyers were right that a minimum price would do nothing to stabilize the situation," says Gilles Thériault. "I believed that once we had negotiated a fixed price, we would be able to negotiate an increase each year. Over a period of five or ten years, the price would continue to go up, and there would be a lot more stability."

In July, the union's and the buyers' bargaining teams met several times at the Four Seas Motel in Shédiac. Headed by Thériault, the MFU negotiating team included Guy Cormier of Cap-Pelé, Alonzo Robichaud of Pointe-Sapin (president of the southeast local), Maurice Doucet of Richibucto Village, and Fernand Bourgeois of Grande-Digue. On the other side of the table were Peter Dysart, executive director of the Fish Buyers Bargaining Association and, representing the major processors in the southeast, Jim Bateman of National Sea, Yvon Gaudet of Westmorland Fisheries, Joe Landry of Cape Bald Packers, and Tony Vautour of Landry and Landry.

On Friday, August 9, 1985, just as the season was about to begin, the two groups finally reached a tentative agreement.

The union team had accepted a fixed price of $1.80 for canners and $2.60 for markets—prices that it considered acceptable. The other important issue for the MFU had been union security.

One of the first clauses that a union tries to negotiate is a union security clause including "automatic check-off" where an employer deducts dues from employees' paychecks and turns those dues over to the union. There are four types of check-off clauses, three of which apply only to employees who are actually union members. The fourth, known as the Rand formula, applies to both union and non-union members.

Named after Mr Justice Ivan Rand, arbitrator for a major strike at the Ford plant in Windsor, Ontario, in 1945, the Rand formula requires an employer to deduct dues from all people in the bargaining unit. Not everyone is required to join the union, but everyone *is* required to pay union dues. It is based on the principle that the union's gains benefit everyone in the bargaining unit, not just union members. (The Rand formula is not the same as a "closed shop," where every employee has to be a union member in order to work.)

Today, the Rand formula is an accepted labour practice throughout North America. It allows unions to survive financially without having to go door to door to collect dues, as the MFU had done for a decade.

For the MFU bargaining team, the Rand formula was essential.

Companies would deduct dues as they paid fishermen for their catch and remit those dues to the union.

After much debate, the buyers finally agreed to the Rand formula in exchange for a similar security clause for their association. All buyers would be required to pay dues to the Fish Buyers Bargaining Association, or MFU fishermen could not sell them their fish. This, the processors hoped, would either remove the small, independent operator from the buying arena or at least force him to respect the price negotiated by the association.

The agreement also allowed for price adjustments after the season was over—to permit companies to continue the practice of paying rebates to their fishermen—and banned Sunday fishing. (Fishermen, in fact, had only recently been allowed to fish on Sundays, after a Jewish fisherman in Nova Scotia challenged the law in court and won. Most fishermen didn't want to work Sundays, though many thought that they had to, to compete with other fishermen.) The contract stipulated fines of $1,000 per day for buyers and $500 per day for fishermen who violated the contract.

In a flyer, the MFU negotiating team explained the benefits of the tentative agreement—and the fixed price—to fishermen:

> We all know that the buyers would not agree to such a contract, especially when they are not forced to, if there were no advantages in it for them too. They want such a contract because they think it will prevent them from cutting each other's throat. It will also mean more stability for them since they will only have one price to deal with for the duration of the season. They can therefore be more effective in their operations and make more money. This may work to our advantage too. We will be in a better position to negotiate a good rebate if the buyers have had a good year.
>
> Some fishermen have said to us that if the proposed contract is signed they may lose some money since there are always some buyers who are prepared to pay above the going price. This may be true. We are asking you to look at the lobster fishery not just for this year but for the future. A contract will provide recognition of our organization by the buyers, and a way to collect dues for all fishermen who benefit from the work of the Union. Without a contract it will be very difficult to maintain an organization that has real strength to fight for fishermen's rights. If we miss this opportunity to get a contract, we may not have one again.

"For the first time in its history," the Moncton *Times-Transcript* said on Saturday, "the MFU has reached a tentative contract with fish buyers before the lobster season opens in southeast New Brunswick, and the pact promises to go a long way towards giving the union the financial security it has long lacked."

* * * * *

Meetings were scheduled to be held in every major fishing community along the coast on Sunday to allow fishermen to vote on the tentative agreement. MFU staff divided up the work. Réginald Comeau would do Baie-Ste-Anne and Pointe-Sapin; Michael Belliveau, Little Cape; Tim Rogers, Grande-Digue and Cape Tormentine, near the Nova Scotia border; and Gilles Thériault, communities in between.

Thériault left home first thing Sunday morning for Cocagne, where fishermen had gathered at the schoolhouse. It was an orderly meeting. Fishermen were concerned about the fixed price, but Thériault's explanation seemed to make sense, so they voted in favour of the agreement. Thériault then left for Ste-Anne-de-Kent, where fishermen were also waiting at the schoolhouse. Again, he outlined the contents of the contract, and again, fishermen voted in favour. The next stop was the community centre in Richibucto Village, where fishermen had always been strong supporters of the union. They, too, approved the contract by a large majority.

By now, it was past noon. Things had been going surprisingly well. But Thériault was not prepared for what was to come.

Wharf representatives in each community had organized the meetings. In the next three locations, fishermen wouldn't be in schools or community centres. They would be on the wharves. By the time Thériault arrived in Richibucto, a crowd had gathered. Forty fishermen, some who had been drinking since before noon, were already milling about. They were angry that they hadn't been allowed to go fishing that day. Some didn't agree with the fixed price and believed that the union, and Gilles Thériault in particular, had sold them out. One fisherman offered to hang the union's executive secretary from the nearest telephone pole. The vote, when it was finally taken, was tight but lost.

Unnerved, Thériault moved on to Loggiecroft, where he met the same scene—25 fishermen on the wharf. Some had been drinking, one was drunk and threatening violence. There was also a buyer who had told his fishermen, on advice from Thériault, that they couldn't fish that day or they would face fines, as would he if he bought from them. As a result, his fishermen had all stayed home. But others had gone fishing, and the buyer turned out to be the only one in the village who didn't make money that day, thanks, he felt, to the union. He had been drinking on the wharf with the fishermen, waiting for Thériault to show up, and was feeling less than charitable. "I explained to him what had happened," Thériault says today, "that no one was supposed to go, but some went anyway. I apologized to him. He had a right to be pissed off."

For Thériault, the day culminated in St-Louis-de-Kent, where the meeting on the wharf was to follow the blessing of the fleet, an annual ritual before the start of lobster season. Fishermen had been waiting all afternoon in the hot sun. Tempers were on edge, helped along by liquid refreshments and a sense of betrayal. After years of talking about a "minimum" price, the negotiating team was prepared to accept a "fixed" one. The more some fishermen talked, the angrier they became. Once Thériault arrived, he became the butt of insults and threats. At one point, with most of the town crowded around the wharf and the mood growing ugly, it was questionable whether a vote could even be taken. In the end, the priest managed to calm things down, and surprisingly, the vote was won, as it had been in Loggiecroft.

For the other MFU staff, the day had been much the same. When Réginald Comeau arrived in Pointe-Sapin, half the fleet had already left to go fishing. The other half had waited around, though not too happily, to vote on the contract. In Little Cape, fishermen were already being offered a better price than that in the contract. "There was a lot of debate about whether fishermen could afford to trade off a first collective agreement for a price that seemed to be too low," Michael Belliveau recalls. The vote was lost, 35 to 4.

But it was in Cape Tormentine where the die was cast. In other communities, the turn-out had been low. Only a small percentage of fishermen anywhere had voted. But in Cape Tormentine, all 52 fishermen showed up and voted against the contract. None were union members. MFU staff were well aware that the area had long been disenchanted with the union. But the union knew that Cape Tormentine fishermen had to be given the chance to vote. Otherwise, the contract would be virtually unenforceable. Even though the vote had been won in almost every other community along the coast, the overwhelming opposition in Cape Tormentine decided the issue.

On Monday, the Moncton *Times-Transcript* reported, "A contract which would have ended financial instability for the union, set uniform prices for lobster and banned Sunday fishing was turned down by fishermen Sunday by a 126 to 113 vote." With that, prospects for a collective agreement for 1985 evaporated.

It was clear that there was a lot of opposition to a fixed price. But it was also clear that time had just been too short—with a tentative agreement signed on the eve of lobster season—for MFU staff and fishermen on the negotiating committee to explain the concept properly, to allow for discussion and debate. Combined with the confusion over whether fishermen could go out on Sunday—and the anger and bitterness that understandably resulted when some made money that day while others didn't—it is not surprising that the 1985 contract was defeated.

The experience was, in a sense, a practice run for the following year. In the spring of 1986, the union succeeded in signing contracts in the northeast for both lobster and herring, contracts that were virtual duplicates of the 1985 tentative agreement, except for higher prices. By then, fishermen were more open to a fixed price. Both sides had more experience in the art of negotiating. And there was more time.

For the union, 1985 had provided several valuable lessons. Meetings were no longer held on wharves. Drinking during discussion of a contract was not tolerated. Nor were meetings held in individual communities. In 1986, fishermen from all over the northeast had a chance to discuss and then vote on both contracts at the Fisheries School in Caraquet after a presentation by the MFU bargaining committee.

In 1986, the price negotiated for lobster was $2.00 a pound for canners and $2.80 for markets. A year earlier, prices had started at $1.70 and $2.00 respectively. For fishermen on the Acadian Peninsula, they were the highest prices ever offered at the beginning of the season, and they sent out a signal to the rest of the Maritimes. "When that contract was negotiated in the northeast," recalls Hasse Lindblad of the MFU's Northumberland local in Nova Scotia, "I had guys coming up to me—guys who had always refused to join the union because they didn't believe it could work—saying, 'I'm going to join the union now.' That was the first time the two-dollar mark had been broken for canners. I don't know if it was because of collective bargaining or because the Canadian dollar started to drop, but it really had a lot of effect, a great sense of binding things together, showing the fishermen that it could work."

Having a first contract also buoyed the spirits of fishermen on the Acadian Peninsula. "There had been higher prices here before," says LeGoulet fisherman Paul-Aimé Mallet. "I remember once having $3.50 for markets for the last two days of the fishery. But you can't catch 100 pounds in those two days."

Finally, after more than a decade of struggle, the Maritime Fishermen's Union had signed its first collective agreements.

*   *   *   *   *

For fishermen in the northeast, the 1986 contracts for lobster and herring were landmarks in other ways. One, their signing meant that buyers had finally accepted the Maritime Fishermen's Union as the official bargaining agent for the inshore. Two, at least in theory, the contracts put in place a methodical system of dues collection.

There were, however, several drawbacks. The contracts proved hard to enforce. The lobster season had barely begun when there were already complaints that buyers weren't respecting the prices negotiated. Some buyers, in fact, were offering more. Each side complained that the other was ignoring the contract.

"The union had agreed that its members would only sell to accredited buyers," says National Sea's Jim Bateman. "That meant members of our association. So if somebody came on the wharf who wasn't a member, really it was the union that should have assured us that the fishermen wouldn't sell to him. But the union couldn't control that." MFU organizer Michael Belliveau blames the processors. It was the processors, he says, who were offering more. Fishermen shouldn't be blamed for accepting higher prices. The issue would be a major stumbling block when negotiations rolled around the following year.

Some companies also didn't respect the union security clause. Several companies didn't collect dues at all, and others deducted them but then didn't turn them over to the union. They either didn't believe in it or complained that it was too much of a bookkeeping hassle, even though they were already making similar deductions for unemployment insurance. The Rand formula, which many had hoped would finally provide the union with financial stability, was obviously not working.

In the fall of 1986, the union took seven companies to arbitration to try to collect money owed. Six of them didn't show up, and the union was forced to go to court, where it won its case. The sheriff eventually collected some of the money, but this was the beginning of a long process that would see the union in and out of arbitration and in and out of court many times. It would be costly and, in the end, very discouraging, especially for those fishermen who had voted for the contract because of the union security clause, even though they disagreed with the price.

"In 1986, companies knew it was the union security clause we were after," recalls Belliveau. "By 1987, they thought they could use that against us again to come up with a fixed price that was lower than what was already being offered on the wharves. We just told them to stuff it. We were prepared to take our chances. We couldn't continue to ask fishermen to support the organization with some kind of union security clause while at the same time selling them out on the price of fish."

As the prospects for negotiations the following year crumbled, the MFU realized that the issue of the union's financial survival had to be separated from the process of collective bargaining. "In reality," Michael Belliveau wrote to provincial fisheries minister Doug Young, "this normal union security requirement [the Rand formula] has been turned against us in the bargaining process by the buyers group who know our weak financial position and who have used the check-off requirement as a kind of 'blackmail' in an attempt to gain our agreement to silly price offers."

Once again, the Maritime Fishermen's Union began a campaign for legislative changes.

MANDATORY DUES DEDUCTION

"We don't want a union but we would like some systematic method for gathering dues from freeloaders."
—Member of the Nova Scotia Fishermen's Association—

"The 'free-rider' fisherman is the one who does not pay his dues: 'Why should I pay,' he says, 'I get the same benefits without paying....' The 'free-rider' is a corrosive force on the whole effort of fishermen to better themselves and the community."
—MFU brief, January 1990—

THE FACES HAD NEVER been longer. In January 1987, the Maritime Fishermen's Union called a press conference at the Hotel Beauséjour in Moncton. The union wanted to outline plans for its eleventh annual convention, to be held in Memramcook at the end of the month. It also wanted to announce that Gilles Thériault was about to resign. At the table alongside Thériault sat MFU president Hasse Lindblad, Guy Cormier, Herménégilde Robichaud, Paul-Aimé Mallet, and Frank McLaughlin. All were original members of the union, and all were still very active. It was clear that all were also very concerned about what would happen to the MFU when Gilles Thériault was no longer involved.

"I don't want to be like an old politician or boxer who never knows when he's had enough," Thériault said as he highlighted the union's accomplishments over the previous decade: battles with the herring seiners, collective bargaining legislation in New Brunswick, a historic working agreement with the United Maritime Fishermen. "In the past ten years," he pointed out, "the MFU has played a major role in assuring the survival of inshore fishermen. A change in leadership will bring a change in direction, new ideas, a fresh approach that will work to the advantage of the MFU."

Later, at the convention, fishermen presented the parting executive secretary with a gift of ski equipment. Réginald Comeau paid a moving tribute to his friend and colleague for 15 years—"a magician who was able to realize grandiose things, who was able to make dreamers out of the most pessimistic, and who was able to achieve the unachievable."

DFO Scotia-Fundy director general Jean-Eûdes Haché also paid tribute in a telegram: "It is rare that one can say that an individual has left his mark in a particular domain. Because of his relentless and unshakeable determination, Gilles Thériault has literally forced a profound change in the forces that control the fishery. Inshore fishermen are now full partners in the industry. The greatest tribute that can be paid to Gilles Thériault is that the MFU will continue to grow stronger even after his departure. It will be an eloquent testimony that all his work will continue to bear fruit for years to come."

With Thériault's departure, Comeau was the last of the three original non-fishermen founders of the union. In February 1987, Michael Belliveau of Nova Scotia took over as executive secretary of the MFU. Belliveau had always been less convinced than Thériault that collective bargaining could work for inshore fishermen. Philosophically, he was more in the camp of the "collective marketers." By now, fishermen, too, were feeling disillusioned, and Belliveau's leadership would reinforce a trend that had already begun. The MFU would move away from the collective bargaining model—in the process, dropping its links with organized labour— and towards a general marketing approach. The MFU would become less of a trade union and more of an organization of primary producers.

One of the first things that Belliveau set out to do was find a way to finance the union that didn't depend on collective bargaining. As Belliveau wrote to New Brunswick fisheries minister Doug Young:

> We question whether, today, our inshore fishery would not look like the farm communities of northeast N.B. or the fishery of the Gaspé had not the MFU sustained the fight for an inshore fishery. Perhaps the most dramatic testimony to our work was the 1987 herring catch by inshore fishermen in northeast N.B. We landed 30,000 tons in 1987 compared to 2,000 tons landed in 1977 when the MFU was founded. It seems outrageous that several million additional dollars have accrued to fishermen in the past year alone from our work in herring and yet our organization remains impoverished for want of an appropriate mechanism for the payment of dues or the equivalent.

In dealing with fishermen who wouldn't pay dues, the MFU was not alone. The Nova Scotia Fishermen's Association eventually collapsed because members refused to pay dues. The P.E.I. Fishermen's Association (PEIFA) struggled continually with the problem and, today, still depends on the provincial government for its survival.

Associations that have had the most success in collecting dues are those that have given fishermen a good reason for paying. An association on Miscou Island, for example, bought a truck for hauling boats, and only those fishermen who paid membership dues could use it. At $10 per year, the dues were not a burden, and even union members on Miscou also belonged to the association. But again, it was a local organization whose goals were limited.

The Newfoundland fishermen's union, touted by many as a grand success, also had problems financing itself. As Gordon Inglis notes:

> ... in the absence of any means of instituting a check-off system, the collection of dues presented an almost insuperable problem. In any case, when the campaign to gain and then to implement collective bargaining rights developed into such a lengthy struggle, it is questionable whether enough fishermen would have been willing to continue paying dues without receiving the usual demonstrable benefits of union membership. McGrath, Cashin, and the union's leaders in Port au Choix were well aware of the problem, and were able to convince the headquarters of the international of the need for heavy initial subsidization. The successively renewed fifty thousand dollar grants, the supplying of mainland personnel for assistance in organizing, and the provision of strike pay—especially during the crucial strikes at Burgeo, Marystown and Bonavista—constituted an essential base for the organization.
>
> Even after all this expenditure, and after five years of the union's life, the NFFAWU was in extremely precarious financial condition during the trawler strike of 1974-75. In short, it had to win its major battles before it could become a self-supporting institution, and it seems most unlikely that it could have won them if it had been dependent solely upon the money that could be generated locally.

The MFU's foes always put forward the same argument—the MFU's failure to collect dues was a reflection of the fact that it

In February 1987, Michael Belliveau took over the helm of the MFU.
(COURTESY MFU)

didn't have the support of fishermen. In response, the union argued that most fishermen's organizations faced the same problem, except for the Eastern Fishermen's Federation, which had a million dollars in the bank and didn't require fishermen to pay dues. The union also maintained that any voluntary system would have the same results. By analogy, it often argued, let the government try to collect taxes on a voluntary basis. It was a credit to the union's tenacity that it had hung on this long.

For the MFU, the events of 1988 brought the issue to a head.

Just as the fall herring fishery was about to begin, inshore fishermen in northeast New Brunswick tied up their boats. Japanese buyers for herring roe, considered a delicacy in their country, were offering $20 a barrel, down from $30 a year earlier. Fishermen believed that there was no reason for the drop, and they refused to fish for that price. They stayed ashore, and were soon joined in their strike by herring fishermen in Prince Edward Island and the Northumberland Strait area of Nova Scotia.

It was a bitter strike that lasted two weeks. In the northeast, union fishermen had not wanted to go on strike. "Our fishermen were more willing to discuss what was happening," explains Réginald Comeau, "to try to understand what was going on in the market. They were used to discussing things because they were part of the union."

But fishermen from the surrounding area who had voted in favour of the union in 1982 but who had never paid dues "didn't want to listen," says Comeau. "They didn't want to understand what was happening. They had no logic or rationale. They just wanted to force everyone to go on strike." Because they were in the majority, they did.

The bitterness was compounded when the fleet in the northeast finally put to sea. After weeks with no income, fishermen were desperate to get back to work. Despite forecasts of strong winds, the fleet sailed on a Monday night. Strong winds turned into gales, and by Tuesday morning, one vessel had been lost. Three fishermen from Miscou Island died.

The whole experience left fishermen in the northeast feeling burnt out and resentful. For years, they had struggled to build an organization, on their own time and with their own money, without the help of some fishermen who were nonetheless more than willing to come to meetings during a crisis and tell them what to do. Fishermen were fed up with such "free-riders" who didn't mind using the union when and if it suited their purpose.

By the end of 1988, downcast and dispirited, fishermen in northeast New Brunswick were prepared to let the union go.

*   *   *   *   *

There are many examples of individuals having to belong to an organization—association or union—in order to be able to work in their profession. Lawyers are required to join law societies, and doctors, medical societies. Ironically, a year after the government in Nova Scotia refused collective bargaining legislation for fishermen, it amended the Medical Act to require doctors to pay dues to the province's Medical Society. A lot of fishermen kept up their membership in construction unions so that they could find work in the off-seasons.

But inshore fishermen, some maintain, are not professionals. If they want an organization—if they think that they need a common voice and a group to fight on their behalf—then they should be willing to pay voluntarily to support it.

Throughout the 1970s and 1980s, both levels of government pushed the idea that inshore fishermen needed to organize, that inshore fishermen needed to speak with one voice. In order to facilitate that happening, governments pumped money into fishermen's associations, though that did not help unite fishermen.

In 1986, the government of Prince Edward Island, wanting to cut funding to the PEIFA, drafted The Fisheries Act, which required all fishermen to pay dues to a "certified organization." The legislation went through second reading, and a round of public hearings in early 1989. Although both the MFU and the PEIFA liked the idea, they did not support the bill itself, because it gave the government too much control over setting and dispersing the dues and in choosing which organization would receive the money. In the end, the bill died.

But there was nothing wrong with the overall concept of legislating compulsory dues. In 1988, in New Brunswick, the MFU suggested something else.

It asked the Department of Labour to amend the Fisheries Bargaining Act so that all fishermen would be required to pay dues to a certified bargaining agent whether or not a collective agreement was in place. It was a kind of statutory Rand formula, less common in the labour movement but not unheard of. But the labour minister was not interested, so the union turned to the Department of Fisheries. Michael Belliveau wrote to Fisheries Minister Doug Young:

> We would like to work out a resolution to our organizational dilemma that is also shared by others in the rest of the Maritime inshore fishery. We think that it is patently unfair that bonafide, democratic, and broad-based inshore fishermen membership organizations are faced with constant financial instability because there is no generalized requirement for fishermen to pay despite receiving the same benefits as the dedicated ones. Virtually everyone associated with the industry says publicly that it is good that fishermen be organized but they leave us with a burden that neither organized labour, doctors, nurses, woodlot owners or a host of other professional and trades people must face.

In the fall of 1988, Doug Young stepped down to run as a candidate in the federal election. He was replaced in the portfolio by Aldéa Landry, also the minister for intergovernmental affairs. A lawyer and the first female Acadian to become a cabinet minister, Landry came from the Acadian Peninsula. Her father was one of the fishermen who had attended the leadership training course in Inkerman sponsored by the MFU in 1976. She knew what it meant to be a fisherman.

Landry agreed to meet with MFU members in Shippegan. "The fishermen were very impressive," recalls Belliveau. "They had a clear idea of what they wanted, and a clear idea of their demands." Landry could see that there were serious problems, but she also realized that there was support for the MFU. She agreed to act. "I've always been a strong believer in making the fishery more professional," she explains today, "whether it's the fishermen, the plant workers, or the processors. Unlike the old days, the fishery is now a very complex profession. You're dealing with two levels of government. Fishermen need to have a united voice to protect their interests, and to do so in a well-organized fashion. I thought that it was only fair to give them the financial means to do that, so that they could survive and grow."

In the spring of 1989, Landry introduced a bill in the Legislative Assembly. The Inshore Fishermen's Deduction of Dues Act said essentially that where a fishermen's organization was certified, all inshore fishermen in the bargaining unit had to pay dues through a system of check-off carried out by buyers, even if a collective agreement was not in place.

Later that afternoon, Landry returned to her office, bearing a single yellow rose. She presented it to Omer Chouinard, who, by this time, had returned to New Brunswick and was working for the provincial Department of Fisheries. "There," she said. "Now the reconciliation is complete."

It had been Aldéa Landry who had gone to court several years earlier, on behalf of her husband and partner, Fernand Landry, to seek the injunction during the MFU's lengthy battle with the Lamèque co-op.

*   *   *   *   *

The Law Amendments Committee began hearings on the Inshore Fishermen's Deduction of Dues Act in Shédiac in January 1990. The N.B. Fish Buyers Bargaining Association made its presentation first. "We strongly disagree with the underlying assumption that government should somehow ensure the well-being and continued existence of fishermen's associations," National Sea Products' representative, Ron Carrier, told the committee. "Where a representative body is not dependent on the voluntary contributions and active support of its members, human nature dictates that it runs a grave risk of becoming less sensitive to member direction or their needs and desires." The New Brunswick Fish Packers' Association also opposed the bill. But ultimately, after much prodding, both groups agreed to support it if a majority of fishermen were in favour. (The legislation would, in fact, require a vote to prove that a majority of fishermen in each region were in favour.)

During a break, Camille Thériault, Gilles' brother, who by now was a Liberal MLA and a member of law amendments, shook his head. "Both processor associations agree to go along with it if it's what fishermen want, if fishermen vote in favour," he said slightly bewildered. "What are we doing here?"

Fishermen's associations from Little Cape and Cape Tormentine and the Eastern Fishermen's Federation also made presentations against the bill, arguing, as had National Sea, that dues contributions had to be voluntary if an organization was truly to reflect the wishes of its members.

The intent of the act was to enable a "certified" fishermen's group to finance itself. But because of the language used—because there were references in the legislation to the Fisheries Bargaining Act—there was some confusion about how the bill would fit into a collective bargaining framework. Michael Belliveau, when his turn came in the afternoon, was quick to clear up the confusion.

With Réginald Comeau on one side and fisherman Paul-Aimé Mallet on the other, Belliveau said that the union was prepared to eliminate any mention of the Fisheries Bargaining Act in order to separate the two concepts—collective bargaining on the one hand and mandatory dues deduction on the other. The union also agreed to a government-supervised vote to determine which fishermen's group would be "certified." (Fishermen's support for the MFU had, in fact, already been proved in the certification votes of the early 1980s.) Said Belliveau:

We would not be here today if we did not feel we had the majority of the fishermen behind us. I think this question of a majority has been well tested in the past. We can test it again. We are open to taking that risk. If the fishermen are not behind us, fine, but the legislation is *enabling* legislation, just as a lot of other legislation in this country is. Any group electing to use it does so according to democratic procedure.

The question of being forced to join the MFU should be addressed as well. No legislation in Canada that I know of forces you to belong to an organization. The principle built into this kind of legislation is the same. You pay the equivalent of organizational dues. If you are not a member of the MFU and the MFU happens to be certified for southeast N.B., all fishermen would be compelled to pay the equivalent of dues. However, they do not have to be a member of the MFU unless they so choose. Nor does their association have to go out of existence.... We are not abashed to ask for union dues of $151 a year from a non-union member if he is in a geographic zone in which the majority of fishermen want to have a broad-based organization and want to pay those dues.

Belliveau pointed out that management of the fishery was now extremely complex. The MFU had representatives on 56 federal fisheries committees, some of which met several times a year. "Who is going to cover them all?" he asked. "The fishermen are out fishing, and that is the most fundamental reason they are prepared to pay someone else to work for them. They cannot possibly be on all of these committees, and watch over all of this elaborate fisheries management process day in and day out."

It was a forceful presentation. In reality, Belliveau was fighting for the union's life.

Later, there were questions from the Law Amendments Committee. The final one came from MLA Bernard Thériault, who represented a fishing riding in the northeast. "I realize, like most of the people involved in the fishing industry, that it is very hard to bring all the people together: the coastal fishermen, the midshore guys, the processors," he said to Belliveau, Comeau, and Mallet. "What do you think is the solution to the problem?"

Réginald Comeau responded. "I think," he said, "that it will take the same kind of political courage as a certain man had during the 1960s in New Brunswick, and I think you can guess who I'm talking about. If he had waited for a big smile from everyone before introducing his program of Equal Opportunity, we wouldn't, perhaps, be here today."

"You gave me a good answer," replied Thériault. "Spoken like a real politician."

There was a second day of hearings, in Fredericton. Then the committee retired to deliberate. The Maritime Fishermen's Union could only sit and wait for its fate to be decided one way or another.

CONCLUSION: BIGGER BATTLES YET TO COME

"Like all human institutions, the MFU wasn't perfect, but it contributed a great, great deal to the professionalization of the industry.... I think if you ask DFO managers in Moncton today, 'What do you think of fishermen's organizations?' they'd say, 'We couldn't manage the fishery without them.'"
—Former federal fisheries minister Roméo LeBlanc—

THE MARITIME FISHERMEN'S UNION started out against enormous odds. Born when the inshore fishery in the Maritimes seemed to be disappearing, the MFU, in the beginning, was really a protest movement that sought to bring together fishermen to defend their way of life. It was an attempt to organize what was—and still is—the only union of inshore fishermen in Canada. Most of those involved had never, as a rule, participated in democratic organizations and had little money to support one. They were unused to the discipline of collective action. They were widely separated by geography and ethnic background, and they were even at odds when it came to fishing. They were inshore fishermen who competed for the same, sometimes scarce resource. They were mostly men who had grown up on the sea and for whom competition came more naturally than co-operation.

In the story of the MFU, there are two central themes: Inshore fishermen wanted to have a word to say about the price of fish in the face of growing concentration and monopolization in the industry. And inshore fishermen wanted a word to say in the management of the resource in the face of the growing hegemony of the federal Department of Fisheries.

The MFU arose because no fishermen's organization at the time was fighting for either.

The United Maritime Fishermen (UMF), for many years the only organization that attempted to bring together inshore fishermen across the region, had given fishermen their first taste of "economic liberation." But as time wore on, it became clear that the co-ops had little influence on the price being set by the large companies. As the UMF began to concentrate its operations in a bid to compete, as UMF management became more entrenched, and especially as the UMF bought offshore trawlers, many inshore fishermen felt increasingly alienated from the organization. To boot, the UMF was strictly a marketing agency. It never claimed to be a voice on issues of resource management.

There were also fishermen's associations, but many were local groups formed to fight specific issues. Most were crisis-oriented, and participation in them was sporadic. Some were dominated by harbour "bosses" who were closely tied to local politicians, wanted to protect their own interests, or favoured the status quo. Fishermen's associations didn't talk about collective bargaining for the price of fish before the 1980s, and even then, some began to do so only to compete for membership with the MFU. Nor did associations have the resources or clout to combat increasing government regulations affecting fishermen across the region, not just on one wharf.

Even when associations joined together under the Eastern Fishermen's Federation (EFF), which was formed with government help, they remained largely ineffective. The EFF opposed collective bargaining for inshore fishermen. It did participate on government advisory committees, but its membership was so diverse—including inshore, midshore, and offshore groups—that it often had difficulty speaking with a clear voice.

For the MFU, the desire to have control over the price of fish was expressed in its fight for collective bargaining legislation. Given the trend at the time—growing monopolization—many believed that fishermen would eventually be forced out of the industry altogether or, at best, into direct employment with the large companies. Fishermen, therefore, the analysis went, had a lot in common with other workers who had achieved job security and wage gains through unionization.

In Nova Scotia and Prince Edward Island, success was limited. Perhaps the most incomprehensible part of the MFU story is the refusal of governments in both those provinces to grant fishermen collective bargaining legislation, even though 10 studies in five years had recommended it. Both governments claimed that the MFU didn't represent fishermen. Neither seemed capable of grasping the concept that the union was asking only for *enabling* legislation—legislation that would require it to prove majority support before it could be certified. There always seemed to be a fear that despite its supposed lack of support, the union would somehow have the power to force fishermen to join.

In New Brunswick, on the other hand, the fight was won. Fishermen finally convinced the government to enact legislation, only the second province in Canada ever to do so. Yet even in New Brunswick, the fight took eight years, wearing down the union, its staff, and the fishermen. By dragging its feet, the government forced the union to function for years on a shoestring budget. Few organizations would have been capable of doing so much on so little for so long.

In 1986, for the first time in its history, the MFU negotiated contracts with the major companies on behalf of fishermen in northeast New Brunswick. But to date, collective bargaining has had limited success. One reason is that the trend towards increasing monopolization wasn't realized. No one could have predicted it at the time, but the major companies did not get bigger and bigger. By 1982, they were all bankrupt. The successful companies turned out to be the small and medium-sized ones. There were also a lot of independent buyers and sellers who did not have processing facilities, who sometimes sold lobster out of the back of a truck.

The presence of a lot of small and medium-sized operators threw a wrench into the analysis. What it meant, in effect, is that a traditional collective bargaining model no longer fit. It wasn't clear who should negotiate with whom. Not everyone belonged to the N.B. Fish Buyers Bargaining Association. Even with contracts in place, buyers paid more than the price negotiated, and fishermen accepted. There seemed to be no way to enforce the contracts. No contracts were signed after 1986, and prices continued to fluctuate, sometimes wildly.

The situation was particularly bad in the lobster fishery, where, in New Brunswick alone, there were more than 100 buyers. In 1988, fed up with a situation that it could not control, National Sea Products Ltd sold its lobster operations throughout the Maritimes. "The nature of the business seems to make collective bargaining extremely difficult," says Jim Bateman, who took over the company's plant in Shédiac. "Until we have some kind of regulations in the industry in terms of who can buy and sell fish, it is going to be very difficult to put together a contract between buyers and fishermen."

It is also true that the unwillingness of lobster fishermen to go on strike undercut the union's bargaining power. The irony, of course, is that fishermen go on strike all the time. What fishermen were and are afraid of is someone else telling them what to do. This was the rationale, in the early days, for not wanting to join a larger union. Fishermen were genuinely afraid that someone who wasn't a fisherman and who came from somewhere else would arrive to tell them to tie up their boats. The decision not to join an international union had major implications for the MFU, almost all of them financial. The Newfoundland fishermen's union was able to organize fishermen in that province—a job that cost millions of dollars—only because its affiliation with a Chicago-based union meant funding. In reality, in the Maritimes, the MFU never had the resources to do a proper job.

The decision not to affiliate with an international union goes to the heart of the MFU itself. Right or wrong, especially in the early days, the MFU always put principles and ideology ahead of strategy, something that is not necessarily true of other unions. As Michael Belliveau says today, "Ideologically, Cashin and his union looked bad when they decided to join the Meat Cutters, but strategically it turned out to be a good move." The Newfoundland union later joined the Canadian Auto Workers, which put it even more in the forefront of progressive trade unionism.

People often point to the Newfoundland and B.C. unions to prove that collective bargaining can work for inshore fishermen. This ignores the fact that both have trawler and plant workers in their membership.

Including plant or trawler workers in its membership was never an option for the MFU, because the fishery was already fragmented when the union began. It has, no doubt, suffered as a result.

Yet there is another side to the coin. In Newfoundland, inshore fishermen have frequently grumbled about not being properly represented. In a CBC Radio commentary in 1990, Petty Harbour fisherman Bernard Martin talked about how the offshore fishery was booming while the inshore was suffering. "Keep in mind that the inshore and offshore are fishing the exact same stocks," he said. (And both, he might have added, are in the Newfoundland union.)

"In response to this crisis, inshore groups sprang up all over the island, quite correctly identifying overfishing by the offshore as the main problem. Some of us even tried to start our own inshore fishermen's union."

Says Cape Breton fisherman and MFU member Herb Nash, "Richard Cashin may be God to some of them, but he's not God to all of them. You can't represent both the inshore and the offshore." More than a dozen years after the official founding of the MFU, its members are still committed to the idea of a Maritime-wide organization that represents only inshore fishermen.

Today, the jury on collective bargaining is still out. Some believe that it can work under certain circumstances. "It seems to me," says MFU executive secretary Michael Belliveau, "that wherever fishermen demonstrate a broad-based willingness to tie up their vessels and withhold their product, then there is a chance for collective bargaining. It's as simple as that."

Even without negotiated contracts, however, the union has influenced prices. "I don't think people have ever given the union enough credit for pushing up the prices," says Big Bras d'Or fisherman Stuart Squires. "It's something that is hard to measure, but just the fact that fishermen were getting together and talking to each other forced the companies to react."

Yet if the MFU has had limited success in bargaining collectively, it has given fishermen more than a word to say about the management of the resource. The union's role in returning the herring fishery to the inshore sector was a remarkable example. So, too, was its involvement in policing lobster poachers, in developing the bonafide fisherman's permit policy, and in getting quota increases. Many gains have been made through the union's participation on Department of Fisheries and Oceans (DFO) committees. "The role that the MFU played was a determining role in bringing issues forward and dealing with them," says Jean-Eûdes Haché, today the DFO's assistant deputy minister for the Atlantic Region. "Putting pressure at the right place, getting their influence heard. In that sense, the progress that was made by inshore fishermen from the mid-1970s to the mid-1980s was due, by and large, to the efforts of the MFU. In my mind, there is no doubt about that." Says Dalhousie University professor Rick Williams, "Back in 1977, we thought that the enemy was National Sea, and that the inshore fishermen would eventually all become waged workers or be pushed out of the fishery altogether. In 1990 … it's the state that is, in effect, the employer because of its regulatory management authority.

"If you look at the decade from 1975 to 1985," he continues, "it is a period when the union made very little progress in terms of collectively bargaining with the companies. But it *did* collectively bargain with the state over the conditions of the management of their industry, and it made *tremendous* progress. The MFU won all kinds of victories for its fishermen, and equally, probably more importantly, it blocked the destruction of their industry, or at least slowed it down."

*　　*　　*　　*　　*

A third, though more minor theme threads its way through the MFU story: culture and nationalism. The MFU was born in an era of rising Acadian nationalism, through a merger of two groups: young intellectuals fighting for the social recognition and the economic survival of their people, and fishermen who realized that they must fight or watch their industry die. The new Acadian nationalism was compelling, and it wasn't surprising that Acadian fishermen thronged to join the union. They were, in fact, among the poorest of the poor in the region, and they had little to lose.

"It was always easier to organize Acadians than anglophones," says Réginald Comeau. "You'd call a meeting in an Acadian village and you'd get 200 guys. In an anglophone one, you'd get 20 or 30 fishermen." It explains, in part, why fishermen in the Cape Tormentine area, the largest concentration of anglophone fishermen in eastern New Brunswick, or in the Bay of Fundy were never as loyal to the union as fishermen in other parts of the province.

"There was always a perception people had of the difference between Acadian and anglophone cultures, that Acadians are much more communal," says Michael Belliveau. "If there's any validity to the theme, I still see it in the way things happen. There's still more collectivity in eastern New Brunswick than you find in the other provinces. For example, I went away for two weeks, and Réginald met with the fishermen, all up and down the coast, and they all decided that they wanted a minimum-size increase for lobster. We had been working on the idea for a couple of years, but just like that, they made a decision across the board, and it seems to hold."

In New Brunswick, there was always an undercurrent of nationalism in the MFU, in the fight with the co-operative movement and in the willingness of people like Jean Gauvin, Aldéa Landry, and Denis Losier (fisheries minister when mandatory-dues legislation was passed) to consider legislation for inshore fishermen when politicians in the other two provinces wouldn't. Many observers believe that Acadian nationalism was the key factor in fishermen winning collective bargaining legislation in New Brunswick. In that sense, it seemed that the MFU was an Acadian union.

Sometimes it still seems that way today. During Law Amendment Committee hearings in 1990, for example, almost all of the groups that opposed the mandatory-dues legislation were anglophone, a fact not lost on Réginald Comeau, who, in frustration, told the media that the issue was "a battle between the two cultures."

Yet at the same time, Acadian fishermen were able to draw anglophone fishermen into the union. Some of the most steadfast members over the years have been fishermen like Percy Hayne, Jr, Hasse Lindblad, and Stuart Beaton in Northumberland; Jamie Ellsworth, Fred Pigott, and Terrence MacDonald in Prince Edward Island; and Con Mills and Kevin and Stuart Squires in Cape Breton. None of them would say that the MFU is an Acadian union. For them, it's an *inshore fishermen's* union that happens to have Acadian and anglophone members. It's *their* union, which they have helped fight for and build over the years.

The MFU has done well in servicing both groups. Literature has been produced in both languages, and meetings have been translated. For an organization critically short of money, that is a major accomplishment. The MFU is one of the few organizations in Canada that has successfully brought together the two linguistic groups. In that sense, it has been a model of co-operation between the two cultures.

The union has also been involved in a number of other areas. In 1985, it set up an insurance program for its members, many of whom had had difficulty finding a company willing to insure them. "It is worth being a union member just to belong," says Baie-Ste-Anne fisherman Elmer Martin. The MFU has led the way in research on accidents at sea—fishing has the highest rate of death and injury of any occupation in Canada—largely through the work of Rick Williams. The MFU has fought changes to the unemployment insurance system and has tried over the years to involve women in the union, recognizing, in effect, that inshore fishing is really a family occupation.

The MFU has also reached out to fishermen in Third World countries. In 1983, Val Comeau fisherman Herménégilde Robichaud and Réginald Comeau went to Nicaragua on a study tour organized by Oxfam-Canada. In 1985, Gilles Thériault also visited the country and, following that trip, helped organize a project to link fishermen from Atlantic Canada with their counterparts in Nicaragua. In 1986, a group of Atlantic Canadian fishermen returned to Nicaragua to talk about specific projects. In 1988, Guy Cormier, his wife, Alfreda, and their four children spent eight months there, helping fishermen to learn how to fish for lobster. For several years in a row, fishermen in the region collected second-hand gear to send on the Tools for Peace boat. Michael Belliveau, too, has been involved in international work, linking fishermen in the developing world with their counterparts in eastern Canada.

For many, the involvement in international affairs has been enriching. "In order to understand our problems," says Herménégilde Robichaud, "we have to be able to understand the problems of others. For me, personally, seeing what inshore fishermen were up against in Nicaragua has made me more committed to our fight here."

Many former MFU staff are now viewed as experts in the fishery. Gilles Thériault is an independent consultant on Canadian as well as international projects; Omer Chouinard works for the New Brunswick Department of Fisheries. Of the original three organizers, only Réginald Comeau remains with the union. Comeau has been the rock in northeast New Brunswick that has kept many fishermen loyal to the union through difficult times. He, too, is beginning to get the recognition that he deserves as an expert in the province's fishery. Comeau's dedication to the union merits a book in itself.

The talent that has been attracted to the MFU over the years—paid and unpaid—has been nothing short of remarkable. The list is long and includes organizers Ron Stockton, Ed Frenette, Fred Winsor, Ron Crawley, Michael LeClair, and Bernie Conway, who were young and inexperienced, though hard-working and devoted. Others include Sandy Siegel, whose role in establishing the southwest Nova Scotia local was crucial; Rick Williams, a close friend and advisor to the union for more than a decade; lawyer Raymond

Larkin, who provided hundreds of thousands of dollars of legal work over the years and who never asked for a cent; Maureen Larkin, the only woman to work as an organizer with the union; Rachel Goguen, who, as office manager, took the wrath of the union's frustrated creditors; and Edmond Drysdale, who has been the organizer and steadfast dues collector in southeast New Brunswick for the past seven years.

Perhaps the most important and the most lasting contribution that the MFU has made has been in the personal development of fishermen and the professionalization of the industry. Says Senator Roméo LeBlanc, "In the long run, I look at the quality of the people who emerged from that experience, and I use Guy Cormier as an example. Basically, you have remarkably decent human beings who also became decent not only in terms of negotiating the price of fish but in exercising real leadership at the local level. If five Guy Cormiers had been the result of Gilles' and all those guys' work, it would still be worth it. But in fact, there are more than five. The next generation of fishermen is already a new species of human being." (In 1990, Guy Cormier ran for the NDP against Jean Chretien in the federal by-election in Beauséjour and cut the Liberal majority from 12,000 in the previous election to 4,000.)

"Like all human institutions," LeBlanc continues, "the MFU wasn't perfect, but it contributed a great, great deal to the professionalization of the industry. The bonafide policy was only one example. I think if you ask DFO managers in Moncton today, 'What do you think of fishermen's organizations?' they'd say, 'We couldn't manage the fishery without them.' The days when bureaucrats thought they could manage the fishery from headquarters are, thank God, over."

*   *   *   *   *

One of the most telling comments in Stephen Kimber's book on National Sea Products came from the company's chairman, Bill Morrow. "If you go back over the years," Morrow told Kimber, "you'll find that every seven or eight years, the industry seems to just go bust. There's always a good reason, but it's never the same reason. One time, the cause might be high interest rates. The next time, it might be poor catches. The only thing that seems certain is that just when you start feeling good about everything, that's the time you should learn to duck."

By 1990, inshore fishermen were, again, beginning to duck. The good times of the mid-1980s were over. Groundfish quotas were slashed dramatically—after biologists realized that they had vastly overestimated the size of northern cod stocks—leading to plant closures that threatened to wipe out entire communities. Fishermen everywhere were complaining that codfish were small and that landings were low. The American Mitchell Bill, which limits the size of lobster entering that country, was also threatening to wreak havoc in the lobster fishery throughout Atlantic Canada.

Once again, inshore fishermen in the Maritimes began to talk about survival.

From an outsider's point of view, it is an incredible state of affairs. Even in the short period covered by this book, the "busts" have arrived with alarming regularity: 1968, 1974, 1981, 1989-90. But no one—neither the governments nor the large companies—seems capable of learning how to prepare for them or to cope with them when they come.

Once again, everyone is talking about a crisis—a crisis that many predict will be the worst since the 1920s. In 1981, the focus was on saving the large companies. At least in 1990, there was some talk, however hesitant, about saving the communities that face extinction. Whether this talk will prove fruitful remains to be seen.

One consequence of the crisis—one that the MFU has grown to expect—is that membership in the union is at an all-time high. Today, the MFU has 1,200 dues-paying members, more than any other dues-paying fishermen's organization in the Maritimes. Yet that number falls far short of the total possible membership. The question that haunts and frustrates many MFU fishermen today is: What will it take for the majority of fishermen to unite? Are fishermen just too independent, too fragmented, or, as some say, too lazy to fight for their rights?

For its part, the Eastern Fishermen's Federation has all but disappeared in Nova Scotia, except for a small presence on the Eastern and Northumberland shores. "I haven't heard the EFF mentioned since Alan Billard resigned three years ago to go into municipal politics," says National Sea's Jim Morrow. In New Brunswick, Cape Tormentine fishermen had joined the EFF, though in 1987 fisherman Rod Pauley said that his group hadn't seen Billard for three years. Yet the EFF surfaced again in the province in 1990 to oppose the MFU's bid for mandatory dues deduction. The EFF now has its headquarters in Prince Edward Island, where most of its support seems to be based. It is, perhaps not coincidentally, the province where the MFU is weakest.

Despite the lack of participation, MFU fishermen are determined to keep the union alive. That seems more possible now since the mandatory-dues legislation was passed in New Brunswick in the summer of 1990. That legislation, expected to be in place by the spring of 1991, should provide a measure of financial stability for the union. Many still see involvement in the organization as the only way to defend the inshore fishery. If the MFU dies, they say, it won't be long before the inshore fishery dies as well.

The DFO does not want the union to collapse, either. The report of the Scotia-Fundy Groundfish Task Force in December 1989 called on government to implement a licence levy to raise funding for fishermen's organizations. "Having strong fishermen's groups," admits task force chairman Jean-Eûdes Haché, "makes our job much easier."

The crisis of 1990—if it is indeed as bad as people say—may be the turning point for the MFU. It may be what finally brings inshore fishermen together and what makes them realize that strength is, after all, in numbers. Some of the Maritime Fishermen's Union's biggest battles may be yet to come.

APPENDIX

Studies on Collective Bargaining for Inshore Fishermen

June 1977
The first report of the New Brunswick Select Committee on Fisheries recommended that "the province should encourage fishermen to increase their participation in the marketing of their products and foster mechanisms whereby fishermen can collectively bargain prices."

June 1978
The second report of the New Brunswick Select Committee on Fisheries said, "The committee has reviewed the matter of unions and fishermen's associations as it applies in Newfoundland and Nova Scotia and holds with its recommendations suggested in last year's report."

September 1978
A Plan for the Development of Human Resources—New Brunswick Fishing Industry recommended to the Department of Fisheries "that a mechanism be found whereby fishermen can negotiate in advance for the price of fish."

1979
The Labour Act Review Committee, set up to review the P.E.I. Labour Act of 1974, wrote a one-page memo to Fisheries Minister George Proud recommending that fishermen be given collective bargaining rights.

October 1979
The Task Force to Study the Commercial Relationships between Fishermen and Fish Buyers in New Brunswick recommended that "the government ... pass the necessary legislation to allow unions and associations of fishermen to become accreditted [*sic*] and to negotiate collectively with fish buyers."

October 1980
The Nova Scotia *Fisheries General Policy* stated, "The concept that fishermen should associate for their own advancement should be supported. Such an association or associations could ... allow them to negotiate such matters as fish prices."

January 1981
Part I of the *Report of the Commission of Inquiry into the P.E.I. Fishery* recommended "that provision be made for collective bargaining legislation at the earliest practical date and in consultation with fishermen's and processors organizations."

June 1981
The interim report of the Joint Committee on Primary Marketing and Commercial Relationships in the Fishing Industry in New Brunswick stated, "While there was no consensus on the need for legislation to give collective bargaining rights to fishermen and fish buyers for the bargaining of fish prices and other conditions of sale or purchase of fish at the primary level, the committee is prepared to recommend the adoption of its proposal entitled: 'An Act Respecting Collective Bargaining Between Fishermen or Fishermen's Organizations and Fish Buyers or Buyers' Organizations in the Province of New Brunswick' as a model for legislation."

April 1981
Fishermen's Collective Bargaining Alternatives, the report of the Interdepartmental Committee, Nova Scotia Department of Fisheries, stated, "The committee recommends that the government endorse the development of collective bargaining legislation for those fishermen who wish to unionize."

December 1982

Navigating Troubled Waters: A New Policy for the Atlantic Fisheries, the report of the Task Force on Atlantic Fisheries (Michael Kirby, chairman), recommended, "Provincial governments that have not adopted collective bargaining legislation for inshore fishermen should do so. The federal government should support such collective bargaining by providing unequivocally for it, in all its forms, when new competition legislation is introduced."

SELECTED BIBLIOGRAPHY

Books, Articles, and Unpublished Manuscripts

Abella, Irving, and David Millar. *The Canadian Worker in the Twentieth Century.* Toronto: Oxford University Press, 1978.

Allain, Greg, and S. Côté. "Le developpement régional, l'état et la participation de la population: la vie courte et mouvementée des conseils régionaux d'amènagement du N-B. (1964-80)." *Egalité,* No. 5, 1984-85.

———, et al. "Regional Development Councils in New Brunswick: Planning or Mobilizing Agencies?" Paper presented to the twelfth annual conference of sociologists and anthropologists. Wolfville: Acadia University, 1977.

Antoft, Kell. "Labour and Legislation." *Dalhousie Labour Institute for the Atlantic Provinces,* June 11-15, 1979.

Arsenault, Georges, et Cécile Gallant. *Histoire de la pêche chez les Acadiens de l'Ile-du-Prince-Edouard.* Summerside, P.E.I.: La Société Saint-Thomas d'Aquin, 1980.

Barrett, L. Gene. "Development and Underdevelopment and the Rise of Trade Unionism in the Fishing Industry of Nova Scotia, 1900-1950." Masters thesis, Dalhousie University, 1976.

Brun, Régis. *De Grand-Pré à Kouchibougouac: L'histoire d'un peuple exploité.* Moncton: Editions d'Acadie, 1982.

———. *La ruée vers le homard des Maritimes.* Moncton: Michel Henry éditeur, 1988.

Calhoun, Sue. "A Wandering Acadian Looking for the Truth." *Atlantic Insight,* May 1989.

———. *The Lockeport Lockout: An Untold Story in Nova Scotia's Labour History.* Halifax, 1983.

Cameron, Silver Donald. *The Education of Everett Richardson: The Nova Scotia Fishermen's Strike, 1970-71.* Toronto: McClelland and Stewart, 1977.

Chaussade, Jean. *La pêche et les pêcheurs des Provinces Maritimes du Canada.* Montréal: Les Presses de l'Université de Montréal, 1983.

Clement, Wallace. *The Struggle to Organize: Resistance in Canada's Fishery.* Toronto: McClelland and Stewart, 1986.

Daigle, Jean, ed. *The Acadians of the Maritimes.* Moncton: Centre d'études acadiennes, 1982.

DeGrace, Eloi. "Document: origines du mouvement coopératif chez les acadiens." *Société historique acadien,* Vol. 18, No. 1, 1987.

Donham, Parker Barss. "H.B. Nickerson and Sons: The Big, Big Fish in Canada's Pond." *Atlantic Insight,* October 1981.

Doucet, Paul, ed. *Vie de nos ancêtres en Acadie: La pêche.* Moncton: Editions d'Acadie, 1981.

Fraser, James A. *A History of the W.S. Loggie Co. Ltd. 1873-1973.* Fredericton: Provincial Archives of New Brunswick, 1973.

Fraser, Raymond. *The Fighting Fisherman: The Life of Yvon Durelle.* Toronto: Doubleday Canada, 1981.

Gallagher, Delbert W. "The Commercial Fisheries of New Brunswick: 1926-53." Masters thesis, University of New Brunswick, 1955.

Gallant, Cécile. *Le mouvement coopératif chez les Acadiens de la région Evangéline (1862-1982).* Wellington, P.E.I.: Le Conseil Coopératif de l'Ile-du-Prince-Edouard, 1982.

Gauvin, Monique. "Le mouvement coopératif acadien: Fondements ideologiques, histoire et composition actuelle." Masters thesis, University of Moncton, 1976.

Godin, Pierre. *Les revoltes d'Acadie.* Montréal: Editions Québécoises, 1971.

Hughes, Gary. *Miscou and Lamèque: Two Islands and Their State of Bondage, 1849-1861.* n.p., n.d.

Inglis, Gordon. *More than Just a Union: The Story of the NFFAWU.* St John's: Jesperson Press, 1985.

Innis, Harold A. *The Cod Fisheries: The History of an International Economy.* Toronto: University of Toronto Press, 1954.

Kimber, Stephen. "Michelin Tire Rolls On." *Financial Post Magazine,* April 26, 1980.

———. *Net Profits: The Story of National Sea.* Halifax: Nimbus Publishing, 1989.

Lamson, Cynthia, and Arthur J. Hanson, eds. *Atlantic Fisheries and Coastal Communities: Fisheries Decision-Making Case Studies.* Halifax: Dalhousie Ocean Studies Programme, 1984.

Landry, Nicolas. "Les Acadiens et la pêche dans les Provinces Maritimes." *Demain. La francophonie,* 1987.

Ommer, Rosemary E. "From Outpost to Outport: The Jersey Merchant Triangle in the 19th Century." PhD dissertation, McGill University, 1978.

Richard, Alvin. *Une véritable paroisse coopérative: La caisse populaire du*

Village de Richibouctou Ltée, 1939-1989. Caisse populaire du Village de Richibouctou, 1989.

Robichaud, Donat. *Le Grand Chipagan: Histoire de Shippagan.* Beresford, N.B.: Société Historique Nicolas Denys, 1976.

"Roméo LeBlanc: A Poor Boy's Crusade for the Fishermen." *Saturday Night,* May 1979.

"Rough Voyage: A Report for the Fishermen of Nova Scotia." St Francis Xavier University Extension Department, April 1978.

Roy, Michel. *L'Acadie perdue.* Ottawa: Editions Québec/Amérique, 1978.

Saunders, Roy. *The Escuminac Disaster.* London: 1960.

Savoie, Donald J. *Regional Economic Development: Canada's Search for Solutions.* Toronto: University of Toronto Press, 1986.

Stanley, Della M.M. *Louis Robichaud: A Decade of Power.* Halifax: Nimbus Publishing, 1984.

"The Sudden Boom in Atlantic Fish." *Saturday Night,* May 1979.

Surette, Ralph. "A Grim Year for the Fishery." *Atlantic Insight,* November 1981.

Thériault, Bernard. *Les Robins: presence jersaise en Acadie 1767-1958.* Presenté au departement des ressources historiques au Nouveau-Brunswick et à l'administration du Village Historique Acadien, Caraquet, N.B., 1975.

Thériault, J. Yvon. "Développement dépendant et pénétration coopérative." *Revue de l'Université de Moncton,* janvier/mai 1980.

———. "L'autonomie aujourd'hui: La question acadienne sous le regard des idéologies politiques actuelles." *Egalité,* automne 1986.

Thibodeau, Martial. "Comment devenir son propre patron." *New Brunswick,* June 1976.

United Maritime Fishermen. *Cornerstone of Co-op Fisheries Movement.* 1975.

Watkins, Lyndon. "Effects of National Sea Products Takeover Being Studied." *Globe and Mail,* April 7, 1977.

———. "Fishermen Test Inshore Waters in Union Drive." *Globe and Mail,* October 13, 1979.

Wells, Kennedy. *The Fishery of Prince Edward Island.* Charlottetown: Ragweed Press, 1986.

Williams, Rick. "Inshore Fishermen, Unionisation, and the Struggle against Underdevelopment Today." *Underdevelopment and Social Movements in Atlantic Canada.* Edited by Brym and Sacouman. Toronto: New Hogtown Press, 1979.

———, and Gilles Thériault. "Bend and Be Strong: An Analysis of Ten Years of Experience in Building an Inshore Fishermen's Organisation in the Maritime Provinces." Presented to the International Working

Seminar, Social Research and Public Policy Formation in the Fisheries: Norwegian and Atlantic Canadian Experience, 1986.

Wood, Chris. "Unsettled Weather Ahead for the MFU." *Atlantic Insight,* July 1984.

Documents and Reports

Atlantic Provinces Economic Council. *Atlantic Economy.* Yearly reviews and outlooks. Halifax, 1985-89

Canada. Department of Fisheries and Oceans. *Commercial Fisheries Licensing Policy for Eastern Canada.* Ottawa, January 1989.

————. Department of Fisheries and Oceans. *Navigating Troubled Waters: A New Policy for the Atlantic Fisheries.* Report of the Task Force on Atlantic Fisheries. Ottawa, December 1982.

————. Department of Fisheries and Oceans. *Program Options. The Southern Gulf Licensing Policy.* Ottawa, June 1988.

————. Department of Fisheries and Oceans. *Report of the Scotia-Fundy Groundfish Task Force.* Ottawa, December 1989.

————. Department of Fisheries and Oceans. *Toward an Atlantic Coast Commercial Fisheries Licensing System.* Prepared by C.R. Levelton. Ottawa, April 1979.

————. Department of Forestry and Rural Development. *Life and Poverty in the Maritimes.* Prepared by Pierre-Yves Pepin. ARDA Project 15002. Ottawa, March 1968.

————. Fisheries and Marine Service, Environment Canada. *Policy for Canada's Commercial Fisheries.* Ottawa, May 1976.

————. Fisheries Research Board of Canada. *The Lobster Fishery of the Maritime Provinces: Economic Effects of Regulations.* Prepared by A. Gordon DeWolf. Bulletin. Ottawa, 1974.

————. Parks Canada. *Report of the Special Inquiry on Kouchibouguac National Park.* Ottawa, October 1981.

————. *Report of the Royal Commission Investigating the Fisheries of the Maritime Provinces and the Magdalen Islands.* Ottawa, 1928.

Centre de Formation au Développement. *Situation de la pêche et organisations des pêcheurs.* Richibucto, N.B., décembre 1975.

Citizens' Committee in Support of Collective Bargaining Legislation for Inshore Fishermen. "A Brief Concerning Collective Bargaining Legislation for Inshore Fishermen in N.S." Submitted to the Nova Scotia Interdepartmental Committee, January 22, 1981.

CRAN. Files. Available at the Centre d'études acadiennes, Moncton.

CRASE. Files. Available at the Centre d'études acadiennes, Moncton.

Maritime Fishermen's Union. *Annual Report.* Richibucto and Shédiac, N.B., 1980-1990.

————. *Evaluation Report of the Lobster Protection Project.* Presented to the Department of Fisheries and Oceans. Richibucto, N.B., November 1980.

―――. "Fishing Industry Bargaining Act for N.S." Submission to Interdepartmental Committee of Deputy Ministers on Fishermen's Organization. January 1981.

―――. *Lobster Fishery and Lobster Markets 1976-80.* Richibucto, N.B., May 1980.

―――. *The Voice of the Maritime Fishermen's Union.* Newsletter. Richibucto and Shédiac, N.B., 1977-1986.

―――. "Submission to Law Amendments Committee, Province of N.S. re Bill 110: 'An Act to Provide for Associations of Independent Boatowner Fishermen.'" June 1982.

New Brunswick. Department of Fisheries. *A Plan for the Development of Human Resources—New Brunswick Fishing Industry.* Prepared by Marine Resources Limited and Training Branch. Fredericton, September 1978.

―――. Department of Fisheries. *Annual Report.* Fredericton, 1960-1988.

―――. Department of Fisheries. *Report on the Sea and River Fisheries of New Brunswick,* by Moses Perley. Fredericton, 1852.

―――. Department of Fisheries. *Study of the Feasibility to Develop a Herring Reduction Industry in the Gulf of St. Lawrence.* Prepared by John D. Koppernaes Engineering Co. Halifax, 1965.

―――. Fishing Industry Relations Board. Certification Order. March 22, 1984.

―――. Fishing Industry Relations Board. Transcript of Proceedings. August 2-3, 1983.

―――. Joint Committee on Primary Marketing and Commercial Relationships in the Fishing Industry in New Brunswick. *Interim Report.* Fredericton, June 1981.

―――. *Journals of the Legislative Assembly,* 1977-1982.

―――. Law Amendments Committee. Submissions and Transcript of Hearings on "Deduction of dues act." Shédiac, N.B., January 1990.

―――. Law Amendments Committee. Submissions by the Association Professionnelle des Pêcheurs du Nord-est, Fundy Weir Fishermen's Association, Maritime Fishermen's Union, New Brunswick Federation of Labour, New Brunswick Fish Packers' Association. Hearings, October 1981.

―――. *Report of the Task Force to Study the Commercial Relationships between Fishermen and Fish Buyers in New Brunswick.* Fredericton, October 1979.

―――. Select Committee on Fisheries. Reports. Fredericton, June 1, 1977; June 28, 1978.

Nova Scotia. Department of Fisheries. *Annual Report.* Halifax, 1960-1988.

——. Department of Fisheries. *Fisheries General Policy.* Halifax, October 1980.

——. Department of Fisheries. *Fishermen's Collective Bargaining Alternatives.* Report of the Interdepartmental Committee. Halifax, April 1981.

Prince Edward Island. Department of Fisheries. *Annual Report.* Charlottetown, 1960-1988.

——. Department of Fisheries. *Report of the Commission of Inquiry into the P.E.I. Fishery.* Prepared by E.P. Weeks. Charlottetown, 1981.

Professional Fishermen's Association of Southeast New Brunswick. Files. Available at the Centre d'études acadiennes, Moncton.

Newspapers
L'Acayen, 1975-76
The Chronicle-Herald (Halifax), 1978-84
L'Evangéline, 1966-80
The Guardian (Charlottetown), 1970-84
Sou'wester, 1980-89
The Times-Transcript (Moncton), 1969-85
Union Forum, 1971

Films and Videos
Meetings of the Maritime Fishermen's Union. Centre de Formation au Développement. Available at the Centre d'études acadiennes, University of Moncton.

Robichaud. Dir. by Herménégilde Chiasson; prod. by National Film Board. Moncton, 1989.

Toutes les photos finissent par se ressembler. Dir. by Herménégilde Chiasson; prod. by National Film Board. Moncton, 1987.

INDEX